THE
EXPEDITION

THE EXPEDITION

TWO PARENTS RISK LIFE AND FAMILY IN AN EXTRAORDINARY QUEST TO THE SOUTH POLE

CHRIS FAGAN

SHE WRITES PRESS

Published September 2019
Printed in the United States of America
Print ISBN: 978-1-63152-592-6
E-ISBN: 978-1-63152-593-3
Library of Congress Control Number: 2019930415

For information, address:
She Writes Press
1569 Solano Ave #546
Berkeley, CA 94707

Interior design by Tabitha Lahr
Map by Mike Morgenfeld

She Writes Press is a division of SparkPoint Studio, LLC.

For Marty and Keenan.
Thank you for sharing this adventure of life.
I am so much more because of you.
I love you beyond words.

Tell me, what is it you plan to do
with your one wild and precious life?

—MARY OLIVER

CONTENTS

FOR THE EXPEDITION

Listen.
The world invites us to adventure
every day.
Say yes.
Across expanses of snow,
cold, and relentless winds.
Say yes.
Across the far-flung seas
and rock-strewn shores.
Say yes.
As we leave the boundaries
of what we know to meet
the mountain, the jungle, the glaciers
that drop from the pole.
Say yes.
And here, in the still heart of now, listen.
The world invites us to adventure
every day.
Say yes.

—BENJAMIN CURRY

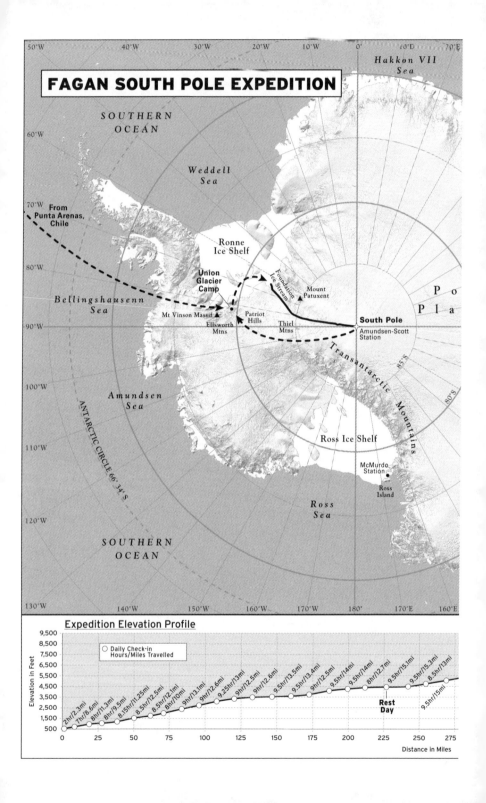

FAGAN SOUTH POLE EXPEDITION

50°W 40°W 30°W 20°W 10°W 0° 10°D 70°E

Hakkon VII Sea

SOUTHERN OCEAN

60°W

Weddell Sea

70°W **From Punta Arenas, Chile**

Ronne Ice Shelf

80°W **Union Glacier Camp**

Foundation Ice Stream

Mount Patuxent

P o

P l a

Bellingshausenn Sea

Mt Vinson Massif ▲ Patriot Hills

Ellsworth Mtns Thiel Mtns

90°W **South Pole** Amundsen-Scott Station

85°S

80°S

Transantarctic Mountains

100°W

Amundsen Sea

Ross Ice Shelf

110°W

McMurdo Station

Ross Island

120°W *Ross Sea*

SOUTHERN OCEAN

130°W 140°W 150°W 160°W 170°W 180° 170°E 160°E

ANTARCTIC CIRCLE (66° 34'S)

Expedition Elevation Profile

○ Daily Check-in Hours/Miles Travelled

Elevation in Feet: 9,500 8,500 7,500 6,500 5,500 4,500 3,500 2,500 1,500 500

2hr/2.3mi 7hr/8.6mi 8hr/11.3mi 8hr/9.5mi 8.15hr/11.25mi 8.5hr/12.5mi 8hr/10mi 9hr/13.1mi 9hr/13mi 9hr/12.6mi 9.25hr/13mi 9hr/12.6mi 9.5hr/13.5mi 9.5hr/13.4mi 9hr/12.5mi 9.5hr/14mi 9.5hr/14mi 8hr/12.7mi 9.5hr/15.1mi 9.5hr/15.3mi 8.5hr/13mi

9.5hr/15mi

Rest Day

Distance in Miles: 0 25 50 75 100 125 150 175 200 225 250 275

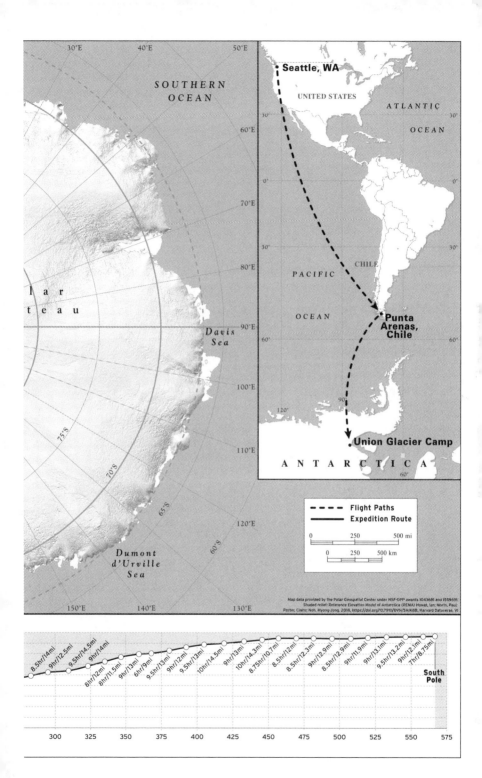

AUTHOR'S NOTE

To write this book, I've relied on my journal notes, voice blogs dictated while in Antarctica, personal memories, researched facts, and discussions with individuals. Others may remember certain details and events differently. Any errors or misinterpretations are mine alone.

I have changed the names of a few people to preserve their privacy and the order of a few events to help with narrative flow, but there are no composite characters or events in this book.

I've reported all temperatures in Fahrenheit (read: I'm American). While we tracked our miles in both nautical and statute (land) miles while in Antarctica, all miles reported in the book are land miles for ease of understanding. Note that nautical miles are used for charting and navigating, and one nautical mile is equal to one minute of latitude, or 1.1508 statute miles. If you think in kilometers, like most of the world outside America, one mile equals 1.6 kilometers.

INTRODUCTION

January 2014

Come on, you can do this. Mind over body.

My body stiffened against the blasting wind that threatened to blow me over—again. The bitter cold searched for a way past my layers of protective gear. Squinting to see through the slice of my goggle that wasn't frozen over, I turned my head left, then right. The coyote-fur ruff on my red anorak danced back and forth in front of my eyes. White nothingness swallowed me. A whiteout. Snow and sky melting into one. The cold penetrating my fingers told me to keep moving—my insurance against the constant danger of hypothermia and frostbite. It was minus 22 degrees Fahrenheit with winds gusting to 15 miles per hour, an average summer day in Antarctica.

I edged my ski forward with bulging sled in tow, slowly feeling my way over chaotic chunks of snow, then lost my balance. Stabbing my pole into the ice, I barely stayed upright. I stared down at my black ski tips as they disappeared into the whiteness. Only my compass could show the way; I had lost all sense of direction after hours of moving through the jumbled mess—with no up or down—and my head felt tangled. I strained to keep the red dot that was Marty in sight as the whiteness threatened to separate us. *No matter what, stay with him.* With just the two of us skiing through the remote interior of Antarctica, there was no margin for error, no easy way out.

I had grown sick of the blank white slate that bore no resemblance to our lush green life back home in the Northwest and tired of being hundreds of miles from anything civilized. I longed to see our son, Keenan, hear his infectious laughter, and feel the warmth as I hugged him close. I worried about how he was coping with the pressures of middle school life in our absence.

Today I felt the weight of the chilling truth. After skiing 460 miles over the past thirty-nine days, Marty and I still had over 100 cold hard miles to go. Attempting to ski from the edge of Antarctica to the South Pole—without guide or resupply—was stretching us beyond our physical and mental limits. Our bond of marriage felt frayed. The bone-deep exhaustion and isolation threatened to break me. If only I could have reached back in history to gain wisdom and strength from the explorers who had completed this arduous endeavor before us. Maybe they would have told me that the usual nine or ten hours of work per day—fighting through whiteout conditions, slogging over slow sticky snow, navigating between jagged ice blocks, and battling with blow-you-over winds—would be worth it. Maybe they would have helped me release the burden of my slow pace and the mounting pressure to ski more miles per day.

As I heaved my 160-pound sled forward with everything I had, I thought: *How long can I keep this up?* I found myself fantasizing—not about the savory taste of Thai food or a steaming hot shower or the decadent feeling of a soft down bed, but about a way back to happy, energetic, smiling Chris. But the route back was as invisible as blue sky during a whiteout.

CHAPTER 1:

ADVENTURE MATTERS

One Sunday morning in November of 2010, Marty casually walked into the kitchen, where I was unloading the dishwasher, and asked, "What do you think about going to the South Pole?"

I stood motionless, staring out at the driving rain. Without looking at him, I knew this was a serious question—just as serious as the times he had asked me if I wanted to train for another ultramarathon. For most other families here in the foothills of the Cascade Mountains outside Seattle, going to the South Pole would be an armchair adventure accomplished only by reading a book.

I didn't know where to begin to answer his question.

Panic rising, I turned and looked into Marty's soft blue eyes, and in a forced-calm voice said, "I'm not sure, I'll have to think about it." I bent over, grabbed a clean plate, and placed it in the cabinet.

"Okay," said Marty, raising his eyebrows. "Lately the idea keeps popping into my head and I'd like to chat about it sometime soon."

As Marty strolled back into the family room, my brain flooded with questions: *Did he just say the South Pole? Isn't that in Antarctica? Isn't it really cold there? That's the pole at the bottom of the earth, right? How in the world do you get there? Can we afford it? How will we be able to take enough time off from work? What about Keenan?*

A FEW DAYS LATER, as Marty and I cooked dinner together and Keenan built a multicolored Lego castle in the playroom, Marty said, "You know, hon, I wasn't trying to convince you to go to the South Pole. I just wanted to start a conversation about it."

"Why are you so interested in the South Pole?" I said, with a tense grip around the spatula.

"I've imagined going there ever since I read books about great polar explorers like Amundsen and Shackleton." Marty began to chop up a red pepper. "When I was just getting into mountaineering, I thought you had to possess supernatural physical powers to be a polar explorer. But we've climbed in harsh conditions and run for twenty-four hours straight in ultramarathons."

I was following his thinking, but wasn't sure how to respond because I knew how much Marty liked to drive toward decisions. If I showed any interest, then maps and books about Antarctica would arrive at our doorstep the next day.

He continued, "So lately I've begun to think . . . why not us at the South Pole?"

"You know I'm all for big adventures—but honestly, I'm not sure what I think, especially given Keenan is only ten years old." I threw the onions into the frying pan and listened to them sizzle. While still squirming at the notion of heading to the bottom of the earth, I could sense Marty's idea wasn't going away without a thorough vetting. I stirred the onions. "I will definitely give it some more thought."

Weeks later, curled up on the couch in front of a warm fire and contemplating an expedition to Antarctica, I realized that while the idea of going to the South Pole had caught me off guard when Marty first brought it up, maybe it wasn't so crazy. Marty and I met while on separate self-guided climbing expeditions to Denali in remote Alaska; we honeymooned in Zimbabwe by canoeing down the hippo-laden Zambezi River; we biked through remote Tanzania with seven-year-old Keenan in tow; and we had run tens of thousands of miles through rugged mountain terrain for over a decade. The irresistible attraction of human-powered adventures in wild places sets our hearts aflutter—throw in a tough physical challenge, and we might explode with excitement.

MY LIFE'S PATH crossed with Marty's in 1998 on Denali, the highest peak in North America. The most northerly mountain in the world over 20,000 feet, Denali boasts arctic winds in excess of 100 miles per hour, temperatures of −40 degrees, miles of heavily glaciated terrain with gaping crevasses, and renowned storms that pin teams in tents for up to a week at a time. The unpredictable weather coupled with the high altitude requires technical snow and cold-weather skills, as well as extreme patience and endurance to move through the five camps on the way to the summit.

I stepped out of the plane at base camp that May, transported to what felt like a secret climber's lair, with snow, rock, and ice walls towering above the makeshift landing area. My jaw gaped wide. Standing among massive peaks like Denali, Foraker, and Hunter with a view straight down the Kahiltna Glacier— the longest glacier of the Alaska Range with endless cracks and pressure ridges created from the ice mass moving over rocky terrain—I felt small.

Under sunny blue skies, we slogged through slushy snow in 39 degrees to arrive 5.5 miles up the mountain at Camp 1. My teammates, Susan and Alyson, and I set up our tent. Three guys from the tent next to us walked over to introduce themselves.

"Hi, I'm Marty, and we're Team Hawaii."

Team Hawaii included Marty, a strapping blond-haired six-foot-tall police officer from Honolulu, Hawaii, and Kevin and Brian.

After a quick exchange of our vitals, we parted ways and got down to the business of melting snow for water on our first night on the mountain. There was no time to be distracted by ruggedly attractive guys.

Susan, Alyson, and I had honed our climbing skills on Mount Rainier, a tough 14,411-foot glacier-covered mountain a two-hour drive outside Seattle, where we all lived, with similar winter conditions of whipping snow and blasting winds. I learned safe crevasse travel on Rainier and dangled deep inside a gaping crack in the ice while trusted teammates pulled me to safety during a crevasse rescue course. This was where my mountain-girl vocabulary expanded to include words like bowline-on-a-coil, self-arrest, boot belay, and Z-pulley. This was where I learned to climb like a girl.

Marty's life had been steeped in its own breed of adventure. Marathon running buoyed his confidence to take on other long endurance challenges. His friendship with a famous Denali mountaineer, Dave Johnston, brought him to Denali twice before. On this attempt, his third, he was determined to reach the top.

While we weren't technically climbing with Team Hawaii, we happened to move up the mountain at a similar pace. Over the first week, harsh weather kept both our teams tent-bound. In those early days, Marty would shout over from Team Hawaii's tent, "How are you girls today?" as a conversation starter. By week two of the climb, a subtle but noticeable shift occurred when he said, "*Chris*, how are things over there?"

"What, are we invisible now?" Susan quipped.

It wasn't until we began moving up from 14,300 feet to high camp, seventeen days into the expedition, that my skills and mental game were truly put to the test. After negotiating the fixed lines from 14,300 to 16,200, we stuffed our packs full with gear cached there a few days earlier and continued on to high camp. With a sixty-pound pack on my back, I labored to lift my legs and find stable foot placement among the rock and ice. Sluggish, I couldn't find a smooth breathing rhythm. I moved in slow motion as my peripheral vision narrowed to a tunnel, then moments later, widened again. Concern washed over me. *Is it the altitude?* As usual, we were all roped together for safe glacier travel—today Susan was leading, I was in the middle, and Alyson brought up the rear. One misstep, one unintended tug of the lifeline between us, and my weary legs might give way. I fought to keep my balance, and confidence, with each step.

Then the terrain turned from rolling uphill to scary steep. The temperature started to drop to below freezing as the sun hung low in the sky. I gazed up at the rock-and-ice-filled gully, worried that I might be the weak link. I didn't want to prevent us from making high camp by nightfall, or worse, from eventually summiting. *What is wrong with me? Susan and Alyson don't seem to be as exhausted as me.*

As if sensing my thoughts, Susan asked, "Are you okay?"

"Yes," I said, choking back tears behind sunglasses.

I loathed feeling weak and vulnerable. Despised being the focus of concern. Summoning every ounce of strength left in my five-foot-four-inch frame, I high-stepped up the wet, slippery granite.

I staggered into high camp at 17,200 feet, shattered from the ten-hour day. I dropped to the ground like a rag doll, staring blankly into the cold, thin air, straining to breathe, with a bulging pack still teetering on my back. To my right, Susan and Alyson sprang into action and dug into backpacks searching for the tent, vestibule, and poles, while to my left, Marty—who had arrived at high camp with his team a day earlier—kneeled down and asked in a gentle, caring voice, "Are you okay?" *There is that question again. I must not look okay.* I slowly gazed up at him, but instead of responding, I fished into the pocket of my Gore-Tex jacket for a frozen piece of Clif Bar, hoping it would jump-start mind and body into action.

It didn't.

Marty reached under my arm to help me stand up, then Susan and Alyson ushered me into our tent. We thawed our bodies, melted snow for water, and finally, at 11:00 p.m., ate dinner. Since high altitude can suppress your appetite, I had to practically force-feed myself to regain my strength.

Two days later—after bad weather kept us tent-bound and gave me a full day to recover—I peeked out the tent door. Clear skies. Summit time. I led us out of camp about 30 minutes behind Team Hawaii. I found a smooth climbing rhythm, moving quickly enough to keep warm while maintaining steady, even breathing. Susan, Alyson, and I pushed forward as one long roped-together snake. As we approached a wide flat area at 19,000 feet, nicknamed the "football field," I noticed clouds blowing in from the east, with visibility diminishing and wind picking up. We stopped for a short consultation.

Huddling close to my teammates, I said, "The weather's changing, but I can see rays of sun trying to peek through the clouds. I'm okay moving ahead. We've been out in worse. What do you think?"

"I agree. Let's go for it," said Susan.

With her head tightly enclosed in her Gore-Tex jacket, Alyson nodded in agreement.

I turned back into the wind, fighting fatigue and thin air that are common on top of big mountains.

I moved deliberately, confidence growing with each step. At the bottom of the final six-hundred-foot summit slope, warm tears rolled down my cold cheeks as I finally let myself believe that we'd stand on top. After nineteen days of perseverance and team unity and faith, the summit was ours. Just then the clouds began to lift, revealing an incredible summit ridge perched above an array of snowcapped mountains and glistening glaciers that spread for miles in every direction. I savored each step, soaking in the enormity of what we were about to accomplish. My body felt weightless. As I blinked to clear my vision, I noticed a light-blue jacket coming down toward us from the summit—Marty, leading Team Hawaii. When Marty and I came face-to-face on the ridge, we instinctively hugged each other tight. In a shaky voice, he said, "I haven't stopped crying since I summited."

Susan, Alyson, and I spent just five minutes on top due to the high altitude and harsh conditions. As we moved down the mountain, I spontaneously began singing "Amazing Grace" out loud to myself, over and over. With each repetition, I sang more fully, more confidently, more from the heart. The words "was blind, but now I see" warming me from deep within. I moved with ease, present in the moment, filled with peace and joy. I became one with the mountain, with the wind, with my teammates, with everything—suspended in a moment that held the key to everything.

SEVERAL DAYS AFTER summiting Denali, Susan, Alyson, and I pulled into base camp. It looked completely different from when we had arrived twenty-four days earlier. I was different too.

While I arranged our flight departure off the glacier, I noticed Marty strolling over to help Susan shovel snow to dig up our post-summit treats of smoked salmon, cracked-pepper crackers, and craft beer we'd buried when we first arrived. According to Susan, as Marty reached for a shovel, he blurted out, "Does Chris have a boyfriend?"

"No," said Susan.

"You just made my day!"

Back in Talkeetna at our hotel that night, when I had finished taking my first luxurious energy-reviving shower and dressed in fresh-smelling clothes, there was a knock at the door. I opened it to Marty's beaming smile and bright glow. He exclaimed, "I knew you were gorgeous under all of that Gore-Tex," and handed me a hot cheeseburger that I inhaled in four bites. Our teams shared celebratory beers and more burgers, and Marty and I chatted long into the night. I felt there was something uncommonly beautiful brewing between us. The next morning, after riding a bus back to Anchorage, our teammates left for home, but Marty and I hatched an escape plan: we rescheduled our flights so that we could spend one day alone together to vet our new feelings.

We shared 24 precious hours, lively conversation, an intimate dinner, and a hotel room. The next afternoon at the airport, I steered the conversation clear of the uncomfortable fact that we lived in different cities. We hugged tightly. There were no words to soften the impact of that moment. *How can I feel so strongly about a man that I just met?*

"I'll call you," he said with a smile, then turned and walked away.

Sitting on the plane before departure, I was struck by a sinking feeling that I might never see Marty again. *Is this all just a beautiful ending to my expedition? Or is this the beginning of something awesome?*

I closed my eyes and remembered being in Marty's presence, the ease of our conversation, the intense connection made on the mountain by simply moving through nature together. We had met on equal ground doing something we both loved. I wondered if he was the type of man described by essayist and memoirist Anais Nin when she wrote "I, with a deeper instinct, choose a man who compels my strength, who makes enormous demands on me, who does not doubt my courage or my toughness, who does not believe me naïve or innocent, who has the courage to treat me like a woman."

The next morning, I called Mom and said, "I met someone. I think I'm in love."

Six weeks later, Marty quit the police officer job he had treasured for eleven years. He sold most of his belongings and moved into my West Seattle home, trading warm weather and bad-guy hunting for cold rain, job searching, and a new life with me. He followed his heart and never looked back.

Three months later, we strolled into a restaurant near the waterfront in downtown Seattle. Marty, in a charcoal gray suit, held hands with me, in a timeless black velvet dress. At our table in the corner, a dozen red roses rested next to an open bottle of champagne. Midway through our fancy French dinner, Marty dug into a bag he'd brought with him and handed me the November issue of *Climbing Magazine*.

"What is this?" I said.

"Open it and you'll see."

I opened to the page marked with a Post-it note and scanned until I spotted a black-and-white photo of Marty and me taken at base camp on Denali at the end of our expedition, just before we flew off the mountain. Beneath it were these words:

> *When my expedition to the summit of Denali began, I never dreamed I would meet the person I would want to spend the rest of my life with. Chris, you have touched my heart, soul, my very being. You are my best friend and I can imagine no greater gift than for you to be my wife. I will love you forever, Chris Keenan. Will you marry me?*

One year after meeting on Denali, Marty and I stood on the lawn of Hope Island Inn in La Conner before our family and close friends. As the sun reflected off the Puget Sound, we declared our love for each other and promised to share a life of adventure.

TWELVE YEARS LATER, at midlife, Marty and I were at a stage when people typically set aside dreams of major adventures for the more serious pursuits of building careers and families. Marty was the director of international facilities and real estate at F5 Networks, a technology company in Seattle, where he had worked for eleven years, and I co-owned an innovation consulting business with my business partner of sixteen years, Michelle. Our son, Keenan, was the center of our lives, but to us, adventure wasn't mutually exclusive from working and raising him.

One night as Marty and I lay in bed reading, I closed my book, turned to him, and said, "If we decide to go to the South Pole, maybe we should wait until Keenan is in college."

"I know . . . leaving him now would be so hard."

"Maybe *too* hard. I'm not even sure I *could* leave him; just the thought makes me feel nervous, and selfish."

"Selfish?" said Marty as he leaned in toward me. "Maybe we are being selfish, but if we wait eight years, I think we may miss our chance."

We were in our late forties, and our bodies were starting to show wear from past adventures—especially Marty's knees. He'd endured a meniscus tear, surgery, and the occasional shooting pain of bone-on-bone while running down a rocky trail—each jolt a humbling reminder that while others sometimes labeled him as superhuman, he was a mere mortal pushing his aging body to the edge. To cope, he lubricated his knee joints with an injection of wonder potion called Euflexxa from the doctor every nine months or so. Though we were in top physical shape, both of us could be one injury away from the sidelines.

"A lot could happen in eight years," I said. "Dad was just fifty when he had the quadruple bypass." I also thought of my sister-in-law, Bev, sixty years old and suffering from stage-four breast cancer.

"I guess a serious illness could strike. Luckily, we're really healthy," said Marty.

Besides our health, we knew the health of Antarctica could change drastically in eight years. The tourism industry had recently discovered the continent and begun attracting those willing to pay a bundle to fly in a small plane directly to the geographic South Pole, take a few photos, and then dash off to the Antarctic coast to camp with penguins. Then there was the possibility that global warming might melt the mammoth ice cap covering the continent that we wanted to travel across. If we waited, the pristine, wild, frozen landscape of Antarctica might change forever.

"Still, leaving Keenan is such a big hurdle," I said with

tightened eyes. As I looked out the window at the glow of the moon, I felt the tension between the responsibility of parenthood and the possibility of adventure.

I thought back to how much Keenan had matured during the past five years of summer vacations paddling the waters of the Broken Island Group near Canada's Vancouver Island. I smiled remembering the trip we'd recently taken.

"Fish on!" Marty had yelled, gripping his reel tight while trying to keep the double kayak stable. "Keenan, get the net."

Sitting in the front seat of the wooden kayak we'd built from a kit, Keenan reached forward, pulled the green net out from under the bungee cord, then held it up triumphantly.

"Feels like a big angry one. We're having rockfish for dinner tonight," said Marty.

As Marty wrestled the fish on the line, Keenan hung the net low near the water, patiently waiting, while I stowed my fishing pole and paddled my single kayak next to the double to raft up and stabilize it so Marty could focus on the fish.

"Here he comes," said Marty as the fish's head broke the surface of the water.

It flopped around madly while Keenan tried to scoop the net under it before it could wiggle off the hook. After one miss, Keenan shifted higher in his seat, stretched his arm out again, and said, "I got him." Marty put down his pole as Keenan held on to the flopping fish and yelled, "Dad, it's going crazy. Take it."

Marty grabbed the net, removed the hook from its mouth, and dropped the fish into a shallow bucket held between his legs. Then came the whack from the big stick Marty used to put the fish to sleep for good.

Back on the shore of Clark Island, we got to work preparing our feast. Keenan stood close, like an intern watching a surgeon, as Marty talked through the cleaning process.

"Can I touch his eye?" said Keenan.

"Sure . . . hey . . . here's his stomach. Let's cut it open and see what he's been eating."

Out popped a small quarter-sized crab and other nondescript slimy green substances. Keenan held the contents in his hands, examining them closely to see if he could identify anything else.

We gathered wood and built a fire, and Keenan waded in the tide pools, flipping over rocks and collecting hermit crabs in his orange plastic bowl as part of his temporary sea aquarium, touching the yellow and pink sea anemone along the way to see them contract and close tight.

As the flame died down and the coals were hot and ready for cooking, I said to Marty, "I love taking Keenan on multiday adventures like this, away from the modern world."

"Me too."

"And exposing him to new experiences." I had come to believe that the joy in life comes from an openness to adventure—having an adventurous mindset.

Over those years of vacationing in the Broken Group Islands, Keenan had grown from a somewhat timid kayaking passenger to a full-on paddling partner. While he used to avoid eating fish, he now loved any fish we caught; and in the dark of night, he was no longer scared to take a flashlight and go to the bathroom by himself.

He was learning firsthand what I'd learned over and over—that adventure expands who you are. Adventure helps us step out of the ordinary to realize the extraordinary qualities that we all possess. Since a polar expedition could do this for me, I began warming to the idea.

A FEW WEEKS after our first conversation about going south, Marty and I topped out at 4,167 feet on Mount Si—the trailhead for which is just a mile from our front door. Below, I could see the valley where our town lay alongside the South Fork of the Snoqualmie River. Out in the distance, the glacier-covered peak of Mount Rainier sparkled in the sunlight against the powder-blue sky. We'd set out at dawn to avoid crowds; Mount Si is hiked each year by upwards of a hundred thousand people looking for a challenge due to its rugged trails, 3,000 feet of elevation gain, and proximity to Seattle.

As we turned to run back down the trail, Marty said, "When it comes to Antarctica, we don't know what we don't know."

"Well," I panted, running down the next switchback. "Between Denali, your climb of Aconcagua, and Mount Rainier, we know what it takes to climb in extreme conditions."

"For sure," said Marty. "And with all the ultramarathons that we've run, we know how to use our mental strength to push through."

I took a sip from my water bottle. "I bet skiing for hundreds of miles through Antarctica would use all of those skills, and more." We passed a group of day hikers on their way up the trail. "I wonder if there are any books that tell you how to ski to the South Pole?"

"I'd like to start researching to get a better sense of what it might take," said Marty.

I heard the question in his statement: Was I willing to seriously consider this trip? We hadn't yet brought it up with Keenan.

"Let's do it—dive into more of the details," I said.

During the next few months of winter, we got to work reading books about polar expeditions. As I waited to pick up Keenan from elementary school, I sped through *Race to the Pole* in awe of the story of Norwegian Roald Amundsen, who became the first in history to stand on the geographic South Pole, on December 14, 1911. Thirty-seven days later, British explorer Robert Falcon Scott, who had competed against Amundsen for this honor, reached the Pole and found the Norwegian flag flapping in the wind. He and his team struggled to return to their ship carrying the added weight of defeat and national disgrace. With physical and mental conditions in steady decline, two of Scott's men died. Soon overwhelmed by cold, hunger, and heartbreak, Scott and his two remaining teammates starved to death inside their tent just 13 miles from their food depot.

Once Marty finished our copy of *Endurance: Shackleton's Incredible Voyage*—the epic 1914 story of Sir Ernest Shackleton's expedition that intended to cross the Antarctic continent from one coast to the other—I spent lunch breaks reading the book in our front yard, feeling the bitter cold of the winter pack ice, though it was spring in the Northwest. I laughed when I read Shackleton allegedly had recruited teammates by running an ad that said: "Men wanted: For hazardous journey. Small wages, bitter cold, long months of complete darkness, constant danger, safe return doubtful. Honour and recognition in case of success." I was swept away on one of the most incredible adventure stories of all time. After they sailed to Antarctica, the pressure of the winter pack ice trapped and then slowly crushed Shackleton's ship. With no chance of rescue, a team of 28 set sail in ill-equipped lifeboats and, after a harrowing ordeal, landed on Elephant Island. Next, a team of six men, including Shackelton, took one lifeboat in search of help. After surviving hair-raising seas and painful frostbite, they hiked across massive snowcapped mountains wearing only threadbare clothes. The entire team miraculously survived the two-year ordeal—and the story left me inspired by Shackleton's tremendous leadership.

As spring transitioned to a hot and dry summer, and our weekends filled with day hikes with Keenan in the Cascade Mountains, we leapt forward in time to modern stories like *Crossing Antarctica*, about Will Steger's 3,700-mile journey on foot across Antarctica in 1990; *No Horizon Is So Far*, an inspiring crossing of Antarctica by ski and kite in 2001 by Liv Arnesen and Ann Bancroft; and *Call of the White*, the story of Felicity Aston leading six women to the South Pole in 2009. I cleared space for our growing polar library and gained insight from those who went before us. One thing seemed clear—Antarctica remained a remote, harsh, and unforgiving place a hundred years after Amundsen had first arrived at the geographic South Pole. Of all the places we could journey in the world, Antarctica was unique in its remoteness and otherworldliness—and in my mind, provided an opportunity to experience what traveling to another planet might feel like.

I also noticed that polar explorers seemed to possess common traits of courage, stamina, technical skill, a high level of strength and fitness, and commitment to years of meticulous pre-trip planning and training. But some teams with vast polar experience who fit this profile failed to reach the Pole because of team dynamics. Extreme physical and mental challenges could cripple expeditions. Months of struggling to survive harsh conditions and living in close quarters could wear relationships thin as teammates placed blame for a slow pace or bristled at the sound of each other's voices. I tucked this information into the corner of my married brain, wondering if our team of two would fare differently. We had been trapped for days at a time at camps high on Denali in extreme cold and high-wind conditions, but the camps had been full of other climbers. In Antarctica, it would be just the two of us in a tent, and no one else for hundreds of miles around us.

Though we could hire a guide to lead us to the Pole, we were hoping to test our own skills, make our own decisions, choose our own direction—ultimately realize success or failure on our own terms. We wanted to journey in the true spirit of polar expeditions, like the early explorers, who relied on skill and self-sufficiency to venture where no others had before. It would be like progressing from medical student to surgeon. After years of medical training and supervised hands-on surgical experience, one day you pick up the scalpel and *you* decide how to proceed—the patient's life completely in *your* hands. When it comes to acquiring experience in the outdoors, you travel with mentors and learn new skills—and decades later find yourself standing on a mountain of knowledge built one experience at a time. You are ready to become your own guide. Your life in your own hands.

CHAPTER 2:

ONE-HUNDRED-MILE MINDSET

"This is it," declared Marty, staring at his computer screen. "What?" I looked up from the photos I was sorting of our recent honeymoon in Zimbabwe.

He had stumbled upon a description of a 100-mile trail race called the Western States 100-Mile Endurance Run that started in Squaw Valley and ended in Auburn, California. It was like the Boston Marathon of 100-mile races, attracting top runners and covering remote terrain in the Sierra Nevada. The 100-mile race was the pinnacle of ultrarunning, a sport in which runners compete in distances beyond marathon length, typically 50 kilometer (31 miles), 50 miles, 100 kilometer (61 miles), or 100 miles. Marty had begun running when he was deployed on a guided-missile cruiser in the Persian Gulf, during the Iran-Iraq War in the eighties. He ran laps around the perimeter of the ship, seven laps to a mile, and pedaled a stationary bike that lived in a stuffy utility closet. On a whim and a personal dare, he ran his first Honolulu Marathon with little training, and within a year brought his marathon time down to 3:15. Running was a key motivator for him.

"I'm going to enter a hundred-mile race," said Marty with a playful smile.

Ten months later, in June 2000, Marty toed the line for the Western States. At 5:00 a.m., he raced into the morning and up the first of many mountain passes. He fell into a pace he thought he could hold for 24 hours—which seemed like an impossibly long time to me. As the sun rose high in the sky, the scent of sagebrush filled the air. The first 40 miles of the race went smoothly for Marty—which sounds crazy since most people will never even walk 40 miles straight. Then the miles began to take a toll.

As he ran into the aid station at mile 45, one of many refueling stops placed every 10 miles or so along the racecourse, I rushed over and asked, "How are you doing?"

"It's so hot. I don't know if I'm eating or drinking enough," said Marty as he slumped over with hands on knees.

"Have you taken enough salt tablets?" We had just learned about salt tablets, used to keep the body's electrolytes in balance, at the race briefing the night before.

"I don't know," he said as he stuffed a bite of a peanut butter and jelly sandwich in his mouth. "My legs are killing me."

I wondered how he would make another 55 miles on a tough mountain trail that gained 17,000 feet in its entirety. After all, the longest distance he'd run before the race was 50 miles on a pancake-flat course.

As his only support crew, I felt clueless as I drove my rental car from aid station to aid station. Most crews, made up of friends and family, traveled in packs between aid stations, enjoying conversation and company as they ferried around extra clothing, first aid, and runners' favorite snacks—plus acted as cheerleaders. I sat alone in silence, sitting in the dirt among the ants because I wasn't equipped with a chair or blanket like everyone else. I felt completely inadequate, like an outsider crashing a reunion of old friends.

After hours of waiting, I spotted Marty coming down the trail into the Michigan Bluff aid station at mile 55.7. He was shuffling along at a slow pace with his head down and face strained; it appeared his 24-hour goal was slipping away.

"I feel nauseous," he murmured. "I just threw up a few miles back."

"Want some Tums?" I glanced at my watch. He'd been running in the heat for 14 hours.

"How much time until cutoff?" he asked. Runners must pass through certain aid stations by certain cutoff times in order to continue the race.

"You are ninety minutes ahead of cutoff." This didn't give him much cushion.

Marty limped out of the aid station, like an injured animal on the African plains waiting for the inevitable doom to strike.

While I waited for Marty at the next aid station—Foresthill at mile 62—the crowd burst into cheers as they caught a glimpse of a tall, wiry guy with curly brown hair and a steely look of determination. He appeared to be in first place. His crew ran next to him, handed him a thick green drink, a giant burrito, and a full bottle of water—and he was off in less than 30 seconds. I later learned the guy was Scott Jurek, the iconic ultrarunner on his way to his second Western States victory. Back then he had yet to win seven Western States in a row, or star in the national best seller, *Born to Run*, by Christopher McDougall, or write his own best-selling memoir, *Eat and Run*. I didn't know at the time that he lived in Seattle and had just started an ultrarunning coaching business, and I couldn't have anticipated the impact he'd soon have on our lives.

When Marty arrived, the sun hung low in the sky. He grabbed watermelon from the aid station table, and I refilled his water bottles with an electrolyte drink.

I told him, "I'm going to start pacing you now instead of at mile eighty." I was hoping to help him make the next cutoff time and keep him in the race. I'd run a full marathon a year earlier, and according to race rules I could have paced him for the last 40 miles of the race, but at the time felt I was trained enough to run only about 20 miles with him. My role would be to motivate him, help ensure he stayed on course, tell silly stories, and generally keep him company through the night and into the morning. Marty nodded in agreement.

I threw on my headlamp and a backpack full of Marty's emergency clothes, and together we ran through the darkness toward the trail that gradually descended 16 miles to the American River. We passed groups of cheering fans, clusters of racers resting in chairs, and a handful of runners lying on the ground getting patched up before they headed back into the night. As the intense heat of the day gave way to a more tolerable temperature, I remembered what I had overheard someone say to a runner, "Things get better when the sun goes down."

As I ran behind Marty, I tried to bolster his spirits with an occasional "Good job" and "Nice work."

"Uh-huh," he grunted in exhaustion.

After a while, I took the lead so Marty could mindlessly follow. I gradually increased my pace, trying to pull him along and put more cushion between us and the cutoff time. The sound of the rushing river grew louder with each passing hour. Finally, huge spotlights revealed the edge of the river and the route that went right through it. After pausing to look at the rushing water, we plunged in, holding tight to the rope stretched across. The strength of the current threatened to take our tired bodies down.

Marty yelled an excited "Oh yeah" when the cold water jolted him awake and invigorated his weary legs.

Once on the other side, he changed into dry shoes and socks that I'd been carrying in my backpack. Blister prevention.

"You can do this," I said, then I kissed Marty goodbye.

"Thanks."

"You're now three hours ahead of cutoff. I love you. Go!"

I watched Marty run down the trail and into the darkness. He still had 20 miles to go, and I knew my body wasn't trained to take him all the way to the finish line.

Shivering in my damp clothes, I pondered how to get myself to the Highway 49 aid station at mile 93 to connect back with Marty. I had left our rental car back at mile 62. I rocked back and forth with my arms wrapped around my knees to try to keep warm. Two hours later, I hitched a ride with another crew. Just after sunrise, Marty appeared with bloodshot eyes and a forced smile at the last aid station.

"My legs are completely spent, and my feet are killing me," said Marty.

"Can I get you anything?"

"No. I can't run anymore. I think I have enough time to walk the last seven miles."

Since he'd be going slowly, I decided to accompany him to the finish line to make sure he didn't fall asleep or fall over on the final stretch. Finally, we entered the track at Placer High School in Auburn, where the race ended, and completed the last quarter mile. Marty crossed the finish line in 29:09, staggered 20 yards further, then lay down on the track and instantly fell asleep.

Despite setbacks and struggles, Marty had found a way to finish his first 100-mile race. I had witnessed again and again how he kept digging deep, resisting the voice in his head that screamed, *Why am I doing this anyway? Why don't I just stop and end the pain?* I had witnessed how important a support team was for him to ultimately cross the finish line.

My eyes were opened to an incredibly raw and real and rare experience.

OVER THE NEXT few months, I couldn't stop thinking about our time at Western States. *Do I have what it takes to run 100 miles?* I wondered. That would be nearly four times the longest race distance I'd run so far. *Can I train my mind and body to suffer through the hard times? Can I become an endurance athlete?* I wanted to find out. The hair on my neck stood up with excitement.

Just when I was ready to dive deep into the belly of the ultrarunning beast, deep in my own belly, a baby began to grow. My life took a detour to focus my energy on my pregnancy instead. While Marty continued racing ahead and competed in the Marathon des Sables, a 155-mile stage race through the Sahara Desert in Morocco, I power walked my way through the next nine months, hoping I'd be able to catch up with him later.

Parenthood arrived with gusto. My new norm became pureed peas drying on the kitchen floor and a half-edited report beckoning from my home office. Instead of waking to the sound of my alarm clock, a baby's cry jolted me multiple times a night. I wondered: *How do people do it?* Be parents. Both work. Both run. Both sleep.

It took all of me.

Shortly after Keenan was born, I strapped him into a new running stroller and took to the streets in search of my pre-pregnancy strength and stamina. As we got accustomed to the beautiful chaos of parenthood, running added a slice of sanity, a way to do a little something for myself each day. I'd return from a run feeling renewed, alive, and mindful—at least until the endorphins wore off. While it wasn't my time to tackle a 100-mile race, I was consumed by the question of how far I could go. I could inch my way toward the possibility by simply lacing up my shoes and running out the door every day. I could still dream big by setting smaller goals for now. Maybe as I grew as a parent, I could grow as an ultrarunner.

Five months later, I toed the line of the Mount Si 50-Mile Relay race with Marty and two others as teammates. I liked the sound of it: *Mount Si Relay Mama.* I was slotted to run three segments, each 5 miles. After my first segment, I dashed off to the privacy of the back seat of my Ford Explorer and pumped my breasts free of milk. After my second segment, I did the same.

As I approached the end of my third segment, my teammate who was supposed to run the last leg of the race wasn't at the exchange.

"Have you seen anyone from my team?" I asked the race attendant.

"Your husband told me your last runner hurt his foot and had to drop out. He and your son are waiting for you at the finish line."

Crap. Suddenly I was staring down 4 additional miles to get my team to the finish line. My body felt tired and weak, and my boobs threatened to burst. Like a child resisting medicine, I begrudgingly marshaled onward.

A half mile down the trail, I found myself running in stride with another woman. I asked, "How's your race going?"

"Great, how about you?"

Since she seemed genuinely interested, I said, "Well, I hadn't planned for these last four miles. My body is rebelling."

After we chatted for a while, I said, "Feel free to run ahead." I sensed she had much more left in her tank and had slowed down to keep me company.

She shook her head. "I love the fact that you're running this race only five months after your son was born. You inspire me."

We happily ran side by side until we crossed the finish line together.

After the race, I felt hopeful that I could juggle being a breastfeeding mom and a runner and a business owner all at once. It was the beginning of a lifelong balancing act.

TIME PASSED, KEENAN began to toddle, and Marty and I got wise to the ways of ultrarunning and 100-mile races. We read books, talked to experienced ultrarunners, and began training with Scott Jurek, the guy I had seen running at Western States. Scott revealed his secrets of workouts, nutrition, and hydration. Tempo running, speed workouts, and back-to-back 6- to 10-hour runs, two days in a row, became regular fare on our training menu. At our house, running became a shared hobby, daily practice, and weekly religion.

Running through the forest, I chased the possibility of peace and clarity that comes with moving through the wild. On good days, the wind kissed me hello as my body warmed to the trail. The air cleansed my mind, sweat christened my body, the pulse of the earth beat inside me. Leaving the heaviness of life behind, I floated weightless over rocks and roots while the trees stood witness to my hard work. My spirit connected to everything.

During our monthly coaching sessions with Scott, we plotted our training using periodization methods, making sure we peaked for major races—at that time 50-milers for me and 100-milers for Marty. Based on Scott's recommendation, we completed a VO2 max test, a measure of aerobic capacity. Heart rate monitors helped us train in specific zones to maximize workouts. A naturopathic doctor helped us dial in nutrition and monitor important levels of iron and ferritin (iron stores), vitamin D, and more. We fueled our bodies with a primarily plant-based diet. We frequently plunged our legs into a bath of ice, suffering through the cold to help muscles recover after long runs. After two years of Scott's coaching, we had improved all aspects of our running. I had gained confidence to put myself through the big test.

I SCANNED THE scene as I waited to line up for the start of the race. The sweet smell of summer in the Northwest mixed with the scent of fresh pancakes hot off the griddle. The Cascade Crest 100 started and finished at the rural fire station in Easton, Washington, and the volunteer firefighters treated runners to a prerace pancake breakfast. After we finished eating, a volunteer asked if Keenan would like to take a quick ride in the fire truck. He placed an adult-sized firefighter helmet on Keenan's four-year-old head; Keenan looked like he'd either explode with excitement or crumble from the weight of the hat. Keenan, Marty, and I climbed into the fire engine and rode through town like we were in our own private parade. Afterward, I mingled with my running friends, chatting about their latest races and goals for the day. Other runners sat quietly staring off into space, as if contemplating the seriousness of the long day and night ahead.

The Cascade Crest 100 captured the true spirit of ultra-running with its sweeping views, 21,000 feet of elevation gain, one-mile downhill bushwhack with rope support, two-mile run through the complete darkness of an old railroad tunnel, and super tough trails on the second half of the course. It was hard, it was beautiful, and it promised to test me to my limits.

Under a sunny blue sky, the group of 120 runners and their support teams gathered in a big circle outside the fire station. My sixteen-year-old niece, Jessie, stepped into the middle of the circle, and the national anthem flowed out of her with the power and ease of a mighty river.

Cheers erupted from the crowd as runners packed into a tight cluster behind the starting line. The clock counted down the last five minutes. I fiddled with the straps on my running vest one last time and thought back to what it had taken to get to this moment: four hard years of perseverance, dedication, and training; weekends of rising early and missing breakfast and cartoons with Keenan; Saturdays running up and down Mount Si—twice—for a total of 16 miles and 8,000 feet of gain; Sundays dragging my tired body up the Twelve Summits of Tiger Mountain, a 33-mile out-and-back course; vacations carefully scheduled around yearly races. After all that effort, only minutes away from the start, I still wondered: *Have I trained hard enough to run 100 miles?*

I glanced at the pack of fans lining the start of the course and saw Keenan sandwiched between Grandma Vicki and Grandpa Tom, holding their hands. They were in town from Ohio to help watch Keenan while Marty and I ran, and to experience a 100-mile event firsthand. Since Keenan was already a veteran of the racing scene, I figured he'd show them the ropes at aid stations.

A gunshot rang out and we were off. After a few miles of gentle terrain, we hit our first big climb. I downshifted into slow-and-steady mode, avoiding getting swept up in the stream of enthusiastic runners racing ahead. I picked a pace that I knew from training I could keep for a long time. I focused on eating and drinking. Time melted away.

When I ran through the aid station at mile 30, someone said, "Go, Chris. Marty is only ten minutes ahead of you." Adrenaline shot through me. *Was I actually on pace with Marty?*

By mile 41, fatigue overwhelmed me. As I ran into Meadow Mountain aid station, I saw Keenan wearing a dirt-covered T-shirt and mischievous grin. He ran up and hugged my sweat-streaked, dusty legs while I grabbed a few pierogies (delicious Eastern European dumplings) and refilled my water bottles. I left the aid station with a shot of Keenan-induced energy coursing through my veins—and Keenan and crew drove 45 minutes back home to North Bend to grab a little sleep. His unbridled enthusiasm reminded me to push pain out of my mind and focus on the simple pleasure of running through the lush green forest. With each step, I worked to stay present and positive, breathing in the freshness of damp air mixed with mossy pine.

Moving alone through the darkness, with my headlamp lighting the way, I felt like my body was starting to betray me. *Just keep moving. You can do it. Mind over body.* I continued riding waves of fatigue followed by bursts of energy. Runners occasionally snuck up on me in the darkness and passed by as I continued at a sleepy pace.

At midnight, I pulled into the Hyak aid station at mile 53, where my neighbors Laura, Lori, and Jill yelled in unison, "Go, Chris! Great job!" then offered me a buffet of grilled cheese, French toast, and homemade chocolate chip cookies (my favorite). After stuffing my face, I turned to leave, and one of them said jokingly, "You stink!"

After 68 miles, further than I had ever run, I was joined by Jamie, Marty's running friend from work, who would pace me through the rest of the night and into the next day.

Together we entered the Trail from Hell, a five-mile section that I knew from training runs was full of downed trees and gnarly roots and rocks. Right away we lost the trail and fumbled around searching for race markers. Frustration filled the space between each breath. Back on the trail, the constant straddling and jumping over huge downed trees amplified the devastated feeling in my legs. I stumbled along and battled to keep my mind on task. At one point, I stopped and stared down with my headlamp at a steep rocky section of trail, wondering if my legs would crumble when I scrambled down.

Snapping me out of my trance, Jamie said, "Put your foot here," as she pointed to a spot on the rock.

I felt like a toddler trying to stay upright through a sleepless night.

Thrilled to complete that section, I began marching up a long, grinding hill. As the first sign of sunlight peeked over the mountain, a spark of hope surged through my legs. The terrain eased; I picked up the pace. But after an hour, my legs fizzled and I felt exhausted and nauseous—not surprising after running for 20 hours straight.

I struggled on despite Jamie's effort to distract me with interesting stories and boost my morale with the occasional "Great job" and "Way to work." My mind was operating like a backup generator after a power outage; it supplied energy only to vital places. Talking wasn't essential. I lacked the focus to process and respond. Instead of carrying on a conversation with Jamie, I had one with myself. *Embrace the lows. Just keep moving forward. You can do this.*

Then I remembered what another experienced ultrarunner had said, "Finishing a 100-mile race is a mental game." I'd prepared my mind to override its primal reaction to pain and intense desire to stop. I had come to terms with the reality that running 100 miles was going to hurt. Time to kick in my 100-mile mindset.

After hours of relentless tough climbs and slow progress, I finally reached mile 90. While I usually love the fun and freedom of ripping downhill—surrendering my body to gravity—this time, I dreaded it. My aching feet and shattered quads begged for mercy with each step of the rocky five-mile stretch.

Approaching the last aid station at mile 95, I yelled "Woohoo" to fire up my supporters, who'd likely been waiting for hours. Amidst all the clapping and ringing of cowbells, Keenan ran up and hugged my legs again. Grandma Vicki, Grandpa Tom, my sister Sue, and Susan (my Denali climbing friend), along with her husband, Danny, and daughter, Hannah, jumped up and down as they cheered. Marty, who'd completed the race a few hours earlier, had grabbed a ride from the finish line to catch a glimpse of me before I finished.

"How are you doing, hon?" he said as he took my empty water bottle out of my hand to fill it.

I stared into his eyes, telling him without words that I could hardly go on. I gulped down a cold electrolyte drink and held back hot tears percolating just below the surface—tears that told the story of all the physical and mental pain I'd pushed myself through again and again to get there.

Marty handed me a full water bottle and a piece of watermelon and said, "You're doing awesome, hot baby. See you at the finish line. I love you."

As I shuffled out of the aid station, willing my stiff legs to work again, I looked back to see Marty and Keenan holding hands, and Keenan waving and smiling at me.

My tank was on empty and I still had 5 miles to go—miles that seemed daunting. I was desperate to stop beating up my body. I struggled to hold back a mountain of emotion—a toxic concoction of agony and anticipation of the end. Jamie started joking to lighten the mood, but her enthusiasm couldn't penetrate my bubble. I put my head down. *Keep moving.* Minutes dragged on like hours.

Finally, off in the distance, giant arches came into view. As I crossed the finish line, my dusty, sweaty body fell into Marty's arms. I held Keenan's hand tightly in mine. After running for more than 28 hours, I'd completed what years ago seemed impossible to me, and the immensity of my own potential—of *human* potential—shocked me. I felt suspended in the perfect moment.

AFTER THE PAIN and suffering faded, what remained was the thrill of the race. I scheduled my next 100-mile race and set new goals, imagining that next time I would be smarter, faster, better.

Over the next seven years, I completed six more 100-mile races, and even once took second place at the Arkansas Traveller 100. By then, Marty had crossed the finish line of eleven 100-mile races and proudly taken first place at the Boulder 100. While delighted to improve our rankings, we ultimately competed against ourselves in tough races that were at once extraordinary and dreadful, friend-filled and lonely. In this sport full of unknowns, I thrived on unsavory conditions to endure and unexpected challenges to overcome. I remember being so cold after running in driving rain for 24 hours that I wore two trash bags for the last 10 miles to avoid hypothermia. I remember being so hot running through stifling summer heat that I sat down in every trickle of a stream I crossed in hopes of reducing my core temperature. I remember the 10-mile stretch of trail littered with over a hundred trees downed after a windstorm—I counted them as I climbed over each one. I remember startling a black bear foraging for wild blueberries and freezing myself in place until he slowly padded away through the thick brush. I remember scooting on my butt on an eight-inch-wide log across a raging river in the dark at 3:00 a.m., afraid I might lose my balance and fall in if I tried walking across. I remember being out of water for hours in sweltering sun and miraculously stumbling upon a full bottle of water left by a trail angel. I remember lying down on a dusty trail at 2:00 a.m. to settle my stomach and gazing up at the sparkling clear night sky.

While running consumed much of our time, our top priority was always Keenan. On most weekends, one of us shared one-on-one time with him while the other rose at dawn, ran through the forest for hours, and returned home for a family lunch. About once a month, Marty and I went on a long run together while my sister Sue watched Keenan or he played over at a friend's house. Of course, if Keenan were sick, we'd drop our plans in order to spend the day caring for him. On weekends when we didn't take long runs, we'd share family hikes in the forest or card games by the fireplace. And Marty and I always made time to attend Keenan's after-school events, band concerts, or basketball games together.

Still, ultrarunning was always part of our schedule. The longer I stayed in the sport, the more I learned about myself and the deeper connection I felt to Marty, my running friends, and the wild environments I moved through. The trails were where Marty and I cemented our bond as a united team, defining what it meant to be *the Fagans*. The trails were where Marty and I learned to master a 100-mile mindset—knowing how to persevere with physical and mental discipline, to ride the highs and dig ourselves out of the lows, to keep moving forward when all we wanted to do was stop, to celebrate life as we moved through nature. And the trails were where we learned the delicate balance of being adventurers and parents—and to model for Keenan what it meant to follow uncommon dreams.

The trails were also where we unknowingly prepared our minds and bodies for the harsh conditions of Antarctica.

CHAPTER 3:

A DARING DECISION

The thing that truly binds Marty and me to our core, that brings us tremendous pride and joy in life, is Keenan. His slender, athletic build, bright-blond hair, and curious blue eyes remind me of a photo of Marty when he was a child. His infectious smile melts my heart. Nothing is more important to us. His happiness is our delight. His pain is our burden. Every day since we first imagined an expedition to the South Pole, I wondered: *Will going to Antarctica somehow hurt Keenan?*

If we decided to go, we'd be away from Keenan for two months—ages in kid time—and we'd miss sharing our Thanksgiving, Christmas, and New Year's traditions with him. Up until then, the longest Marty and I had both been away from Keenan was four days to attend an ultrarunning training camp on Orcas Island. At the time, I had wondered if Keenan felt left behind or less important to us than ultrarunning. Those same feelings were now magnified tenfold. Marty and I would miss Keenan's basketball practices and games; the entire season would be completed while we skied across Antarctica. Would he feel a void when he looked up in the stands and saw everyone else's parents? We'd miss helping him with his nightly homework, pancake Sundays and pizza Fridays, and all the other interactions that make up daily life. Would he feel a loss of belonging, a loss of our love?

'Ihe question of how our expedition would affect Keenan had taken up permanent residence in my mind, causing sleepless nights.

After dinner one night while Keenan worked on homework at his desk in the playroom, I said, "Marty, do you think we'll hurt Keenan by going to the South Pole?"

"What do you mean, hurt him?"

"It's not normal for parents to leave their child for two months."

"Yeah, but our lives aren't ordinary. We've always wanted to be so much more than average—and I think it's good for Keenan to see us take on big goals."

"Sometimes when I think of leaving him, I feel guilty," I said, looking down at the floor.

"Do you love him any less because you want to go to the South Pole?"

"No. But can we do this and still be good parents?"

"I hope so," said Marty. "If anyone can, it's us."

Still the thought lingered: *Is it possible to leave our son for two months and still love him more than anything in this world?*

"HELLO?"

Though Steve was in another hemisphere, in Punta Arenas, Chile, it almost sounded like he was sitting on the other side of my desk in the playroom with us.

"Steve, this is Marty and Chris Fagan," Marty said into the speakerphone.

We had discovered that modern-day polar explorers traveled to Antarctica not by ship, but by plane. Steve was head of operations with Antarctic Logistics and Expeditions (ALE), the only US company that flew commercially to Antarctica. ALE was also a full-service expedition company that supports trips to Antarctica. Private government planes flew scientists to the continent to conduct research—but they didn't allow civilians to hitch rides.

Marty said, "So, Steve, we've read a bit about your planes, but can you tell us more about how you land in Antarctica and how we'd get to the start of our expedition?"

"Sure. ALE charters a large transport aircraft capable of landing on a natural ice runway, and a few twin-engine ski aircraft for remote flights beyond base camp. To support flights to the interior, we pre-place caches of fuel at strategic locations throughout the continent."

I'd read that in recent years, ALE had put together an entirely self-sufficient, staggeringly complex operation in Antarctica that runs from November through January and then closes down for the Antarctic winter while the continent goes into a deep freeze. With no public transportation infrastructure in Antarctica (besides systems created for government scientific bases), all of the equipment, fuel, and food for ALE operations were transported there from South America.

Steve continued, "We maintain a base-camp infrastructure—like a mini pop-up village—with kitchen accommodations, sleeping quarters for staff, bathrooms, communications and meteorological equipment, and heavy machinery for transporting gear and removing snow. A small staff maintains the camp."

"Would we begin and end our expedition at your base camp?" I asked.

"Yes. That's right. It's possible you'll spend a day or two at base camp when you arrive and before you depart as you wait to get a weather window to fly out to your starting point or back to Punta Arenas."

"Steve, as we evaluate the expedition, we need to understand your fees," said Marty.

"Given the logistical challenges and the expense of building and maintaining the infrastructure on the continent, traveling to Antarctica is expensive—there is no way around it." He went on, "For a flight to Antarctica and all of the base-camp support, including rescue if necessary, the cost is fifty-five thousand dollars per person."

Marty and I stared at each other with wide eyes. I wrote down $110,000 in my notes, then, trying not to gasp into the phone receiver, said, "Okay."

Trying to process this giant number, I thought of Everest. A guided climb of Mount Everest would cost $65,000 or more per person. Needless to say, the price tag to adventure to Antarctica would require months of serious consideration.

"So are you guys thinking of going guided or unguided?" asked Steve. "Safety is our top priority, so we carefully vet clients who plan to travel without a guide."

"I think we're interested in unguided—if we're qualified— otherwise we aren't opposed to guided," said Marty.

How would we figure out if we were qualified to travel unguided? Soon after talking to Steve, we found Chicago-based Polar Explorers, a company that not only guides teams to the North Pole, South Pole, and Antarctica's Mount Vinson, but also offers a five-day Polar Shakedown Training Course created for their guided clients. After we explained our potential project to them, they invited Marty and me to join the course. The training would help us assess our overall skills and ability to lead our own self-guided expedition.

A YEAR AFTER Marty first mentioned the possibility of an expedition, I arrived at Diamond Willow Lodge, a rustic getaway in northern Minnesota nestled among spruce drooping with fresh snow. Winter there promises cold, windy conditions— the perfect place for Antarctic training. Marty stayed home on parent duty with Keenan; he would attend a separate training.

As I entered the cabin, the lead guide from Polar Explorers, Keith Heger, stretched his hand out to mine. Standing over six feet tall, dressed in faded khaki Carhartt pants and a blue fleece jacket, he wore an easy smile on his weathered face, looking his part having guided in Antarctica eight times and to the North Pole fifteen times. Keith stood confidently and spoke with a strong voice, as if ready to take control should the situation turn south. He introduced me to his assistant guides, then to a father and son from London scheduled for a ten-day guided trip to the North Pole, and to a retired executive from Florida considering a ten-day guided trip to the South Pole. I stood alone as the one contemplating a forty- to forty-five-day self-guided expedition to the South Pole.

The next morning, Keith outfitted each of us with a harness, sled, boots, and skis. My body pulsed with anticipation as our group prepared to set off on the frozen Boundary Waters—a famed region of wilderness straddling the US-Canada border that hosts canoe trips through a network of lakes during the summer. I strapped on the harness and clipped into the sled, feeling like a dog ready to mush. I skied forward, pulling my sled for the first time while envisioning myself gliding straight into our South Pole dream.

The wide-open white landscape of frozen lake and blowing snow looked arctic-like, but instead of the expected minus-20-degree temperature, we skied along in a balmy 26 degrees above zero. A few miles later, I struggled to keep moving while opening armpit and leg zippers to cool off. I was overdressed and trying to avoid sweating—the enemy in polar environments as sweat can freeze into unwelcome ice clumps inside clothing. Once I found a comfortable pace, time melted away. After six hours of skiing, we stopped as the sky turned orange. We quickly set up tents before the cold curtain of black descended. That night, the temperature dropped to 13 degrees. Frost formed on the inside of my tent and outside of my sleeping bag. Nestled inside, I wondered what Keith thought of my performance so far, hoping my experience and fitness placed me closer to guide than client.

The next four days of training provided a glimpse into life on the ice: the daily routine of packing and dragging a heavy sled, scraping skis against snow and ice, and navigating through low visibility. Each day, I tested gear and fine-tuned my clothing system. My body adapted to the new appendage dragging behind me as I found a rhythm of movement on my skis. Keith mentioned that he could tell I had already mastered my winter outdoor skills—changing clothing layers to match conditions, setting up the tent in snow, managing the stove and melting snow and ice for water, sleeping in cold weather. He assigned me to kitchen duty while he taught the others how to use the stove and shared tips for preventing frostbite.

Back at the lodge on our final night before heading home, Keith took me aside and said, "Chris, I think you have what it takes to safely go with Marty to the South Pole without a guide. Your past experience will be invaluable, especially your ability to endure extreme physical and mental stress."

I almost hugged him, but instead said, "Thanks!"

"I just have one concern. You need to gain some weight. You'll likely lose ten to twenty pounds during your expedition."

Gaining weight for an endurance adventure—that will be a first for me, I thought.

A few months later, Marty flew to remote Longyearbyen, Norway, the world's northernmost town located well above the Arctic Circle. Longyearbyen is a launching point for North Pole expeditions—and an ideal environment to ski across glaciers and frozen fjords in freezing conditions. Because of the high concentration of polar bears, each night the team from Polar Explorers set up a portable trip-wire fence around tents as a barrier of protection against curious intruders. Lucky for us, polar bears don't roam the wild in Antarctica. While the coast is teeming with emperor penguins, Adélie penguins, leopard seals, and sea birds, there are no animals living in the cold, desolate interior of the southern continent. It's even too cold for bacteria to grow.

Marty's training covered much of the same ground as mine—and as he prepared to fly home, Keith said, "I believe you and Chris both have what it takes to expedition to the South Pole. Like I told Chris, you need to gain some weight."

With Keith's endorsement, we'd jumped over a major hurdle in our vetting process. With no guide, now every decision we made before and during our journey would weigh heavily upon us. We would not have the on-the-ground knowledge of a professional. There was no way around the stress of calling our own shots while in Antarctica for the first time. Every mistake was ours to make in a place where there is no room for errors.

ONE DAY THE phone rang in my home office. It was Michelle, my longtime business partner who consulted with Fortune 500 clients with me. After a bit of catching up, Michelle said, "I don't see myself working for our company anymore."

Wow. A chill swept through my body. Change was coming. Scary change.

Admittedly, thoughts of shaking up our business had plagued me for a while. Although business was good, we both felt stuck. After a decade and a half of being in the innovation business, the world had dramatically changed, and I wished for new ways to inspire creative thinking. After a long heartfelt discussion, I hung up the phone.

Gazing out the window at a hydrangea bush bursting with purple blossoms, I thought back to when Michelle and I first met right out of graduate school while working at Leo Burnett advertising agency in Chicago. She had inspired me to ask for (and receive) a leave of absence to travel through New Zealand, Australia, Indonesia, and Thailand. I arrived back in Chicago four months later with a renewed sense of confidence and clarity—and a deep need to live in a place with daily access to the smell and feel of nature. Then I moved to Seattle, and in 1995, at a retreat on Orcas Island, we birthed our company. We landed our first client, Pepsi, before purchasing computers or printing business cards. Despite living on separate sides of the country, in Seattle and New York, we built a thriving business.

Now Michelle seemed so confident in her decision to move away from what we had built together. I felt up in the air—with no clear landing sight.

Soon we worked through the details of shutting down our company while simultaneously trying to preserve our friendship. At times, I struggled to find my identity and purpose separate from our company. *Who am I if not part of this company I've created?* After sixteen years, the company and I had grown intertwined as one.

But it wasn't long before I began wondering if Michelle had actually handed me a gift—the motivation to redefine what success meant in my life. While success had meant tackling challenging goals and helping people and companies become more creative, perhaps there was something more. What would be my significant contribution in my second half of life? And how might I feel even more satisfied?

Big questions.

Deep down, I had always wanted to inspire people, something I seemed to do naturally but had never given my full focus. I ended up launching a new company a year later— SparkFire—that was similar to my previous one, only this time I wanted to focus more on public speaking and training. But my new company had yet to feel very new as I took on some of the same old types of projects. I wondered if my fresh start—in work and life—would begin with traveling to the wide-open space of Antarctica.

SIXTEEN MONTHS AFTER Marty first mentioned the idea of journeying to the South Pole, a complex array of variables— fitness, expedition skills, jobs—came into alignment. We still had to consider Keenan, our finances, and a laundry list of unknowns—but a vision of us standing at the South Pole began to seem possible. And that's when it started becoming real.

Ten miles into a long Sunday run, I stopped on the trail in front of Marty, turned around, looked into his spirited eyes, and said, "There's a lot we still don't know about an expedition to the South Pole, but I think we'll figure it out."

"So you think we should go?"

"Yes!"

Marty leaned over and kissed me, then we ran down the trail with a new shared purpose vibrating through each step.

That night over dinner, I said, "Keenan, you know Dad and I have been doing a lot of research to try to figure out if we should take an expedition to Antarctica. Well, now we believe we have what it takes to go."

Keenan looked down and took a bite of spaghetti.

Marty continued, "To do this, Mom and I will be gone from you for about eight weeks. We still have a lot of planning and details to figure out, and we'll fill you in along the way. Our top priority is to make sure we are safe and that you are safe and comfortable at home."

Keenan looked up and said, "Who is going to watch me when you are in Antarctica?"

"We aren't sure yet . . . probably Aunt Sue and Aunt Jean and other family members too."

Keenan went back to eating and talking about the latest *Lord of the Rings* Lego set he wanted. It would likely take time for the full gravity of what we told him to sink into his eleven-year-old brain. It would for us too. But we believed now was the time, and we were all in—there was no halfway. In my experience, once you are committed, stars align and the world conspires to help you succeed.

WHEN THE IDEA of a South Pole expedition had first come up, I used my friend Leni as a sounding board. Leni and I had met five years earlier at the bus stop waiting for our kids. At that time, Leni noticed I always showed up looking like I had just finished a run (which I had). She peppered me with questions about trail running—the vest I wore to carry my phone and snacks, the water bottle strapped to my hand, the type of trail running shoes I wore.

"Wanna join me on a short run up Little Si sometime?" I asked.

"Sure."

A few miles from our neighborhood, the technical, rocky trail that gains 1,100 feet in 2.5 miles was no match for her fast footwork. Soon Leni and I were running together a few times a week and became fast friends. At the same time, her son, Ryo, and Keenan became friends too.

When our kids were at school or Marty was on parent duty with Keenan—Leni and I logged hundreds of hours running through beautiful lush forest on world-class trails in the foothills of the Cascade Mountains. We ran well past small talk. Our runs were part social hour, part counseling session, and sometimes just pure fun. I learned that Leni had a researcher's mind and was intelligent, intuitive, and insightful. She cared deeply about those in her life and was always ready for adventure. And during those five years, she turned herself into a serious ultrarunner—completing a number of 50-kilometer and 50-mile races.

One day, in the midst of working out trip details for Antarctica, I ran next to Leni on the Snoqualmie Valley Trail. The sun had yet to reach over the trees, and the tall green grass lining the trail was still wet with morning dew. I said, "Now that our South Pole trip is starting to feel real, Marty and I need to figure out how to take off two months from work."

"Since you have your own company, can't you just take off whatever time you want?" Leni's ponytail bounced back and forth to match the rhythm of her stride.

"In theory, yes, but I don't have Michelle as a business partner to cover for me anymore." I felt the gravity of my words lodge in my chest. "I have to shut things down the whole time I'm gone."

Leni looked over at me with her curious brown eyes as we ran side by side. "What about Marty's work?"

"His unused vacation carries over from one year to the next. He's already built up four weeks and should be able to save nine weeks by the time we leave."

We carried on running and talking. I glanced down at my watch; it showed 8 miles. As we headed into our final 2 miles, I said, "You know, I keep wondering how to best support Keenan while we're gone."

"Chris, we'll be here for Keenan—he can come over and play with Ryo while you are gone." The confidence in her voice was comforting. "I'm sure your siblings and other friends will be happy to pitch in and help out."

"It's hard for me to think about leaving him." I paused, feeling the emotions in my words. "It's tough to balance being a parent with heading out on an adventure without him."

"I'm sure it's hard. But I have to believe Keenan will be fine." Leni glanced over at me with a reassuring smile.

I sensed that Leni's friendship would prove to be vitally important to our South Pole expedition.

I SAT ACROSS from Mom and Dad at a cheery café in Hot Springs Village, Arkansas, the retirement community that they had moved to twenty years earlier. I made the trip with the intention of telling my parents face-to-face about our expedition plans.

At eighty years old and five foot five with his shoes on, Dad wore a permanent smile with his comb-over of thinning brown-gray hair. Mom, a year younger and an inch shorter than Dad, had smooth skin framed by dark-brown hair cut short and curled back for volume and height like a modern bouffant style.

Our raspy-voiced waitress had just delivered heaping plates of scrambled eggs, bacon, and toast.

I leaned in, smiled, and said, "I've got some exciting news to share."

"What is it, honey?" Dad asked.

"Marty and I are planning an expedition to Antarctica."

Silence.

I anxiously looked back and forth at Dad and Mom, searching for any hint of understanding. Instead of smiles, I saw bewilderment.

Here I was, a wife and mother in her late forties, sitting in front of her parents looking for approval. I was going to Antarctica with or without their blessing, but the way that I wanted to go was the way that I had always gone—with my parents' unconditional love and support. It mattered to me that they understood. I knew my adventure would likely cause sleepless nights for them, just like when I traveled alone internationally for four months in my late twenties and climbed Denali in my early thirties. They had endured my adventures before, and I hoped they'd find the strength to do that again.

I continued spoon-feeding them a few facts at a time, letting them digest each morsel of new information as they swallowed their scrambled eggs. Granted, most people I talked to didn't have an instant understanding of what it meant to go on an expedition to Antarctica. Most took a while to get their bearings, to determine whether I was talking about the extreme North or extreme South. I wished for a globe, like the one in my bedroom growing up, to use as a visual aid.

After a long pause, Dad said in his eternally optimistic way, "Honey, I think it sounds exciting."

Mom made a half-hearted "uh-huh" noise—either indicating she agreed with Dad or that she'd simply heard what I said—then scooped up eggs with a fork.

Mom didn't make eye contact with me until the conversation shifted away from Antarctica. That wasn't like her. Perhaps age had dulled her ability to disguise her worry when it came to my every-so-often big adventures. Her face looked like she'd taken a bite of exotic food and was deciding whether to swallow or spit.

Maybe Mom thought that if she didn't talk about the expedition, it wasn't real and might disappear with our dirty dishes.

Toward the end of breakfast, Mom said, "Chris, I'm not going to think about Antarctica until your departure date is closer."

Other family members and friends were full of enthusiasm and support with the news. They *seemed* to understand our motivation, *appeared* to trust that we knew what we were doing, didn't *overtly* pass judgment on us as parents.

Then one day I was playing hooky from work with some other moms from Keenan's school. We caught up on each other's lives as we sat outside in my backyard, soaking in the spring sunshine, the smell of fresh-cut grass mixing with the scent of pink azaleas.

When the conversation turned to my future expedition, another mom I saw infrequently said, "I didn't know you were going to Antarctica."

"Yes. Marty and I have been planning it for a while now."

"Really? Hmm. So how long will you be gone?"

"We're not sure. We're estimating about eight to nine weeks, including travel."

"Won't it be dangerous, like Mount Everest? Is it really worth risking your lives?" she asked, pursing her lips.

"Well, there will be some risks, but we're all about safety, and it's much less dangerous than climbing a mountain like Everest."

"Wow. I could never do that to my kids."

Her words cut to my core. What did she mean? Was she implying that she wouldn't want to stress her kids out by leaving or that she wouldn't want to abandon her kids for good? I wanted to shout: *I am a responsible parent! Can't parents follow their dreams?* Instead, I smiled and placed her in the "doesn't get it" category.

Next time, I'd arm myself with stats, load them up, and fire away to combat these types of comments. Based on my research, I discovered that only one explorer had died in Antarctica in the last fifty years. Sure, there would be risks, but we would have contingency plans. It wasn't like we were BASE jumping off a cliff and if our parachute failed, there wasn't any possibility for a plan B.

NEXT THERE WAS PAT.

My brother's tousled brown hair and easy smile reflect his laid-back personality. Growing up, Pat and I had been playmates, and after college—when I moved to Chicago and he headed to Alaska—we regularly kept in touch and made a point of visiting each other beyond family Thanksgiving gatherings at our parents' house. After I climbed Denali, I flew to Homer to recover at his house for a few days by eating ridiculous amounts of steak and salmon that Pat, a chef, made for me. Over the years, marriage and parenthood and running a business had filled my schedule, leaving less time for those special trips. But Pat paid us a visit while we were in the midst of expedition planning.

One morning when he and I were out to breakfast at a local diner, he asked for an update on our progress. After I rattled off the vitals, he asked in an accusatory tone, "So why do you want to go to the South Pole? It's cold, you won't see anything, and it will be really hard. I don't get it."

The sharpness of his tone surprised me.

Pat intimately knew cold and its harsh impact on life. He was the head chef at the Prudhoe Bay Hotel, which housed and fed hundreds of transient oil-field workers in Deadhorse, Alaska, near the Arctic Circle. It was −60 degrees in Deadhorse at the time. Years earlier, he'd worked on the Bering Sea in frigid winter conditions on crab boats—similar to those shown on Discovery Channel's *Deadliest Catch*.

Feeling a bit of a chill in the air from Pat's question, I gave my short answer. "We're going for the adventure. It's one of the last wild frontiers on earth, and we want to experience it before it changes."

Then Pat said, "So who is going to take care of Keenan . . . if you and Marty die?"

Wham! I hadn't seen that stomach punch coming. I struggled to regain my wits. I had thought he was going to ask, "Who is going to care for Keenan . . . *while you are on your expedition*?"

I said, "Keenan's guardians, Leni and Randy, will care for him," then looked away.

End of discussion.

Later that day, as I set off on a trail run, I wondered why Pat had reacted so negatively. As a forty-five-year-old single guy, our expedition threatened what was most precious to him—family. If lost to Antarctica, I would disrupt the balance of our family. The twenty-two members (our parents, five siblings, nieces, nephews, great nephews) sprinkled around the country gave Pat's life purpose. I imagined he just couldn't reconcile how it could be worth the risk.

Despite our conversation, I still believed an adventure to the South Pole would be life-giving—not life-taking.

ONE NIGHT JUST a few months after we had committed to the expedition, as Keenan lay in bed before we went through our regular good-night ritual, I checked in with him. "What do you think about Dad and me going on an expedition to Antarctica?"

He turned his head away, fighting back tears, and mumbled into his pillow, "Mom, I don't want you to go."

I curled up next to Keenan in bed, enveloping him in a hug. Fighting back tears of my own, I whispered into his ear, "Dad and I love you so much. We would never do anything to hurt you."

He didn't respond.

"As I mentioned before, we're going to make sure that all of us—you, me, and Dad—are safe."

"I will miss you too much," he said.

"We'll be leaving for the trip in a year. You are eleven now. That won't be until you're twelve. I'll make sure I keep checking in with you to see how you're feeling about it. Okay?"

"Uh-huh."

I held Keenan close as he drifted off to sleep.

WORD WAS SPREADING about our expedition. A friend of ours told their friend, an employee at KING 5's *Evening Maga-zine*, about our plans. I was most concerned about what people close to us thought about our plans, but still, when *Evening Magazine* asked to interview us, I sensed the heart of our expedition would be put to the test.

On the day of filming, Michael King and his cameraman walked into our family room carrying two giant lights, a sturdy tripod, an oversized camera, and an assortment of cables. The cameraman placed two kitchen chairs side by side facing out from the fireplace. He clipped a wireless microphone on my brown scoop-neck shirt, then said, "Say a few words for me." As he fiddled with his equipment, I wondered: *Will we be portrayed as extreme adventurers?*

Next, Marty threaded the cord of the microphone down his navy zip-neck Patagonia shirt and shifted in his chair. While Michael and the cameraman completed final sound checks, Marty and I looked at each other and smiled.

Michael began the segment by asking, "So who came up with this idea?"

"I planted the seed, and then we spent over a year researching before we committed," said Marty.

"What has been the toughest part of your preparations?"

"There are so many details to figure out . . . food, gear, safety, training," Marty said.

Midway through the interview, we reached the heart of the matter. "What about your son, Keenan?" Michael asked. He was a father himself. "How can you leave him to go on this expedition?"

So there it was, right out in the open for thousands of viewers to judge whether or not we were good parents. How do you communicate your personal beliefs about life, marriage, and parenthood, ideas you've sculpted into the shape of your life for decades, in a few sound bites?

I took a deep breath and calmly answered. "I know there are people who can easily pass judgment on us, saying, 'This expedition is so selfish,' and 'You're being irresponsible,' and 'Why are you doing that?' We have an obligation to our son to be who we are, to be role models for him, and to show him how to live a life you love."

Yes, there was risk, but we would focus on minimizing it. Work with polar mentors to ensure our planning was sound and gear top-notch. Craft contingency plans to handle the worst possible scenarios associated with extreme cold and harsh weather. Build in redundancy. Avoid drama. Be methodical, organized, detailed. Train like crazy—a process that at the time we didn't know would threaten our very identities.

CHAPTER 4:

TRAINING WITH TIRES

"Go, Keenan!" Marty whooped as the Nerf ball swished through the net. Keenan threw his hands in the air and I cheered too as I bent into another lunge. With one year until departure, our South Pole training, gear acquisition, and planning had shifted into high gear. On that October night of 2012, we were all in our garage, which we had transformed into a workout facility, complete with an industrial rubberized floor, weight bench, free weights, aerobic steps, Bosu ball, and treadmill. I was sweating through one hundred lunges while Marty flung thirty-five-pound hand weights over his head. Spending our evenings here while Keenan played Nerf basketball, worked on homework, or helped count reps had become our new normal.

Our expedition plan was to follow a route pioneered by renowned mountaineer and explorer Reinhold Messner in 1989. Messner crossed 1,740 miles from one coast of Antarctica to the other; we would follow the first 570 miles of his route, starting at the Ronne Ice Shelf, one of the largest ice shelves on earth, on the northwest coast of the continent and ending at the geographic South Pole. Our chosen route through remote terrain would skirt the western flank of the massive Foundation Ice Stream, a river of ice that flows over 150 miles across the continent, and the Transantarctic Mountains, the range that divides the west and east sides of the continent and runs longer than the Himalayas. Once past the Patuxent Range, part of the Transantarctic Mountains, we'd turn south toward the Pole.

In addition to being self-guided, we planned to go unsupported, meaning we wouldn't take any outside assistance such as an air-resupply of food, fuel, or replacement equipment. And in Antarctica lingo, going unassisted meant we would be only human powered, with no aid such as dogs—no longer allowed on the continent—wind-powered kites, or motorized vehicles used for significant speed or load advantage.

Being unguided, unsupported, and unassisted on this route promised a test against extreme elements in the true spirit of polar journeys. During our research into previous Antarctic expeditions, we were surprised to learn that only about one hundred people in all of history have ever completed a journey from the coast to the Pole—unsupported, unguided, and unassisted. By contrast, over four hundred have completed a journey supported, guided, and/or assisted.

Building on our years of ultrarunning experience, Marty and I devised a detailed training plan to maintain extraordinary endurance and build what we hoped would be staggering strength. For endurance, we'd continue running 40 to 70 tough mountain miles every week. Our trainer—Courtenay Schurman of Body Results, who had helped me train to climb Denali fifteen years earlier—provided customized strength routines that changed every four to six weeks. She'd have us lift weights, hike hills wearing heavy backpacks, carry sandbags around our front yard, push a wheelbarrow full of sandbags around the house multiple times, and more—all to build strength in our core and legs to handle long days of pulling heavy sleds for weeks on end without incurring injury.

Days and nights were full, with little time for much else than work and training and tending to the hundreds of items on our expedition to-do list. Each time we crossed off an item, two more appeared in its place. Besides ongoing training, we were constantly acquiring gear. Shipments with everything from down sweaters to backcountry skis regularly arrived at our doorstep thanks to the convenience of Internet shopping. When gear wasn't right, I shipped it back—even my custom-made anorak because it had heart-shaped piping on the sleeves instead of generic shapes that seemed more suitable (less cliché girly) for a polar mama like me.

That night, Keenan dropped the Nerf ball in the corner and collapsed on the mat next to me to help me count lunge reps. "Ninety-eight, ninety-nine . . ." I plunged down and up one more time, legs shaking and sweat dripping from my forehead. He sat up and cheered, "Come on, Mom." And in unison we said, "One hundred."

"You got this!" he said.

AROUND THAT SAME time, we gathered at Mary Queen of Peace Catholic Church to say goodbye to Peg, a teacher who had welcomed Keenan into the Saint Joseph School family when he transferred there in second grade, four years earlier. A steady stream of mourners packed into the limited space remaining in the great hall. I scooted down the pew to make a little more room. Quiet whispers filled the space between moments of silence. I nodded at a friend from Saint Joseph School who squished into the pew in front of me. Peg's tribe of family, friends, students, parents, and coworkers radiated a warmth and beauty that permeated every molecule in the church. I wondered if we were all reflecting the essence of Peg to each other.

A hush came over the crowd when Fiona, Peg's seventh-grade daughter that Marty and I had coached in cross-country, and her younger brother walked down the long aisle with their dad. The chilling feeling of death crawled up the skin of my arms and sleeveless shoulders, where goose bumps popped and hair stood on end. I stared at the gaping hole in their family. *How will her kids cope? And what about her husband?*

The priest began describing Peg, the forty-five years-young teacher who had a friendly smile and contagious zest for life, and had unselfishly touched so many students' lives before breast cancer took away hers.

"I know Peg lived a good life—just look at this church and all who she touched and loved," said the priest.

While the priest continued the service, I squirmed in my seat as death found a way inside my chest, clenching its hands around my saddened heart. I gasped for air, glancing left at Marty and then right at Keenan. My eyes welled with tears as I imagined Keenan walking down the church aisle with Marty, and I was the one missing from the picture. Imagining the worst, a gut-wrenching shock wave of grief overwhelmed my body, as if I were experiencing the pain felt by a child who lost their parent too early. Through misty eyes, I wondered again: *Are Marty and I doing the right thing by leaving Keenan for our expedition?*

Just then, I heard the priest say, "We are here to learn to love, and we'll be given opportunities over and over again in this life to love deeply." My mind shifted its attention from death to love.

I pondered his words. *Do I know how to love Marty and Keenan and my tribe—I mean really love at the deepest level?* Maybe while planning our expedition and skiing across Antarctica, I would be given opportunities to open and expand my heart, to give and receive love at a deeper level than ever before.

What does that even mean or look like? I wasn't sure.

All I knew was on that day in that church, the idea of learning to love deeply was tattooed on my brain and would require further reflection to understand its meaning in my life, like studying a beautifully complex piece of art.

WITH WINTER UPON us in the Northwest, we set two new training goals for our limited snow season: test gear in snow, preferably in extreme cold, and become better backcountry skiers.

We stuffed our silver Jeep Grand Cherokee with our new gear—saving just enough room for Keenan and our dog, Kiya—and drove 20 minutes to Snoqualmie Pass.

Kiya raced ahead, nipping in excitement at the snow, while Marty and I pulled our half-full sleds, weighing about 120-pounds each, uphill for the first time. Marty had picked up our custom-made sleds, along with specialized boots and harnesses, in Oslo, Norway. Our light, durable, high-quality carbon-fiber sleds, made by Acapulka, promised low friction and the ability to withstand rough ice conditions common in Antarctica. Measuring seven feet long and two feet wide, they had durable crimson-red bags made of strong, abrasion-resistant material to contain all of our gear.

Keenan, dressed in his navy-blue puffy jacket and green fleece hat, snowshoed behind me, pulling his empty purple plastic sled. After an hour, his pace slowed.

I stopped and said, "Keenan, come here."

Walking up to me with his head down, he said, "What?"

"Let's clip your sled onto mine and you can ride inside. I need the extra weight for training."

Keenan flung his body into his sled and hung on to the rope handle like he was riding a horse. He hooted and hollered, poking at drifts of snow with his mittens as I skied forward.

Ten minutes later, a snowball went flying over my head from in front of me and hit the purple sled only inches from Keenan's leg. He jerked his head up, jumped out of the sled, grabbed a handful of snow, yelled "I'll get you," and threw a snowball back in Marty's direction. Stuck in the crossfire, I ducked out of the way as a full-on snowball fight ensued.

After a few hours more of pulling sleds, we stopped.

"This looks like a fine camp spot," said Marty, pointing at a flat patch of snow surrounded by evergreens with branches weighted down with four inches of white.

I grabbed the tent from my sled while Keenan and Marty stomped down the fresh snow with snowshoes and skis to make a firm tent platform.

After setting up the tent, I said, "I'll grab the rest of the stuff out of the sled."

"Keenan, we're going to stake out the tent by digging small T-shaped trenches," said Marty, "like this." He placed the stake perpendicular to the cord attached to the tent and said, "Pull it tight, put the anchor into the trench, and stomp snow on it to keep it in place." Then Marty showed Keenan how to cut blocks of snow to melt for water. Meanwhile, perched 30 yards above our campsite, Kiya kept watch over her pack.

Later, as we cozied into the tent among our pillowy down sleeping bags, I poked Keenan's shoulder. "Remember camping out this summer in our front yard?" We both laughed at the memory of Keenan deciding to sleep in his new hammock, wrapped in a blanket instead of his down sleeping bag, while Marty and I tested our new tent. The next morning, when Marty and I had popped our heads out of the tent to check on Keenan, he sat up, gasped, and said, "Mom, Dad, that was the coldest night ever. I barely survived!"

On the ski out from our winter training trip, we stopped at our favorite sledding hill and took a few laughter-induced out-of-control runs on Keenan's purple sled. While this practice outing, and a few others that followed, pushed us even closer together as a family, pulling sleds through soft Northwest snow in 30 degrees didn't quite mimic the deep freeze we'd experience in Antarctica.

In search of extreme cold close to home, with no desire to incur the cost or complicated logistics of flying to the Arctic for two weeks, we scheduled a trip to the best place we could find within a 12-hour driving radius—Yellowstone National Park. The networks of snow- and ice-covered roads were perfect packed surfaces for dragging sleds.

But a week before our departure to Yellowstone, the phone rang. Mom said, "Everything is okay . . . but last night Dad felt dizzy, so I took him to the hospital. The doctors are doing some tests now." A few days later, I flew to Arkansas to check on Dad in person. He had been in and out of the hospital over the past year—his defibrillator had zapped him back to life multiple times, and he had recently fallen in the bathroom in the middle of the night. Dad appeared to be slipping toward the unthinkable.

One night after dinner at my parent's house, while we lingered at the kitchen table—the same round oak table our family of seven had gathered around every night while I was growing up—we took bites of apple pie, reminiscing about days past.

My parents met on a blind date in high school in 1950. Dad pulled up to Mom's house in his light-green Ford to take her to the Valentine's dance at his school (they attended different high schools). When they arrived at the dance, Dad opened Mom's car door like a gentleman. Before stepping out, Mom handed him a Valentine's cake she was holding on her lap for the party, and somehow it slipped and frosting was smashed all over his new letterman jacket. Mom thought, *I'll never see him again.* The kiss at the end of the evening said otherwise. Thus began their lifelong romance. After a year of dating, Dad was drafted and sent to Germany during the Korean War. For two years their romance blossomed through long-distance letters, and they married three months after Dad returned home to the South Side of Chicago. Dad's eyes crinkled with a smile as he finished the story. "And now we've been married sixty years." He looked over at Mom, then said, "We are so proud of our family—it's everything to us."

I scraped the last bit of pie off my plate and said, "You should be proud of the family that you've raised."

Even though I frequently told Dad I loved him, I wanted him to feel the positive impact he'd had on my life as his own appeared to hang in the balance.

"I want you to know just how much I love you," I said, looking directly into his kind blue eyes.

"Thanks, honey," said Dad, his face straining to hold back tears.

Later that night as I lay in the twin bed in my parent's guest bedroom, staring at the striped red, white, and blue wallpaper, I pondered the sharp contrasts between my life and Dad's. Dad struggled to maintain his health and independence, while I felt pressure to return home to continue expedition training and planning. Dad labored to complete simple movements with his physical therapist—like standing up from his chair five times in a row—to help him regain enough strength and balance to walk around the house without falling; my rigorous daily training schedule, packed with hours of strength and endurance workouts, would hopefully power me to the Pole. Dad had all the time in the world, his life revolving around simple household activities like opening the mail or watching reruns of his favorite cop show, *Blue Bloods*; I wished for more time to prepare to journey to the end of the earth, my world expanding with possibilities.

BACK HOME IN North Bend, I discovered we were too late. The roads throughout Yellowstone would be plowed before we could reschedule our much-needed training trip. We shifted to a less ideal option—Mount Rainier National Park, a two-hour drive away from home. While the forecast didn't include extreme cold, at least we could test all our gear in snow conditions one last time before we left in mid-November, just eight months away.

Driving down Highway 410, just past the Crystal Mountain Ski Resort turnoff, we pulled over into a parking lot near the northeast entrance to the park, unloaded mounds of gear from the Jeep, packed up our sleds, and began pulling toward the main road into the park.

When we reached the entrance, I looked at Marty, who was wearing his black Gore-Tex bib pants and lightweight jacket, and said, "No way." Even though we'd heard otherwise, the road had already been plowed, just like at Yellowstone.

"Oh well. There's nothing we can do about it now."

To make do, we pulled sleds on a ten-foot-wide strip of soft snow next to the road that led to White River Ranger Station. The unseasonably warm 35-degree weather wasn't ideal. At times, patches of melted snow revealed rocks and mud.

"Ugh—the sound of rocks scraping up the bottom of our new sleds is killing me," I said with a half-smile when we stopped for a break. It gave me the shivers, like fingernails scratching a chalkboard.

"Well, rocks aren't much different than sharp ice, so I don't think it's going to do much harm."

After four hours of pulling, we set up camp on our narrow strip of snow with a beautiful unobstructed view of the plowed road.

Thirty minutes into the next day, we unclipped sleds from harnesses and carried our 170-pound beasts over a small section of road—like portaging overstuffed canoes between waterways. When the terrain turned to steep downhill, instead of pulling my sled, it slid in front of me. I held the rope attached to the sled in my hands and could hardly control it on the small swath of snow next to the road. Steering from behind was like holding on to the leash of a big uncontrollable dog. I awkwardly yanked my sled to make it stay on the narrow strip of snow while it fought to jump the curb and run free.

The terrain leveled out for a while, and my sled slid back into its regular place behind me. Then on the slight downhill, it turned into a red missile threatening to flatten me from behind. I tried to out-ski it, then jumped out of the way as I braced for the force of the sled to jerk me forward as it whipped in front of me again. In Antarctica, we would primarily travel on a gradual uphill gradient, moving from sea level to the Pole, which sits on top of an icy, windswept plateau at an altitude of 9,301 feet. Right now, Antarctica's uphill gradient sounded much more appealing to me than dodging sled missiles launched on the downhill.

After crossing paths with a few backcountry skiers and snowmobilers, we moved deeper into the heart of the wilderness, too far for day excursions. We skied onto a section of unplowed road and christened fresh snow with our tracks. Out of reach of any man-made sounds, I listened intently to the swish of skis and heaviness of breath, the stillness of the forest enveloping me. I found a steady rhythm and ease of movement that grew stronger each hour.

Stopping for a snack sometime later, I pulled out a bar and said, "Oh my gosh, look over at Mount Rainier."

"Awesome," Marty said. Below the orange glow of the sky, the White River wound through the valley, and its roar hung on the gentle breeze.

"How are you doing?" I asked.

"We've really been moving well the last hour or so . . . it's so peaceful tucked back here. And I think we're both moving well."

A quarter mile later, we approached a campsite blanketed in over four feet of snow. I began to recognize the lumps as the bathroom and picnic table where Marty and I had rested at 3:00 a.m. during our trail run a few years ago, when just the two us made our way around the 95-mile Wonderland Trail, which circumnavigates Mount Rainier.

As we relaxed into our sleeping bags that night, I said, "Sometimes it's daunting to think about all we've done so far to get ready, and all we still have to do."

"Yeah, I wonder how many hours we've already put into planning?"

"It's a lot of work to be so adventurous," I said with a smile.

"Sometimes I wish that we were the kind of people who could just feel satisfied, that didn't have to be so driven all of the time," Marty said as he cozied his sleeping bag next to mine.

"I wonder what that would be like," I said with a smirk.

For the next few days, the winter wonderland of Mount Rainier was our training ground. We both developed hot spots on our heels from breaking in our Norwegian boots in temperatures that made our feet sweat. Soft snow constantly stuck to the skins on the bottom of our skis—skins provided traction for skiing uphill—making it difficult to fine-tune our skiing techniques. Marty in particular seemed to be bogged down with these issues. And much of the cold-weather clothing we had planned to test, like goggles with special face masks, down mittens, and balaclavas, never emerged from our sleds.

After four days of training, one less than we'd planned, we arrived back at our starting point and parked car.

"I wish we could have trained in extreme cold," Marty said as he sat on the tailgate to remove his ski boots.

"Yeah, we still don't know how we'll handle negative-twenty degrees or colder while skiing and dragging our sleds." Right now, my hands were toasty warm even after I removed my gloves.

"We don't have time, with everything going on," said Marty.

I sighed, staring at the ground. "And with spring coming."

"This trip was a bit of a bust . . . but it will just have to do."

While I later spun it as a positive outing to friends and family, I agreed with Marty. *It will just have to do.*

Driving home from Mount Rainier, I couldn't wait to call Keenan. My sister Sue and her husband, Frank, who also lived in North Bend, were staying at our house and having their own shakedown training with him. Sue and Frank were scheduled to care for Keenan the first ten days of our expedition and the last week before we returned home, with other family and friends covering the rest of the days.

I dialed. Sue answered and handed the phone to Keenan. "We're coming home a day early because of poor training conditions on the mountain—so we'll see you in two hours!"

Keenan's voice sounded somewhat dejected as he said, "Oh . . . Uncle Frank, Aunt Sue, and I were planning to make mac and cheese with hot dogs for dinner, play dominos, and then watch a movie."

Keenan's shakedown training had gone perfectly.

"TODAY I MAILED our check for fifteen thousand to ALE," I said to Marty as we prepped dinner.

ALE required a deposit six months before departure. Our nonrefundable check would secure our spot on their flight to Antarctica in November.

"No turning back now," I joked.

At first, we had tried to gain major sponsorship to help defer costs. But after limited effort chasing scarce dollars, we decided to focus our time on stockpiling cash from my consulting business and Marty's job at F5 Networks, and fund our own expedition. While it was impossible to rationally justify the cost with the intangible value we'd gain in return, I knew in my heart when I mailed the check that skiing into the unknown held secrets that would shape our future.

Marty said, "Well, today my new boss had a talk with me about our trip."

I stopped chopping carrots and looked up at Marty, as the tone in his voice sounded serious.

"He said that while he'd like to approve my vacation request, he was worried about setting a precedent."

"Wait, what do you mean, precedent?" I asked. "I thought you could carry over vacation year to year without a problem."

"Technically that is true. But they've never given eight to nine weeks off at once to someone at my level."

"But I thought it was already approved?"

Marty shrugged. "It was, but not by my new boss. The executive team is rethinking it."

"You've been at F5 for fourteen years . . . doesn't that carry any weight?"

"I guess we'll have to see."

We pushed forward with planning even though Marty's job was now on shaky ground, trusting that things would somehow work out.

ONE DAY I stopped by Les Schwab Tire Center. "Can I have four tires from the recycle pile out back?" I asked the woman behind the counter. "My husband and I need them to train to go to the South Pole."

"Um, sure," said the woman with a baffled look on her face.

After picking out four similarly sized SUV tires, I heaved them into the back of my Jeep. Back home, Marty screwed fasteners into each one so that we could connect two tires with a short rope, then attach them to a harness via a longer rope. With the mountains snow free, we planned to simulate pulling heavy sleds on snow by dragging these tires on trails. While the two tires together weighed only about seventy pounds, we figured that without the glide that snow provided, they'd feel much heavier.

At first, we dragged tires around our neighborhood on Sunday mornings, covering 2 miles in 60 minutes—not counting all of the time it took to talk to curious neighbors asking, "What are you doing?" By the time we were two months from departure, we were dragging tires for 6 to 10 hours—12 to 20 miles—at a time.

One rainy Sunday, we pulled into the parking lot at Rattlesnake Lake near North Bend, popped open the back of our Jeep, and threw our four heavy rubber "babies" (as we affectionately called them) on the ground. These babies lived outside in the rain by the side of the garage, never crying for attention—although at times the madness of dragging them around for hours almost made *me* cry like a baby. The previous day, we had dragged them for 8 hours, and today we planned another 11 to 12.

Keenan was hanging out with his best friend, Ryo. Marty and I had leaned on Leni's family countless times to help care for Keenan while we trained. Luckily, he loved spending time at their house.

After I clipped the rope stretching from my tires to my harness, I leaned forward and adjusted the various harness straps around my waist and chest to customize the fit and maximize my pulling force. The weight was distributed across my waist, chest, and shoulders. Within a few minutes, Marty and I were pulling down the Iron Horse Trail, an abandoned railroad track turned trail that was relatively flat. We planned to make our way gradually uphill for 22 miles, toward Snoqualmie Pass, our farthest tire-dragging session to date—farther than the 15 miles per day we hoped to average in Antarctica. We had left a car at the other end for when we finished.

We pulled the tires side by side for a few minutes, and then fell into our usual single-file formation. Above, thick clouds and dark skies threatened to soak our day. The loud grinding sound of tires rolling over gravel echoed through the hollow tire chambers and made conversation virtually impossible. I pulled forward with my own thoughts keeping me company.

The world moved much slower at our two-mile-an-hour pace than it did when we ran—slow enough to interact with runners, bikers, hikers, and dog walkers sharing the trail. Over the months, countless people had stopped dead in their tracks as they stared in bewilderment. After we described our pending trip, a curious young girl had asked, "Are you scientists?" Two local elementary school teachers had asked if we would be willing to present our story to the kids at their schools. A personal trainer had told us, "This is the most inspiring training I've seen in years." We had met a father who planned to follow our blog as part of his homeschool curriculum, an Air Force pilot who had flown US scientists from New Zealand to the South Pole, and a gray-haired biker who slammed on his breaks and yelled, "You guys are awesome. I'm *pulling* for you!"

Onlookers had shown so much interest that we made business cards with our expedition website and handed them out. We had named our expedition 3 Below Zero. The 3 represented the different members of our team—Marty, me, and our supporters (family, friends, and followers). Just as football's twelfth man acknowledges fans, we wanted to acknowledge those who helped make our journey possible.

Now, during what seemed like the thousandth tire-dragging session, I was finally at peace with this relentless mode of training. My tires were like Zen masters, quietly teaching me patience and mental toughness; sharing the secrets of staying present. Perhaps before being discarded into the recycle pile at Les Schwab, they had studied with Zen monk Thich Nhat

Hanh, who said, "Smile, breathe, and go slowly." I had accepted the monotony of pulling tires, that there was nothing to do but breathe and go slowly. I was forced to practice being in the moment. Admittedly, on cold, rainy days after hours of dragging tires, it was tough to smile through the struggle, easier to hang my head while just powering through.

After two hours of moving through driving rain, I pulled off to the side of the trail under the shelter of a few trees. Marty and I sat on our tires, leaned in close to each other, and began inhaling snacks. My frozen hands could barely function as I attempted to stash the Clif Bar wrapper into my pack. Just as a chill began creeping deep into my body, I tightened the hood of my jacket around my head and stepped back into the downpour. I turned on my iPod to try to distract myself from the relentless rain. After an hour of music, we stopped for another snack and water break. An episode of *This American Life* kept me company for the next stretch. Then another break. This was the rhythm of the day. Listen to iPod. Snack. Pull. Snack. Daydream. Snack.

The rain finally let up. Soaked brown fall leaves littered the trail. Our tires acted as trail plows and leaves accumulated inside them, adding weight and friction to our workout. As I glanced back, I saw a leaf-free line of trail. A person on a bike stopped and asked, "Do you work for the Park Service? Are you doing a new type of trail cleaning?" I looked up and smiled but thought, *Really, you think this is a good way to clean the trail!*

After we crossed a bridge with a peek view of the Snoqualmie Valley below, I had a flashback to the day we'd been pulling tires here when, unbeknownst to us, the Light at the End of the Tunnel Marathon was taking place. A strong current of hundreds of runners had come toward us as we fought like salmon to swim upstream and out of their way. One runner had joked, "Did you lose your car somewhere?"

I glanced at my watch; it had now been 11 hours. We were moving at a slower-than-predicted pace. I stopped on the trail and waited for Marty to pull up next to me.

"Given the time and our pace, I think we may need to consider our options," I said.

"We don't have a choice, we just have to keep going," he said in his matter-of-fact cop voice.

"If we continue dragging tires for six more miles, it will take us at least three hours. If we stash the tires and run the rest of the way, we'll be done in an hour or less," I said. "I don't want to be so late picking up Keenan at Leni's house."

We opted to stash our four rubber babies safely off-trail under the cover of a cluster of dripping hemlocks, noting their exact location so that we could recover them a week later. Instead of being rooted to the ground by the downward tug of tires, I floated weightless down the trail, rejoicing in my new-found freedom. Soon we arrived at the entrance to the Snoqualmie Tunnel, a two-mile abandoned railroad tunnel that connected us to our car parked on the other side. I had run through this tunnel a decade earlier during my first 100-mile race. Today, we donned our headlamps and slipped into the darkness. Inside the tunnel, I could feel the cool, damp air and hear the periodic dripping of water from the ceiling as I followed the beam of light through complete darkness. About 20 minutes later, a faint pinpoint of light ahead showed us the other end of the tunnel and grew bigger and brighter as we moved closer. On the other side of the tunnel was the end of this long training day.

As I emerged back into daylight, muscles depleted, stomach growling, I smiled, feeling accomplished from a day of hard work.

NOW IN THE home stretch of training, we had an update call with our coach, Courtenay. Marty started out the conversation by giving her an update on our progress. "During our final months of training, we're planning various long tire drags and big trail runs," he said, "like a ninety-five-mile run around the

Wonderland Trail. We are also working around an upcoming vacation to Japan with Keenan."

"Remember the prize is the Pole," Courtenay said, "and running a hundred miles straight, while great ultrarunning training, may ultimately be a bad idea if it wears down your bodies. At this point, super long training runs are not necessary in order to prepare for the Pole."

I thought about what Marty hadn't said during his opening comments. How a month ago his knee had flared, and despite daily ice baths, it continued to swell to the point where he could hardly walk. While the pain had eventually eased, the undisputable warning sign threatened to crack his confidence.

She continued, "I'm concerned about how to keep your muscle mass from diminishing with the endurance running that you're planning to complete. Building muscle and running long can be incompatible activities."

Truth was, we didn't just need to *keep* current muscle mass—we needed to *grow* mass and gain weight in order to counter the loss that would inevitably happen on our expedition. So far, we'd both gained about ten pounds. Once we hung up the phone, Marty looked at me with narrow eyes. "I knew the day would come when I'd have to stop running so much," he said in a serious tone. "I just didn't think it would be right now, when we were in peak running shape."

Our "get real" conversation with Courtenay stayed with me for days. I intuitively knew she was right. We had to reduce our running mileage. Our training needed to focus on strength exercises, hiking with heavy backpacks, long tire drags—with a mix of more moderate runs. It was time to let go of Ultrarunning Chris, at least for now, and fully embrace Polar Chris.

That shift planted a seed of worry. What if Ultrarunning Chris—a part of me I cherished—didn't return after the South Pole trip and vanished for good? My identity, even my tribe of friends, was so tied to running that the thought of losing it rocked my world. If Marty and I were no longer the Ultrarunning Fagans, who would we be?

KEITH FROM POLAR Explorers opened his arms and enveloped me completely in a mama-bear hug. He had arrived at our house at 7:00 p.m. on a Friday night, just in time for dinner. His gregarious personality filled the kitchen as we fell into easy conversation, like old friends catching up on what had happened since our polar shakedown trainings in Minnesota and Norway a year and a half earlier.

With three and a half months until departure, we had invited Keith to fly out to our home to review our gear, navigation strategies, technology, and emergency-scenario planning. We wanted to get answers to lingering questions, eliminate redundancy, reduce overall weight, and squeeze every last bit of expertise out of Keith's polar brain.

The next morning, I placed a plate full of scrambled eggs and turkey bacon in front of Keith. He laughed under his breath and said, "You guys should be eating *real* bacon."

With Keenan at Ryo's house to play for the day, we began assessing each item in our grand pile of gear in the garage. Keith picked up two pee bottles. We had packed two wide-mouth liter-sized bottles as in-tent toilets to avoid having to brave the cold every time we had to pee.

Keith asked, "Do you both really need a pee bottle? Can't you share one?"

"I need my own," I shot back, as if his suggestion sounded ridiculous. Marty looked at me in silence. Then I paused and reconsidered, and set one pee bottle off to the side.

"Let's talk about socks," Keith continued. "Heels tend to rub thin when you're skiing for eight to ten hours per day."

"We were thinking six pairs," said Marty. "We'll change them weekly."

Fresh socks would help us avoid blisters that often start as small inconveniences and blossom into infected wounds.

"Sounds great," said Keith.

Keith continued to challenge the necessity of every piece of gear. We were searching for the sweet spot between must-have and nice-to-have. Pack too many luxury items and risk breaking the back of our expedition.

Finally, I asked the burning question. "How much toilet paper do you think we should bring?"

"I don't bring toilet paper," Keith said. Before I could let out a gasp, he went on, "I bring paper towels because they're more durable and easier to hold with gloved hands." So we packed one paper towel per person per day (forty-five sheets each). In the end, I snuck in a few extra sheets as backup.

For 10 hours on Saturday and 8 hours on Sunday, we meticulously worked our way through the twenty-foot-long party-sized sub sandwich of our expedition until we had gorged ourselves on the minutiae of detail. Most of the time when we asked Keith a question, he responded, "What do *you* think?" As Marty and I talked through options and solutions to various scenarios, he observed our team dynamic. He never told us what to do, only offered his opinion. Comparing duplicate items, we chose favorite Gore-Tex pants, windproof gloves, and down mittens. We left behind our spare set of skis and bindings in favor of a six-inch replacement ski tip. We added one extra collapsible ski pole that could double as a camera tripod, and a two-person bivvy sack (an emergency bag) that we could climb into should we lose our tent.

We talked through possible emergency scenarios. What if we burned down the tent? What if the tent blew away? What if one of us sustained a major injury like a broken arm or leg? What if one of us got frostbite? What if we lost each other during a whiteout? What if one of us fell into a crevasse? Teams can tumble like dominos into tragedy from a series of bad decisions in the wild. In remote situations, there are often no second chances. For each scenario, we created detailed emergency-response plans that utilized all our skills, including Marty's training as an emergency medical technician (EMT) and my training in wilderness first aid.

It felt good to make progress with Keith as our guide, even if it was painstaking at times. Throughout our time together,

Keith masterfully shifted between various roles—polar guide ("These gloves worked best for me"), coach ("I know you guys will make great decisions"), facilitator ("How do you plan to divide team tasks?"), and psychologist ("I see that leaving your son is going to be hard for you")—like an actor playing multiple parts in a play. Married with two kids, Keith was short on ego and long on understanding.

By 3:00 p.m. on Sunday, I checked the last item off our agenda. My head was swirling with the tornado of topics we'd covered. Our garage looked like the aftermath of a raging storm—with clothing items draped over the treadmill and gear scattered across the floor in loosely organized piles labeled "Go," "Customize," "Return," and "Stay Home." After I hugged Keith goodbye, I turned to Marty and said, "That was totally worth it." Our planning was on track.

It seemed we had come so far, yet we still had miles to go—I thought of planning Keenan's time at home while we were gone and felt a familiar surge of anxiety. I would have to say goodbye to him in a couple of months.

CHAPTER 5:

BYE FOR NOW

As Dad aged, somewhere along the line he replaced the word *bye* at the end of our visits or phone conversations with the phrase *bye for now*. The change was subtle yet profound. Maybe saying "Bye for now" was his declaration that despite failing health, he wasn't going anywhere.

I liked the sentiment behind Dad's new way of saying good-bye. It seemed to fit as Marty and I prepared to temporarily leave our lives to set off for Antarctica. But I did worry that this time my goodbye to Dad would be for good. I had begun to wonder: *What will I do if Dad dies while we are in Antarctica?*

Our family had recently gathered for his eightieth birthday, one I feared might be his last. I saw it in the way he shuffled along, trying to avoid dangerous obstacles like the leg of a kitchen chair sticking out into his path or a newspaper resting on the floor. One trip and fall could mean a broken hip, a concussion, another visit to the hospital—or worse, the end.

During a private moment with Mom after the birthday party, I asked her that very question. In a calm and reassuring voice, as if sharing a predetermined plan, she said, "Chris, if your father dies while you are in Antarctica, you will continue on to the South Pole. It will be too hard for you to quickly get home, and I won't want to delay the funeral. Keenan will come to the funeral to represent your family. He will travel from North Bend with Sue."

Captivated by her grace, I said, "Okay, Mom." Then I hugged her for what seemed like a long time. I felt an unexpected rush of relief. While I had no idea how I would react if Dad actually died while I was in Antarctica, or what was expected of me, Mom had a plan. I leaned into her unwavering confidence—finding shelter once again in her unshakable strength—and knew in her infinite wisdom that she was right. I wouldn't want to miss the funeral, but it could take weeks to attempt a hasty return from the end of the earth. Maybe in the back of her mind, she didn't want to risk losing me as I tried rushing home in an emotionally rocky state of mind.

I thought about how death is viewed differently depending on the circumstances. If Mom or Dad died, I'd be deeply saddened—but would feel consoled knowing they had lived a good life, been married for sixty-plus years, and raised a loving family. If I died now, I'd upset the natural order of things, sending shock waves to all corners of my family. Mom and Dad would bear the burden of outliving their child, and the suffering I'd cause Keenan was unthinkable.

I had never taken the time to think in depth about death. Death was something others had to deal with, not me in my bubble of happiness. I had never wanted to have a conversation with death, fearing I might look into its eyes and see a deep sadness that I couldn't escape. But as we planned to head south, that conversation became inescapable.

THE MORNING AFTER Marty returned from a grueling nineteen-day trip to Tel Aviv to open a new office for F5 Networks, he called me from his office. As I sat in my pajamas at the kitchen table sipping my morning coffee, he said, "You'll never believe this. My boss called me into his office. I thought he was going to congratulate me on opening the Tel Aviv office. Wrong.

He said that the executive team met while I was gone . . . and while they respect me and value my hard work, they can't let me take all of my vacation at once to go to Antarctica."

My stomach flipped. "So that's it? There's no way to take all of the vacation you earned?"

"I can take all my vacation, just not at one time. Apparently, the company doesn't permit extended vacations or leaves of absence—especially from someone at my level. This type of request has come up a few times before and it was denied."

"I guess I thought they would make an exception for you."

"Me too," he said.

"So, what do you want to do?"

"There's only one thing to do. We are going on our expedition."

Marty's response didn't surprise me. He lives with calm urgency. He balances a strong sense of responsibility, honor, and dependability with a burning desire for freedom, independence, and exploration. He's driven to live life on his own terms.

That night, when Marty returned home from work and after we had each mulled over this new reality, we continued our conversation as we got ready for bed.

"So you're quitting your job?" I squeezed toothpaste onto my toothbrush.

"Yes. I was told that when I return, if I would like to be rehired, they would find a job for me, even if my current job has been filled."

"Well, that's a positive. And just think, you won't have to answer hundreds of emails that pile up while we are gone."

"Yeah, it will be nice not to have the pressure to jump right back into work the minute we return," Marty said as he grabbed a piece of floss.

"Maybe this is for the best. You're getting tired of all the international travel."

"Maybe," said Marty.

"Maybe when you return, there will be something new waiting for you." I believed that sometimes when you close one door, a new one opens.

Marty had been here before. Back in 1998 after we met on Denali, he quit his job as a police officer and followed his heart to Seattle. Now, with similar conviction, he was following his heart to the South Pole.

MARTY AND I sat next to each other with The Manual laid in front of us on my desk.

"Hello everyone," said Marty into the speakerphone.

"Thanks for taking the time to join the call this evening," I said. "I'd like to start by saying thanks to all of you for agreeing to help care for Keenan while we are gone in Antarctica. Obviously, we couldn't do this endeavor without you. We really appreciate it." Then I continued with a smile, "Any questions so far?"

Laughter blared through the speakerphone.

My brother Jim said, "Anybody need a break yet?"

More laughter.

Preparing to say bye for now to Keenan meant making sure he'd be loved and cared for during our time away. We had meticulously pieced together Keenan's surrogate parenting team of aunts, uncles, older cousins, and dear friends—fifteen people in all, most of whom were on the call. To minimize the disruption to his routine, it was important to Keenan, and to us, that he stayed at our house while we were gone. With the exception of one week during Christmas break when he'd be with Leni's family, everyone caring for Keenan would stay at our house for a week to ten days at a time, including those folks who lived in town and would temporarily abandon their own homes in order to honor Keenan's desire to stay home.

"Tonight, we wanted to highlight some items in The Manual that we emailed you a few days ago and answer any questions that you have," I said.

Marty and I had crafted a detailed thirty-three-page document full of all the information the team needed to care for Keenan and run our household in our absence. The Manual contained everything from Keenan's band practice schedule to which doctor to call in case of an emergency to how to start the generator if the power went out (every winter, strong winds and soggy weather inevitably caused trees to fall on power lines in our neighborhood).

I walked our team through the highlights, with Marty chiming in periodically.

"Keenan wanted me to make sure that I tell you his wake-up routine," I said. "Kiya jumps up on his bed and nudges him awake with her nose—which he loves. He plans to make a video to show you exactly how it works."

After an hour of sharing information and answering questions, I wrapped up the call. "While this manual is comprehensive, I'm sure we haven't thought of everything. You guys are all smart people, and I know you'll make great decisions for us in our absence."

"Thank you, everyone, so much. We are very excited," Marty said.

"Chris, it's great to have all of this information, thanks," said Leni.

"Signing off from 3 Below Zero headquarters," I said with enthusiasm in my voice.

In unison, Marty and I said, "Bye everyone."

Despite all the minutiae in The Manual and the awesome team we'd assembled, that night as I lay in bed, I still thought: *How do we hand over the reins of parenting to a group of caregivers? How do we educate them about the subtleties of reading Keenan's moods so they know when to give him a hug, to cheer him on, or encourage him to try a little harder? How will they know the millions of little things that we've learned by parenting him for the past twelve years?*

THE NEXT DAY, Marty and I strolled into a classroom at Saint Joseph's. Four of Keenan's teachers were sitting in a semi-circle facing two empty chairs. As I slid in, the cold hard surface brought me back to the awkwardness of my middle school days.

I had been on the cusp of finishing elementary school when my parents told us that we were moving from Champaign, Illinois, to the far away land of Des Moines, Iowa. My bubble of comfort and happiness burst. I didn't understand that moving could present an opportunity to step outside my twelve-year-old comfort zone and grow and learn. I didn't know the power of stepping into the unknown. All I knew was that my world was changing, and I was certain it was for the worse.

Just days after I finished the sixth grade, we drove six hours in a sagging blue station wagon without air conditioning to our new home. It was similar in size and shape to the two-story gray house we'd left behind, except that it was white with black shutters. At least it had a basketball hoop mounted on top of the garage. Still, summer dragged on at a snail's pace. I was trapped on a deserted island. The social isolation and lack of new friends were as stifling as the humid air. I couldn't wait for school to start, a chance to meet new people, a chance for a breath of fresh air.

But at my new school, I was a foreigner in the land of merging elementary schools. I felt like everyone except me had an established group of friends. For the first time in my life, I sat alone at the lunchroom table, staring down at my food to avoid eye contact, face turning red, feeling as if everyone were staring at me. I shrunk into loneliness. My confidence unraveled.

Would our expedition to Antarctica cause Keenan to unravel in his own way? He'd been adjusting to middle school for only two months while we prepared to leave.

I snapped myself back into the classroom at Keenan's school as the teachers each took a copy of our caregiver schedule. As I began talking, my breathing shallowed and constricted and my voice sounded like it might crack into pieces at any moment. I felt the cold hard gravity of the situation, of leaving Keenan, descending upon me. *This is no longer a distant dream.* I struggled to keep my composure as I described the details of our plan. Marty gave me a smile of support. I forced a smile back through the stress. *Just keep smiling and you won't cry.*

Keenan's homeroom teacher, Ms. Castle, leaned forward with warmth in her eyes. "Don't worry. We'll keep a special eye out for Keenan to ensure his well-being at school while you are gone." I felt overwhelmed with gratitude.

MAYBE KEENAN WAS also preparing himself to be without his parents for two months. For a quarter of his life, he had watched us plan, train, and sometimes agonize as we worked toward this goal. With four weeks until departure, as he approached his twelfth birthday, there was a subtle shift in my nightly routine with Keenan. Marty sometimes went to bed earlier than Keenan since he rose at 4:30 a.m. to go to work, so it was usually just me who went into his room to say good night. I always said, "I love you, Keenan," as I kissed him good night, and he routinely replied back, "I love you, Mom."

Now, before replying, Keenan paused—taking himself off auto-reply—and said in a warm voice, "I love you, Mom." And then, when I was almost out the door, with urgency in his voice he again said, "Mom . . . I love you." I gazed back at him, my heart in my throat. He continued, "Make sure you tell Dad that I love him too."

That evening, after Keenan was asleep, I sat down with my journal and pen. It was time to confront the question.

Dear Keenan,

This is the hardest letter that I've ever written, and I'm certain it will be the hardest letter that you've ever read. For if you are reading my words, then I must be gone. Something unpredictable and horribly unimaginable has happened to me in Antarctica.

At this moment I wish my arms could reach out from these pages and wrap around you, to comfort you like no other. I would take your hand in mine, whisper in your ear, tell you I love you and everything will be okay.

One of the best moments of my life was the day you were born, the day I became a mother, your mother. From the moment we locked eyes, it was love at first sight. Our special bond was instantaneous, undeniable, everlasting. Of all of the things that I've done in my life, nothing compares to being your mom. Nothing. You live in my core. You've taught me how to be more kind, more loving, more patient, more selfless.

Right now, I'm sure these words feel empty. Right now, you're full of sadness and perhaps anger, with questions that demand answers. How could I leave you? How could I choose Antarctica over spending the rest of my life loving you and watching you grow into a man? I promised to be safe. I promised I would be back.

You deserve answers. Part of living, really living, is to continuously grow and learn and challenge your limits. I believe to my core that the best way to live a good life, a full life, a happy life, is to seek challenge and to take risks, try new things, and push into the unknown. If I hadn't chosen Antarctica, then I might have been trail running on a mountain in Patagonia, or climbing an unnamed mountain in Nepal, or sailing on the Pacific with friends. You may have been there too. You see, don't be afraid of what will happen if you challenge yourself. You must do the things you think you cannot do. For you must live and use your gifts to the fullest, to share your light with the world. You never know what day will be your last, so don't wait for the perfect moment to step out and into your full self.

I know these words sound empty and meaningless, because nothing will bring me back to you. I hope over time this all makes some sense. I didn't die a senseless

death. I died while truly living. And my wish for you in
life is that you find your own path to being fully alive.
Please promise me to live, each day.

Keenan, I spent twelve glorious years with you—
my best years. I know your character. I see your heart.
You are destined to do great things in this world. I
know you will be true to yourself. I will be watching
you, and with you, every step of the way.

All of my love,
Mom

Teardrops sprinkled my journal, smearing some of the words. I cried because I knew without a doubt that I had no regrets about heading south. I didn't fear death, but I didn't take my life and my responsibilities as a parent for granted either.

My conversation with death prepared me to live.

THE BULLETIN BOARD at the entrance of Keenan's school displayed a map of Antarctica that would show students our daily progress. Marty and I walked past it on our way to the gymnasium, where hundreds of students were buzzing with excitement. It was our first school presentation; before our departure, we would present our story to other schools whose teachers we'd met while dragging tires on the Snoqualmie Valley Trail. Additional schools in Ohio, Iowa, and beyond would also be following our journey.

Marty and I stood in front of the audience of kids sitting on the glossy wood gymnasium floor and teachers sitting in metal folding chairs around the perimeter. Our bright-yellow tent, red sleds, and assorted gear were displayed off to the side. After Mrs. Johnston, the principal, introduced us, I began by saying, "It's so great to be here today. Marty and I are headed out on our expedition to the South Pole on November 17. Today we'll share a little about Antarctica and the details of our planning and training as we go after this dream. To start, we're going to get you to think about cold."

Drawing an imaginary line down the middle of the room with my arm, I said, "When I point at this half of the room, you will yell *think*." I pointed at the other side of the room and said, "And this half will yell *cold*."

Like conducting a symphony, I pointed right, then left and the gymnasium erupted with screams of "Think cold!" I repeated the exercise a few more times to pump up the energy in the room.

Next, Marty shared some vitals about Antarctica and the gear we'd take along. "Would any teacher like to volunteer for a demonstration?"

Mr. Eberhart, a six-foot-four fourth-grade teacher, raised his hand high into the air. Marty had him lie down inside our sled, then zipped him into the attached bag. "Ta-da, an emergency shelter," he said. The audience erupted with cheers.

Then Marty called up the principal to taste test various dehydrated meals and grade each as pass or fail. Rice and chicken passed, while chili mac failed.

After the principal sat down, I hoisted a gallon jar containing a white powdery substance above my head and asked, "Can you guess the secret ingredient that we'll take with us?"

Kids in the audience yelled: "Flour?" "Gatorade?" "Protein powder?"

"No. Powdered chicken fat," I said.

"Gross," shouted the kids in unison, and the wrinkled look on the teachers' faces said they agreed. Nobody volunteered for that taste test.

Keith had recommended powdered chicken fat as a lightweight way to add dense calories to our diet. I'd cold-called a company that sold the product in bulk to food manufacturers. After I told a nice man in the research and development department about our expedition, he sent us three gallons free of charge.

Then I said, "We all have talents, and one of ours is dreaming up hard endurance adventures and then making them happen. We all have our own South Pole dream to go after. What is yours?"

The kids' enthusiasm for our journey was contagious. Just imagining them waiting for our latest blog update would motivate me to push through the hard days in Antarctica. I wouldn't want to let them down.

WITH TWO WEEKS until departure, Marty held my hand as we stood before a packed living room at my friend's house. In all, there were twenty-two adults and fourteen kids there. In addition to my sister and her family, who live in the area, many were neighbors who'd grown to be close friends over the eleven years that we'd lived in North Bend. Our kids had literally grown up together. Others were local friends we had known for over fifteen years, who had shared in many outdoor adventures, Thanksgiving holidays, and summer weekends with us. As I stood there watching everyone, I got shivers thinking about how this was our village, our support team who had made this possible.

"Thank you, everyone, for being here," Sue said. "Chris and Marty will be proudly representing the United States while in Antarctica." A large military-style American flag was unfolded and displayed behind us—and our niece Jessie sang a compilation of songs that concluded with "The Star-Spangled Banner." As everyone sang along, the sound of separate voices melted into one. Standing before that flag, before that special group, the words "the land of the free and the home of the brave" took on new meaning. Marty and I swelled with pride, while the eyes in the room swelled with emotion. I knew going on an expedition was not the same as going off to war (I would never compare our adventure to sacrifices that those in the military make for our country), but I felt I'd already experienced some of the same emotions as I prepared to leave home. I imagined I might feel alone as we battled the elements so far away from this life and those we loved so dearly.

Then, one by one, people stood up, poured water into a bucket to represent our cup running over with support, and shared special send-off words. Brett Nunn kicked it off. The Nunns had been friends for over twenty years, ever since I lived next door to them in West Seattle during my single days. Keenan would be spending Thanksgiving with Brett, his wife, Becky, and their daughters, Emillia and Isabella. "As the lone representative of the Nunn family here tonight," Brett said, "I would like to say bon voyage to Chris and Marty and let them know we will be bathing them in the white light of love every moment they are away."

My twenty-seven-year-old niece, Lindsey, Sue's daughter, who would also be part of Keenan's surrogate team, spoke next. "I'm thankful you are entrusting me to take care of Keenan for a week. I'll faithfully update your blog every day while you are gone."

Her husband, Ben, added, "I feel welcomed into the family and appreciate your warm hearts."

Leni said, "After running with you for hundreds of miles, I know how prepared you are for this adventure. I have no doubt that you and Marty will make a great team. I'm thankful to be a part of it all and for our friendship. And while the expedition will test you physically and mentally, I believe this will surely be a trip of the soul."

I smiled at her, uplifted and grateful for her friendship and unwavering commitment to our expedition.

Keenan confidently stood up and said, "I'm glad you're going to the South Pole. I know that you'll do a great job."

I looked over at Marty and could see that he was holding back tears of pride, just like me.

Sue and Jessie each talked about how much we'd supported them through tough times; Maren, Byron, Susan, Danny, Laura, Ted, Jill, Jeff, and Lori recounted stories about shared adventures and provided words of wisdom to take with us; Randy and Frank talked about the quality of the people that surrounded us, and how we enriched each other's lives.

After the bucket was full of wishes, Sue gathered the group into a tight pack around Marty and me, all hands on us. Eyes closed, I could feel the energy emanating from each person and flowing to us in the middle of the pack. "God, please watch over and protect Chris and Marty as they make their way across Antarctica," Sue prayed. While God may have many definitions and names, I believe divine light moves through everything and everyone. *We are one.* Our shared energy connected us, bonded us, lifted us. This was the first time I'd had family and close friends pray over me like this. I felt deeply loved and filled with intense joy and inner peace. Grateful for the intimate moment, I thought: *I will tap this energy on days in Antarctica when my batteries are low.*

When Keenan went to bed that night, I said, "I'm really proud of you."

"Mom, I'm really proud of *you.*" Keenan was growing more confident and mature right before my eyes.

Lying in bed, I thought about all the things I'd miss about him. I loved the peaceful look of his body right before I woke him up for school. I loved hearing about his day over dinner, then playing a game of UNO before he started homework. I loved when the three of us sat in a row on our king-sized bed and read together in silence. I loved hearing him practice his flute in the privacy of his bedroom, snuggling up with a bowl of popcorn and fleece blanket to watch *Harry Potter* (again), and spending much of our time as a close-knit family of three.

A FEW DAYS before departure, I went for a last run with Leni.

As I followed her through a less traveled trail between Mount Si and Mount Teneriffe that I call The Connector Trail, I broke the silence and said, "Leni, while I'm in Antarctica, I'm really going to miss you."

"Aww," she responded without breaking stride, as if that was all I had to say.

I went on, "I mean I'm *really* going to miss you." I wasn't sure what I wanted to say to Leni, but I needed her to know how very important she was to me.

Leni stopped running, turned around to face me, and looked me straight in the eye. "Chris, I've tried to write down my thoughts so many times to formulate what I wanted to say to you before you leave—beyond what I said at your send-off party. I just never got it right." Then, through misty eyes, she said, "I just want you to know that I love you. And those words don't come easy for me."

"I love you too . . . your friendship is so important to me," I said with a shaky voice, my eyes matching her misty ones.

In all those years of friendship, we'd never uttered those three words to each other.

"I've depended so much on your support through the last few years of training and planning," I said. "Thanks for always being there for me and Marty."

Our teary hug communicated the rest.

As I edged my way closer to the unknown, a blanket of clarity surrounded me. People who mattered knew they mattered. Emotions that typically went unspoken were spoken. Love that sometimes hid inside me—behind the layers of defenses I sometimes wore to be strong—spilled out.

SINCE THE INCEPTION of our expedition, Keenan had grown five inches taller, advanced from simple math to algebra, and begun to speak with a lower tone to his voice. I saw him perched at the edge of our nest, ready to take flight as a sixth grader, just as we were about to board a plane for Chile and then Antarctica.

On the eve of departure, I lingered and lounged with Keenan, savoring a few more moments to imprint his facial features in my mind, memorize the sound of his changing voice, seal his laughter inside my heart. He had just turned twelve a few days earlier. Before I said good night, I asked, "How are you feeling about us going to Antarctica?"

"I know you and Dad are going to be okay. And I'll be okay too, Mom."

The last bits of stress drained from my body as it filled with pure excitement, joy, and love—a cocktail of intoxicating emotions. I thought back to twelve years ago, when as a new mom, I was completely sleep deprived, overwhelmed, and filled with anticipation of the future. Life was fresh and new. I was too, though not quite comfortable with my new title as parent. Now I found myself in a similar place, wrestling with new titles like Polar Mom, Polar Woman, and Polar Couple. Would I be able to live up to these new titles while calling upon the wisdom of my ultrarunning self?

It was a lot to take in on the eve of departure. I still needed to pack a few items, download more audiobooks, and copy a few more recent photos of Keenan onto my iPhone.

CHAPTER 6:

HOLDING PATTERNS

Departure day. Sunday, November 17, 2013. As promised, I woke Keenan at 3:30 a.m. before Marty and I set off for the airport for our early flight. I pulled him close and hugged him hard, whispered "I love you" into his ear, then let his tired body fall limp into bed. As I slowly walked out of Keenan's room, I glanced back to see him peacefully enveloped in a mass of warm down. Kiya slept on the floor beside him, her strong, sleek body spilling over the ends of her bed as she stretched out in bliss, unaware that the head of her pack was heading out.

I quietly padded downstairs and placed a handmade booklet entitled *Daily Notes* on the counter for Keenan to discover. On the cover were various photos of the three of us from adventures like our recent trip to Japan on top of majestic Mount Fuji. Inside were handwritten notes from Marty and me to ensure that Keenan would hear from us every day, even if we didn't call. I lingered, glancing at the photos on the wall above the kitchen table of the three of us on other adventures in California, France, and Africa—then turned and left behind my regular life.

AFTER FOUR FLIGHTS and 40 hours of travel, we were on the other side of the world. Glancing down the street as we drove in a taxi to our hotel, I could see a slice of blue water and imagined Antarctica beckoning from afar.

The next morning, we were about to enter ALE's warehouse in Punta Arenas. I placed the key into a padlock on the warehouse's two oversized green metal doors, and it clicked open.

Marty pulled open the hefty door. As I walked in, I scanned the sea of boxes and stuffed shelves like a mother searching for her lost child in a massive crowd. The warehouse served as a storage and staging area for the few self-guided teams like ours, and for ALE's guided expeditions that would ski to the South Pole or climb Mount Vinson, the highest mountain in Antarctica and one of the renowned Seven Summits. Somewhere hidden among this jumbled mess of crates, tubs, boxes, tents, and sleeping bags were our eight heavy-duty blue plastic tubs full of gear and food, and a long wooden crate packed with two sleds. All we had carried on our flights were a few clothes, toiletries, books, and all of our electronics for the trip: laptop computer (which would stay in Punta Arenas while we were in Antarctica), single-lens reflex camera (which would stay at base camp), point-and-shoot camera, two solar panels, solar battery pack, two GPS devices, personal locator beacon, hotspot device, iPhone, two iPod nanos, wind meter, battery charger, extra batteries, and two satellite phones to connect us with home.

Before departing, Marty had investigated the complicated international rules of shipping gear. We had meticulously checked off each item listed on our Customs manifest before sealing the tubs for shipping. A professional company had packed our sleds in a Styrofoam-filled wooden crate to ensure safe passage.

When Marty dropped off our items with the shipping company in Seattle, he asked the manager, "Do you *really* think our cargo will arrive safely in Punta Arenas in four weeks?"

"I hope so," the man said.

I recalled those not so reassuring words as I searched the warehouse, thinking it would take a small miracle for all of our items to actually be there and not mysteriously lost or hung up in Customs.

Just then, Marty yelled, "Our sleds, I found our sleds."

I continued scanning, and then the color blue popped out of the clutter. "Here are our tubs."

As Marty prepared to open the container of sleds, I held my breath. After prying the box open with a screwdriver he found lying on a shelf, he carefully pulled them out. Examining all sides, I could see there was not one scratch, crack, or dent.

Marty and I looked at each other and smiled. Relief.

We moved the sleds and tubs of gear to an empty corner of the warehouse and made a makeshift workstation out of a stray piece of plywood set on top of two small tables. I opened the tubs and after a quick inspection, decided everything had arrived safely without being disturbed in customs.

More relief.

Two other people were working at a similar station nearby. Marty and I took a break to wander over and introduce ourselves.

A blond-haired sturdy-looking young man said, "Hello, I'm Lewis," in a British accent. "I'm skiing the Hercules Inlet route. This is my guide, Carl." Next to Lewis stood a tall dark-haired guy in his midtwenties with a scruffy beard and weathered look of experience.

Instead of beginning their expedition with all of their possessions packed into sleds, they planned to have ALE airdrop two packages of food at designated drop sites. This made the weight of their sleds more manageable—about half the weight of ours to start. If Lewis finished his intended route, he would become the youngest to ever complete the journey. He was sixteen years old, only four years older than Keenan, and had been inspired by the slide presentation of a local man who had gone on an expedition to the South Pole. Afterward, he couldn't get the idea out of his head.

Lewis was scheduled to be on our flight from Punta Arenas to Antarctica. Since we were planning to ski the Messner route, though, we would start in a different place on the continent than he would. I received an email from his mother earlier that day saying that I would likely meet her son and that while she knew from our blog that I was missing Keenan back home, she was missing her son. I imagined one day Keenan would put me in this mother's place, and like my mom had done with me, I would have to fight through unsettling worry while trusting in my son's skills.

CHILEAN IMPORTATION RULES required that we ship all food items in their original packaging, so our goal for the day was to repackage all of our food to eliminate unnecessary weight. I dug out all of our food from the tubs, and soon trash bins overflowed with discarded packaging from freeze-dried meals, ramen noodles, oatmeal, and chocolate bars.

As I worked, I thought back to the morning in early October when I'd hunched over a food scale in the mad-science lab that was our kitchen, weighing every gram and calculating every calorie of each item on our menu so that we ensured we brought the right amount. For fun, Marty had Keenan lie on the kitchen floor and buried him under a huge pile of dehydrated meals—the winners of our month-long taste test of practically every meal on the market.

I unwrapped a package of dehydrated mac and cheese and instantly remembered Keenan's proclamation that day: "Mac and cheese is the best, followed by chicken and noodle. I could eat those every day." I chuckled to myself.

In Antarctica, our diet of ready-to-eat calorie-dense foods and dehydrated meals would starkly contrast the organic fresh fruits and vegetables and primarily plant-based diet we ate at home. Our expedition breakfast menu consisted of oatmeal packed with almonds, powdered whole milk and dried fruit, and an instant mocha—Starbucks Via mixed with hot chocolate. We would eat an assortment of bars, nuts, salami, and cheese for on-the-move snacks during the day, and soup and a dehydrated meal for dinner.

When Marty had been in Oslo to pick up our sleds, he'd met with Norwegian polar expert Christian Eide, who holds the speed record on the Hercules Inlet route. Christian shared spreadsheets breaking down how many calories he recommends per day, and we followed this when putting together our menu. We planned for 5,400 calories (2.5 pounds) of food per person each day. Since we'd each burn 7,000 to 8,000 calories per day, we would fall short by about 1,600 to 2,600 calories, leading to inevitable weight loss. We packed forty-five days of food—for an estimated forty-day expedition plus five extra days of food. This represented about half the weight in our sleds. Every ounce mattered. Bring too much food, and our sleds might prove too heavy to pull. Bring too little food, and we might run out of gas. Much to Marty's dismay, at the last minute we cut our hot chocolate packets from two per person per day to one to save fourteen pounds.

After hours of tedious work, stacks of food repackaged in lightweight plastic bags lined the table. Next, we consolidated smaller bags into larger bags that each contained four days of food. By the end of the day, we found our way back to our hotel, the Ilaia, and fell into bed.

THE NEXT MORNING, I locked our room with the key attached to a star-shaped piece of wood that said "Trust." The cheery red and yellow walls of the hotel, with the phrases "Let's laugh" and "Here and now" painted in crisp white, set the tone for the day. After three years of nonstop running to get to the starting line, this charming hotel seemed like the perfect place to recuperate for a few days.

Sitting at breakfast as we waited for our homemade muesli, yogurt, and fresh fruit, I became engrossed in reading a poem printed on the colorful placemat: "Laugh, dream, celebrate, enjoy, live, breathe, caress, rejoice, sing, dance, listen, advise, relax, kiss, give, amaze, receive, forgive, watch, feel, share, be, hear, imagine, travel, express, create, learn, shine, fulfill, grow, respect, play, risk, do, and most of all . . . LOVE."

I reread the words over and over, as if reading a message from inside a fortune cookie that I hoped would come true.

"I love this placemat," I exclaimed.

"Yeah," said Marty. He looked up at me with a polite smile, clearly not as moved.

While I tend to feel the extreme emotional highs and lows of life, Marty's more even-keeled and practical. We experienced similar waves of anxiety and concern over saying goodbye to Keenan, but my waves were a bit bigger. And now, Marty was right with me as I shifted into the joy of starting our adventure, only I was feeling the nuanced meaning of it all—even this placemat—while he patiently waited in anticipation of the actual experience.

As we split the last bite of melon, Marty said, "In Antarctica, we'll have to stay strong and keep our emotions in check."

I glanced at him with questioning eyebrows.

He continued. "I mean, like when we're running hundred-mile races or climbing in dangerous situations . . . or like when I was a police officer. To stay focused and safe, we don't let emotions get in the way."

"Right," I said politely. I basically agreed. I also knew I wasn't able to compartmentalize my emotions the way Marty could. But no matter how I was feeling, I would give it my all in Antarctica.

We spent the morning hunting down perishable items to complete our expedition menu; at home, we had planned the exact number of perishables (and calories) to purchase—with the help of Christian's spreadsheet. We left the specialty nut store with a cornucopia of almonds, cashews, sugar-coated peanuts, and dried fruits: twenty-four pounds of snacks packed with calories and fat that wouldn't freeze at −40 degrees. At the local supermarket, we cleaned out the supply of hard cheeses, salami, and Pringles. I wondered how our bodies would manage on this new diet.

After hours of shopping, we set up a food-prep and bagging station back in our cozy hotel room. Liz, the bubbly Chilean manager with happy brown eyes and deep wrinkles in her cheeks likely created from decades of smiling, loaned us a cutting board and two flimsy serrated knives, the type you buy for half price in packs of ten from an infomercial. Over the next few hours, we cut twenty-six pounds of hard cheese and sixteen pounds of salami into small cubes, and then packed them into individual plastic bags. I tended to my first expedition blister caused by hours of cutting. Splaying my tired body out on the bed after completing our mission, I smelled the scent of cheese and salami lingering in the air, like smoke after a fire.

With our departure to Antarctica scheduled the next day, it was finally the moment of truth. Marty grabbed the handle on one end of his fully packed sled with both hands, and I grabbed the other end. Bending down, I grunted as I lifted the sled six inches off the ground, just high enough to shuffle over to the oversized scale and hoist it up. The digital reader stopped at 220 pounds. *Holy crap.* I caught Marty's eye for a moment, but neither of us spoke. Forty pounds more than we had originally estimated. My sled ended up weighing 220 pounds too. I wondered how the higher-than-expected weight might impact our journey.

There was nothing we could do about it now.

Relaxing at the hotel, just before turning off the light for bed, the phone rang. Steve, our contact at ALE, said, "Chris? Due to bad conditions in Antarctica, your flight to Union Glacier will be delayed. It'll be at least two days while we wait for a weather window."

I hung up the phone and saw by the somber look on Marty's face that he knew what was going on.

"I was really looking forward to stepping foot in Antarctica tomorrow," Marty said.

"Me too," I said, pulling up the covers. "At least we're done packing and can actually rest for a few days."

To land at the ALE airstrip, pilots needed to have a visual sighting of the runway, which was impossible in stormy weather or low-cloud conditions. A few years ago, ALE had moved their airstrip from Patriot Hills, which was plagued with unfriendly wind shears, to Union Glacier, which provided better landing conditions. They had also installed a sophisticated weather forecasting system to help minimize delays. Still, a stunning array of variables and logistics had to come together to actually allow a plane to touch down in Antarctica.

Two additional days turned into five long days, and we were still in Punta Arenas growing tired of waiting.

WE TOOK REFUGE in a peaceful glass room perched on top of our hotel like a modern tree house. Soft piano music and distant sounds of birds filled the air. The intense Chilean sun warmed my body, relaxed my mind. As I looked out the window to the south, I saw large whitecaps caused by the 30- to 35-mile-per-hour blasting winds that had greeted us earlier during our morning jog along the water. I wondered if those winds were blowing in from Antarctica and causing our flight delay.

Marty sat next to me on the cozy salmon-colored couch. He was learning the advanced features of our new camera.

"Do you think it's going to be worth all of the time and money we've invested?" I asked.

He stared off into space, reflecting on the gravity of my question. It was one we had revisited many times over the past year.

"Yes, I do. As we've said before, we could have spent the money on a rustic cabin in the mountains or a new luxury car, but those are things—not experiences." He paused, and then went on. "We know how much we both love adventure and how close we get as a couple when we're out in the wilderness together."

"Yes. I can't wait to get started . . . for just you and me to be moving across Antarctica."

"Leave all of this complexity behind," Marty said. I understood what he meant: that we could finally let go of making decisions about minute details, trust that we had everything we needed, and lean into the singular focus of skiing to the

South Pole. I was ready to see how the adventure would shape the next decade of our lives, like the way the birth of a child puts your life on a certain trajectory, giving it dimension and depth and meaning.

Marty and I decided to test the satellite phone one last time by calling Keenan. It was Thanksgiving, and back home, the Nunn family was celebrating with him at our house. When I checked email that morning, Brett had written, "I made the cranberry relish and baked the corn bread squares that go in the stuffing, and the pumpkin pie just came out of the oven . . . Isabella is pummeling Keenan with those foam sticks."

Breathless and excited on the phone, Keenan said, "Mom, the smoked turkey was awesome, as usual, and tomorrow we're going to cut down and decorate our Christmas tree." Brett and Becky planned to carry out our longstanding day-after-Thanksgiving tradition by visiting our local Christmas tree farm, the one where we typically celebrated with homemade chocolate chip cookies and apple cider sold at their makeshift store after cutting down our tree. The farm where, in Keenan's younger years, he melted into my lap with my coat wrapped around him to keep extra warm during the haystack ride around the property.

Toward the end of the call, Marty said, "Keenan, how are you doing with us being gone? You know we really miss you." The heartfelt way Marty asked the question instantly brought tears to my eyes.

"I'm fine, Dad. I'm having a lot of fun."

That night as I lay in bed imagining the smell of the smoked turkey and herb-infused stuffing we'd missed, I counted the days that had passed in Punta Arenas—a total of ten, five more than planned. It was the longest we'd ever been away from Keenan—and we weren't even in Antarctica yet. I could not imagine just how tough being apart was going to be.

Then the phone rang. I looked at my watch—10:00 p.m.

Steve said, "There is a small weather window to land in Antarctica. We'll pick you up at your hotel in thirty minutes."

Marty and I jumped out of bed and hugged as if we'd just won the lottery. Go time.

AS I POKED my head through the door of the plane, bitter air blasted my huge blue down jacket. Even though I wore goggles, my eyes strained through the blazing sun to find each step down the metal staircase. I was careful not to slip as my boot touched Antarctic ice for the first time; I had read about someone falling and injuring his back, ending his expedition after one step. I turned and saw Marty in his puffy red down jacket step onto the ice.

"Oh my gosh, this is so crazy!" I said, my body pulsing with excitement to be in one of the remotest places on earth.

"It's awesome!"

I was glad our Russian Ilyushin Il-76 cargo plane had brought us here safely; being aboard the old plane, which had no windows, had been like traveling back in time, and my ears still thrummed from the fury of the engines throughout the four-and-a-half-hour flight. Behind me, more people squinted as they stepped off the plane: a group of Mount Vinson climbers, a tourist group who would fly to the South Pole for a quick look, then head to the coast to observe and photograph penguins, and a few expedition teams like us.

The air was electric.

I walked carefully away from the plane on the blue-ice runway. The relatively smooth, shiny surface with a shellacked look was created naturally by continuous wind that scoured snow off the surface, allowing cargo planes with wheels to land. I stopped open-mouthed and turned 360 degrees to take in the place that I'd been imagining for three years. Beyond the runway, the powdery white of the glacier extended out in all directions. To the west was the Ellsworth mountain range, a semicircle of mountains stretching 224 miles, and home to 16,066-foot Mount Vinson, the highest mountain in Antarctica.

The mountains, with patches of rock peeking through snow and ice on south-facing ridges, looked more like the Colorado Rockies than the Cascade Mountains that I was accustomed to seeing back home. The blazing sun danced off all the white, making it come alive. Our plane seemed strangely out of place, an alien vessel in a wonderfully wild land.

I turned back to see Marty staring off into the distance with a smile on his face. "Hey, let's document our first moment here." I reached into my pocket and pulled out my camera.

We took pictures of each other posing in front of the plane, and then squeezed together, arms around each other, as another passenger took a photo of us.

After standing like penguins in a pack, waiting for an instruction, groups were escorted over to orange four-wheel-drive trucks. We drove along a makeshift road in the snow marked by tire tracks and black flags. Within 10 minutes, we arrived at ALE's Union Glacier Camp.

I exited the truck and saw a snow-packed runway and four small planes off to the left, and to the right, temporary structures dotted the landscape. The driver pointed out a communications building, two main tents for eating and congregating, a bathroom building, and rows of sun-faded red, white, and blue dome-shaped tents—the living quarters for ALE staff and guided clients. We would stay in our own tent. While trucks shuttled gear from the cargo plane to an area outside the main tent, we ventured inside the heated structure to eat a welcome breakfast of scrambled eggs, bacon, pancakes, and fresh fruit. By the time we recovered our packed sleds, it was 6:00 a.m. on Saturday, November 30.

With ideal weather conditions—clear skies, minimal wind, and a temperature of a balmy 10 degrees—we set up our tent, following the process we had practiced at home and would repeat nightly throughout our expedition. Marty unzipped his sled bag and removed the fat six-foot-long sausage that was our tent. With Keith's help, we had rigged the poles to be permanently threaded into one side, and then each pole was folded over to make the whole unit compact enough to fit into the top of our sled bag. This method allowed us to efficiently set up our tent without the chaos of trying to insert poles into tent sleeves with cold hands and in harsh conditions. Our tent, a brand-new dome-shaped North Face VE 25, was the same classic workhorse we both used in Denali fifteen years earlier. It was familiar and comfortable and had stood strong against 60 mile per hour winds at high camp; we trusted its durability for whatever Antarctica would whip up.

Marty clipped a carabiner from the base of the tent to a loop of rope on the sled, anchoring it to prevent it from accidentally blowing away during the setup process. Marty had learned his lesson at 16,200 feet on his first attempt on Denali in 1995. A puff of wind blew into his tent just as he was about to anchor it, picking it up like a kite and instantly sending it over the ledge and tumbling 4,000 feet down the glacier, ending his expedition. In Antarctica, we carefully unrolled our tent and unfolded the poles to their full length. I held on to the back of the tent while Marty pushed the remaining portion of the first pole through the tent sleeve until it made the tent curve into the air. As we connected the remaining four poles in a similar fashion, a bright-yellow dome sprang to life like a structure in a children's pop-up book.

I repositioned the tent on a flat surface, avoiding slopes or bumps to make for a better night's sleep, and faced the back door into the wind. I kicked a few stakes into the crusty top layer of snow to hold the tent in place, then removed the tent fly from the top of my sled bag. The waterproof outer tarp would cover the tent to add insulation and protection from wind. Starting at the back of the tent, I unrolled the fly onto the top of the tent like a giant pancake, then handed over the second half to Marty to finish the job from his end of the tent. We each connected our sides of the fly to the tent and finished staking to secure it against weather. We moved quickly and efficiently without talking, like dancers in a ballet.

We crawled into the tent and I looked around. "Hey, I forgot about all of the writing on the tent walls."

Before our departure, family and friends had scribed notes on the walls; out of town family had emailed their messages to Sue, who wrote them on the tent. I looked around the tent, smiling. This was the first time we would read the messages. Next to Marty's bed, it said, "Every once in a while during the day, don't forget to look up and take it all in," and next to where I lay my head at night, Keenan wrote, "I know you're going to make it! I love you!" I felt that a welcome committee of family and friends had joined us in the tent, the words and drawings, big and small, were scrawled across the yellow walls in an array of colors like cheerful hellos. Marty and I nestled inside for much of the day, lounging around as we waited for a flight to our starting point that we hoped would depart the next day. After dinner in the main ALE tent, it was strange to crunch through the snow to our tent at nine at night with the sun still glaring above us. In the summer in Antarctica, the sun never sets.

The next morning, the continent provided a proper welcome with 30-mile-per-hour winds and a wind chill of −20 degrees. To walk the short one hundred yards from our tent to the food tent, I leaned hard into the wind, bundled from head to toe in layers of insulation, down, and windproof shells. With our sleds packed and ready to go, we were again playing the waiting game. The bad weather had created a backlog of people hoping to be air-shuttled to the start of their adventures. Two weeks since leaving Seattle, and we still hadn't actually started our expedition. Frustration started slipping through the cracks of my patience like crystals of snow finding their way into my face mask.

Back in our tent later that afternoon, I laid in my sleeping bag, staring at the ceiling. "I can't take this waiting, it's starting to drive me crazy."

"I'm sure we'll get to leave soon," Marty said calmly.

All day we'd been anxiously waiting for a break in the weather at our destination, which was plagued by low visibility and high winds. Now I watched through the tent door with envy as the two Twin Otter and two Basler BT-67 ski planes took off in the direction of Mount Vinson and the South Pole.

"I wonder if ALE is shuttling the penguin people first because they have tighter vacation schedules," I said anxiously.

"I'm sure we'll get to leave soon," said Marty, still using his calm voice.

"We should be the ones getting to leave since we are already behind schedule." I was worried that our later-than-expected start date would throw off the schedule for those watching Keenan back home. I just wanted to get started.

To kill time, we pulled out our Iridium hotspot device that worked with our satellite phone and attempted to send a few test photos to our team back home. Despite repeated tries, it failed. The cable connecting the hotspot to the sat phone appeared to be damaged. *Crap!* Aborting that mission, I decided to confirm that our camera battery was fully charged. I inserted it into the charger on our solar panel, and nothing happened—the charger seemed to mysteriously have stopped working. *Really? Come on people!*

"What is happening?" I said, as if Marty should have an instant answer and make it better.

"I don't know?" said Marty, the calm now draining from his voice.

The charge in our battery would likely last only a few days. Without a way to recharge the battery, we wouldn't be able to document our expedition with photos or video. We bundled up and scrambled around camp in search of technical help. In the communications tent, we met Dean hunched over a small desk surrounded by an array of technical gadgets, phones, and maps. After we explained our problem, he fished around in boxes of cables, spliced together two different wires, and fashioned a new connection for our hotspot so we could send photos back home.

Later that day, someone else from ALE donated his battery charger to replace our faulty one so we'd be able to charge our camera battery.

Thank goodness.

In the tent that night, I felt embarrassed about my attitude from earlier in the day. If we had flown out in the morning, we would not have discovered our gear problems and found make-shift solutions.

I zipped myself into my deep-purple down sleeping bag. "Sorry I was so impatient today. I love you."

"I love you too. I hope tomorrow is our day."

CHAPTER 7:

FINDING OUR BEARINGS

The next morning, I pulled open the tent door and peeked outside. I was greeted with clear, sunny skies and low winds, perfect conditions for flying the two and a half hours from Union Glacier to our starting point on the Ronne Ice Shelf. It was finally our day. After stuffing ourselves with our last hot heaping plateful of lunch, we helped the pilot cram our bulging sleds into a small red Twin Otter plane. He strapped them into place like oversized passengers.

Engines revved to life as the plane raced down the snowy runway and a cold draft filled the plane. I looked at Marty and grinned. His eyes lit up and he reached over and held my gloved hand. Now it really felt like go time. Flying away from a shrinking base camp and the expansive Ellsworth Mountains, I marveled at the vast nothingness that would be our playground for the coming months.

Antarctica is a giant land mass draped in ice that has been compressed over hundreds of years, ice that runs one to two miles deep in some places. As we flew along, I saw long parallel lines stretching across the landscape, formed by snow that settled just above the surface of gaping crevasses and created the illusion of stripes on a giant white American flag. Crevasses are cracks that result from thick glacier ice slowly moving over the uneven Antarctic terrain. From my vantage point from above, the cracks looked about thirty feet wide, spacious enough to swallow a skier and sled as a small appetizer.

When the plane leveled out, I fished around for my camera stashed inside my pocket and then tried to find the perfect angle to capture the feeling of limitlessness. My ability to discern any sense of scale was lost to the whiteness of it all. *Is it possible to spot a skier far below from here?* I imagined looking down upon myself, a barely perceptible dot appearing frozen in place. My heart raced. Every ounce of me was bursting to start our expedition.

A few hours later, our plane descended and flew close to the ice as the pilot searched the surface for an ideal spot to land. He lowered to twenty feet above the ice, then suddenly pulled up, aborting the landing. After four passes over the white snowpack, the plane lowered closer and closer until at last—touchdown. My body bounced up and down and sideways as we bumped along to a stop. The pilot intended to set the plane down as close to the coastline of Antarctica as possible, where land meets the Ronne Ice Shelf, a block of ice about the size of Spain that extends to the Weddell Sea. To me, it all looked the same. Snow and ice everywhere.

Marty and I unloaded our sleds from the plane. As the pilot helped, he casually said, "Some years the snow is firm and hard, and others it's soft. This year, everywhere that I've landed, it's been soft." Hard pack meant gliding skis and easier miles. Soft snow meant sinking sleds and heavy pulling. I dreaded the thought of dragging sleds for weeks on end through grueling soft snow.

Within minutes, we bid the pilot and the last remnants of civilization farewell. Watching the plane shrink to a red dot in the sky and then disappear on the horizon, we stood motionless in the piercing silence. We were instantly transported to another world, one like no other on earth. In every direction, a sea of white nothingness and cloudless blue sky. The full weight of the adventure stretched out before us. It was 18 degrees, a warm day by Antarctica standards given the average was −22 degrees from November through January, the summer months on the continent. As it was already late in the day, we had agreed in the plane to ski only a few hours before setting up camp.

With no discernible coastline marking the beginning of our journey, Marty turned on the GPS.

"We are two miles out at sea on the Ronne Ice Shelf," he said. "Our official starting point."

Then Marty took our first bearing. We both dialed the number from the GPS screen into our low-tech compasses held about a foot in front of our bodies by a triangular device that attached to our waists for hands-free use. Marty turned off the GPS to save battery power and stowed it in an insulated container inside his sled. We would only turn on the GPS a few times a day—in the morning to confirm our bearing, once in the middle of the day, and at the end of the day inside the tent. At 4:30 p.m., we snapped on skis and clipped harnesses to sleds.

I turned and gazed deep into Marty's blue eyes, the ones that I'd first seen fifteen years earlier on Denali, the last place that we'd been on a major expedition. I smiled the same smile of unbridled enthusiasm that had captured his heart on that mountain. Marty smiled back, wearing the look of eager anticipation I'd seen at the beginning of other adventures we'd shared. Then we lowered goggles and threaded mittens into ski-pole straps.

I leaned forward in my harness until I felt the familiar tug that meant all slack had been pulled out of the rope attached to the sled. This was the first time we'd feel the brutal 220-pound weight of the beasts.

I yelled into the wind, "Woohoo!" and with great anticipation, I lunged forward. My sled slowly slid into motion. *Hello, adventure, here we come!*

Whether due to overactive adrenaline glands or a fully rested body or the pure Antarctic air rushing into lungs, my heavy sled glided better than expected. Marty and I skied side by side like synchronized swimmers. After about 30 minutes, I glanced back and noticed that our skis and sleds left deep grooves.

"I'm going to drop behind you," I said.

"Sounds good."

In the lead position, Marty navigated while I fell into the single-file formation that we'd practiced back home. In the coming weeks, we would create a single line of tracks across the Antarctic snowpack. The snowpack is composed of a layer of newer snow on top, crusty snow from previous years in the middle, and icy glacier below that is flowing outward and downward from the pressure of its own weight. In my research, I learned that Antarctica is considered a desert with annual snowfall averaging only six and a half inches. More than a foot of snow can fall near the coast, while the interior averages two inches.

After about an hour of skiing through soft snow, I took the lead and Marty dropped behind me. Staring out at the vast nothingness, I imagined that I was the only person in Antarctica, at least for 600 miles in every direction.

There are no permanent residents on the continent, only people working at remote scientific stations separated by thousands of miles of harsh terrain on a landmass one and a half times the size of the United States. More than thirty countries maintain permanent research stations. The Antarctic Treaty, a multicountry agreement that governs the continent, provides a remarkable example of cooperation for the greater good of research. The treaty states that "Antarctica will be used for peaceful purposes only." During the summer months, up to 200 people inhabit the Amundsen-Scott South Pole Station, a US scientific research station located at the geographic South Pole, the southernmost place on earth, on a high plateau at 90 degrees south, and the finish line of our expedition. A staff of about eighty people winter over from mid-February through mid-October. Due to extreme cold, severe winter storms, and 24-hour darkness, all air traffic to and from Antarctica is discontinued for the long winter season. In essence, staff are stranded on a giant white island.

In addition to the South Pole Station, the United States runs another larger base, McMurdo Station, located on the southern tip of Ross Island, on the opposite side of the continent from the Ronne Ice Shelf and about 995 miles from the South Pole.

I glanced at my watch—6:30 p.m., our agreed-upon stop time for the day—and stopped. Marty skied up next to me; we unclipped from sleds.

Gazing out at the white snow topped by endless blue sky, I stretched my back, took a long deep breath, and exhaled.

"This is amazing," I said.

"I still can't believe we've finally started."

With gentle, wide-open terrain in all directions, everywhere looked like an ideal campsite. No worries about unsavory car campers showing up to ruin our night with blaring generators powering TVs and air conditioners, like that Fourth of July on Orcas Island. That night, Marty, Keenan, and I had hastily broken down our tent at 11:00 p.m., stuffed all of our camping gear into our car, and hopped on the last ferry back to Seattle.

Once the tent was securely standing, I grabbed our gear for the night. I sifted through sleds until I found our cooking gear, bedding, clothing and personal items, water bottles, thermoses, and food for the night and next morning. I opened the tent door and tossed in the assorted items.

Marty jumped inside and began the tent organization process.

Staying outside, I stabbed the crunchy top layer of snow with my shovel to create chunks. Then I piled them onto the tent flaps that were custom-sewn to the bottom of the tent fly. The snow would prevent wind from blowing under and lifting the fly into a vulnerable position.

I whacked more chunks from the surrounding snow and stuffed them into the tent vestibule. Our tent fly covered the main living quarters and extended out over the front and back doors, forming two areas called vestibules. In the front vestibule, we stored cooking equipment and food bags, while the back contained the shells of our boots and other stray items.

Plunging inside, I said, "Our first official night on our expedition."

"Come in and get cozy."

Sitting in the doorway of the tent with legs dangling in the vestibule, I removed my boot shells, then liners, and squirmed onto my side of the tent. The inside of the tent felt surprisingly warm, so I put on my light down sweater and stowed the rest of my jackets in my corner. Marty, on cooking duty, set our only cook pot onto the one-burner stove and began the nightly two-hour process of melting snow blocks into water. Cooking for us meant adding hot water to our various dehydrated meals full of noodles, rice, meats, vegetables, spices and sauces.

While snow melted, Marty logged our stats for the day in his small green waterproof notebook—the same flip-from-the-top style he used as a police officer—and plotted our position on an aviation map that showed the most granular detail of our route that we could find. A quarter inch represented about 10 miles on ice. While it would be quite some time before it looked like we had made any progress, I was excited to see our first dot on the map.

Marty poured boiling water into our cups full of dried ramen noodle soup. While I waited for crispy clumps to turn into soft noodles, I jotted a few notes in my journal. Soon the soup was ready, and I quickly slurped it down.

About 20 minutes later, Marty said, "Time for our second course. Can you guess what it is?"

The smell of chicken broth filled the tent. "It's either chicken and noodles or rice and chicken." I opened the lid and took a bite. "Oh, yum," I said with a smile.

"Keenan loves chicken and noodles." I was thinking about him when I picked it.

"What a perfect day for skiing." I shoveled in another spoonful of surprisingly delicious salty noodles. "I thought we moved well. Even though it was only a few hours."

"I'm glad we got some skiing in before our first full day. I can't wait for tomorrow."

"Me too."

After doing dishes by swishing hot water around in the cups and dumping the contents in the corner of the vestibule, I switched on the satellite phone and dialed a number that went directly to a voice mailbox set up for our expedition. Each night we would leave a three-minute voice blog about the highlights of the day. Our team back home would post a link to the audio and transcribe the message on our website so that people could follow along on our journey. Marty called ALE to report our current location (S 82 23.582, W 65 14.296) along with distance and time traveled (2.5 miles in two hours). We would call ALE Communications at 8:10 p.m. each evening to report our daily stats. They would find out how we were doing and provide a general weather report. ALE was our ultimate safety net. With Keenan back home, we wouldn't have gone on this adventure without knowing they could dispatch a plane to help. If ALE Communications didn't hear from us within 24 hours of our scheduled call-in time, they would follow a series of protocols ultimately resulting in a plane searching for us at our last known position, and alert our support team at home that something was wrong.

Of course, there was no guarantee of how quickly a rescue plane could arrive at our destination, especially in unfavorable weather conditions. Their small planes land by sight, eliminating the option of flying through low clouds, whiteouts, or extreme winds—the exact conditions that could lead to trouble for us.

Still, knowing that a plane was theoretically a phone call away provided great comfort. We were trading the purity of a completely isolated experience for the comfort of staying connected with loved ones and the outside world. Our satellite phone was like an umbilical cord connecting us back to Keenan. We could feed him information about our well-being and prevent him from suffering in silence like the families of early explorers. Those explorers were gone for two years with no contact with the outside world along the way, sailing for months through frozen oceans to arrive on the shores of Antarctica, wintering over while waiting for more favorable summer conditions for overland travel, then advancing through harsh terrain and blizzards in their struggle to reach the Pole.

After our evening call, we brushed teeth (spitting into the corner of the vestibule), emptied bladders into our shared pee bottle, and finally dissolved into the comfort of our cozy sleeping bags.

"This feels awesome," said Marty.

While tired from the day of travel, our bodies felt invigorated after our short ski—our first real exercise in a week.

We set our watch alarms for 6:00 a.m. and covered our eyes with hats. It still felt strange to have sunlight shining through the tent at night. No need to pack headlamps.

"I love you," Marty said softly, then leaned over and kissed me. I felt the stubble of his beard against my cheek.

"I love you too."

Within seconds, I was asleep.

IN THE MORNING, I sat up, rubbed the sleep out of my eyes, and stuck my arm out the back door of the tent to check the weather. I chose this more primitive method versus digging out the anemometer—a device the size of a granola bar—that precisely measures temperatures and wind speed. Another temperate day.

Since it was my day to cook, I fired up the stove, which ran on a refillable canister of white gas. Before we left, our woodworker friend, Hugh, fashioned a thin hardwood platform to use as insulation between stove and snow. Without it, the stove would heat up and sink into the surrounding snow, resulting in a tipped-over pot of boiling water. Within 10 minutes, we were eating oatmeal and sipping expedition mochas, one of Marty's favorite moments of the day—he savored every drop of chocolate and caffeine. After melting snow to fill water bottles, we packed up belongings, placed our water bottles in insulated holders (critical to keep water from freezing while stored in the sled), took down the tent, and stowed the gear in our sleds.

By 8:30 a.m., we clipped into our sleds and set off into a sea of whiteness for our first full day. While the surface looked relatively flat in all directions, it felt rough and wavy under foot, with a thin layer of sugary snow on top. Except for a few small white cotton-ball clouds to our left, the sky was powder blue. With little wind and a balmy 10-degree temperature, I felt hot within 15 minutes of skiing. I changed from a heavy wool buff—a tube of cloth worn around the neck like a scarf or pulled up around the head like a balaclava—to a lighter one, but I still started sweating. Pulling heavy sleds was hard work. When you sweat, the cold wind quickly turns damp clothes into frozen hypothermia death traps. Succumbing to hypothermia and the slippery slope of events that happen when you get dangerously cold—slurring of speech, stumbling around like a drunk, frostbite, or loss of fingers and toes—was not an option.

Feeling utterly uncomfortable, I struggled to open pit zips and ventilate while on the move just like during my training in Minnesota. Heat from my body caused my goggles to completely fog over. For two hours, I struggled to see more than twenty feet in front of me despite the clear sunny day.

At break time, I fished inside my sled to find my spare pair of goggles. Both pairs of my specialized dark glacier goggles provided protection from harmful UV rays that can cause sun blindness, a painful temporary loss of vision that can happen when you travel for multiple days in sunny, snowy places. In places like Antarctica, where there is little natural ozone protection against UV rays, we had to not only be extremely careful with our eyes, but guard against potential sunburn caused by sun reflecting off snow. Today the intense sun made every detail pop and shimmer, like the effects of a mirrored disco ball. Five minutes into break time, I realized my liner gloves were sweaty and would soon turn my hands into useless frosty clumps. On mild days like today, I wore fleece liner gloves and shoved hands into pogies, special mittens attached around my ski poles to protect my hands while allowing good hand mobility. When it got colder, I would wear warmer ski gloves over my fleece liners and shove my hands either into my pogies or into big down mittens.

For now, my body registered warm while skiing and cool when we were stopped.

Midway through the day, Marty waved me over and said, "Seems like you're going too fast when you lead. Can you slow down?"

I paused and glanced up at him with a surprised look hidden behind my face mask. He sounded like me when we ran together back home sometimes. Besides, I felt like I was skiing at an easy to moderate pace.

Likely sensing I didn't understand his comment, he continued, "My ankles are rolling outward each time I thrust my skis forward, so that's slowing me down."

"Okay, got it."

I wondered if our lack of experience skiing and pulling 220-pound sleds through soft snow was contributing to Marty's problem. Like a sailor getting his sea legs, maybe he was getting his *ski* legs.

Instead of switching leads, I continued in front so Marty could sort out his ankle-rolling issue without focusing on navigating at the same time. I settled into a slow, steady rhythm, feeling at ease. My mind wandered home to Keenan, where my niece Lindsey and her husband, Ben, had already dropped him off at school. The time back home was three hours earlier. Marty and I could actually set our watches to whatever time zone suited us because, technically, the South Pole is in all time zones at the same time; all longitudinal lines used to define time zones converge at 90 degrees south. The South Pole Station follows New Zealand Standard Time. Marty and I had decided to follow the time zone of Punta Arenas, where ALE headquarters was located.

We were only days into our new routine, but Keenan had been home without us for over two weeks and just started his third set of surrogate caregivers. Each new team had to learn Keenan's routine of being dropped off and picked up at school, attending basketball practice on Mondays and Wednesdays and weekly games on Saturdays. I pictured Keenan's infectious smile and sparkling blue eyes, and heard the sweet sound of his voice the last time he said, "I love you, Mom." I choked down my longing to see him as I listened to the scraping of sleds across ice. Hours melted away.

I glanced behind me and saw Marty's red anorak and red sled cover—two splashes of color against an all-white backdrop. Head down, Marty stared at his skis. The outer edges dug into the snow with each step, preventing his skis from gliding flat against the snow. His movements appeared choppy and labored. Behind Marty, I noticed the tracks of our skis extending off into the distance.

At our next break, I sat down next to Marty on his sled. "I'll just keep leading for the rest of the day so you can see if you can figure out what's going on with your boots and skis."

"Sounds good. Hopefully I can quickly sort this out."

After seven hours of travel, we stopped at our agreed-upon time. Setting and attaining our daily time goals provided a sense of accomplishment and helped keep us from feeling overwhelmed by the hundreds of miles ahead of us.

Inside the tent, Marty turned on the GPS; it said we had covered 8.5 miles (1.2 miles per hour). Not quite the pace we'd planned, but we weren't worried. Over the next few days, we planned to gradually increase our pulling time to nine hours. Within a week or so, we figured our daily average would increase to 15 miles as we became more efficient skiers and the weight of our sleds decreased while we consumed food and fuel.

We completed three hours of nightly duties—hanging an array of gloves, hats, shirts, and goggles overhead to dry; melting snow; stuffing faces with food (trying to devour what remained of our 5,400 calories per day); mapping our progress; calling ALE with our position; and leaving a voice blog.

Then I dialed home. Every other night, we connected with Keenan, and tonight was the first night we would talk to him since we had started skiing.

"Hi, Keenan!"

"Hi, Mom." While Keenan's voice sounded a bit crackly, it came through clearly without any delay.

"How was your day?"

"Good. After dinner, Ben and I battled each other with my Nerf bows and arrows. We were chasing each other all over the house."

"Sounds fun. Dad and I are having fun too. I sure love you and miss you."

"Me too."

I handed the phone to Marty, and after a brief chat he said, "I love you K-man," then hung up.

"Keenan sounds good," I said as I stowed the satellite phone and reached for my toothbrush and toothpaste.

"Yes, sounds like he's adjusting to us being gone."

"I love hearing that he's goofing around with Ben."

As I stretched out in my sleeping bag, I thought about our core team back home— members of Keenan's caregiver team who would also play a unique role in supporting us in Antarctica or sharing our journey with those following along.

Sue was the general overseer—the point person to help manage life back home in our absence. While Sue and I begrudgingly shared a bedroom growing up, as adults we'd grown closer, living in the same small town for the past decade. Her dedication and unwavering sisterly support helped ease the stress of being away.

Lindsey—an experienced marketing and graphic design specialist with website and social media experience—would post our daily voice blog in both audio and written formats, along with Facebook and Twitter updates. Her expertise and perpetually positive outlook were invaluable to the team.

Brett would transcribe our daily voice blogs for Lindsey to post, keep tabs on our location in Antarctica, and email us weekly updates about the world at large. An adventurer and writer with a keen ability to sniff out facts, Brett brought a calm, even demeanor and set of weathered eyes to the team.

Leni would play the role of educational liaison, helping coordinate with schools following along and funneling kids' questions to us. I also planned a weekly check-in call with her in case I needed a cheerleader, counselor, or outsider opinion. We provided only the core team with our satellite phone number and email address to minimize message overload from outsiders and to maintain control of our satellite phone bill. The team could funnel messages to us from others if necessary.

At 9:30 p.m., I closed my eyes, feeling confident our team back home had everything under control.

ON OUR THIRD day, we fell into our normal morning routine. Packed up and ready to start skiing, I left my sled and crunched over the soft snow in my ski boots to Marty, who had turned on the GPS.

"Two hundred ten degrees," he said.

I aligned the needle on my compass to point to 210 degrees and, after stowing the GPS, Marty did the same.

As we headed out, in every direction I saw the same white canvas with no landmarks on the horizon to ski toward. To avoid having to constantly stare at my compass, I spotted a piece of ice that cast a unique shadow on the snow—then skied toward it. I reached the spot in 10 minutes and then scanned for another. To help navigate, I used the shadows cast by my body, the prevailing wind direction, and patterns in the snow sculpted by wind. Navigating required an active, present mind. A straighter course meant fewer unnecessary miles.

At midday, when it came time for me to take the lead, Marty didn't say anything, only hung his head low, his eyes staring at his skis like he had done repeatedly for the past few days. While I couldn't see his expression through his face mask, I imagined that he looked frustrated and was thinking, *I am so done with having this problem!* I led for the rest of the day so that Marty could work on solving the puzzle of his ankle-rolling issue. Actually, it was unclear if his ankle was rolling inside the boot, or if the boot wasn't staying centered on the ski while he moved, or exactly what was going on. It *was* clear that his skis were not staying flat against the snow, which caused his legs to bow outward slightly. I hoped the unnatural position wouldn't cause his bad knee to flare. Meanwhile, I was having minor issues with my persistently foggy goggles. Though my hat wasn't covering the side vents, my hair wasn't stuck inside them, and I was trying to breathe in a downward fashion, foggy goggles prevailed.

Inside the tent that night, as I started nightly chores, I said, "My foggy goggles are driving me crazy. Made it seem like I was navigating through whiteout conditions. But it was clear and sunny most of the day. How irritating."

Marty didn't seem to hear me. He just stared at the map with a confused look on his face.

"Marty, what's up?"

"Nothing . . . I mean . . . I'm not sure . . . just looking at the map," he said without looking up at me.

I took that as my cue that he wasn't to be bothered with my story right now.

I turned my attention away from foggy goggles, picked up my journal, and wrote for a few minutes. I looked up and watched Marty connecting the dots from the last few days on our map. He stared at the line for a long time, as if he was waiting for it to speak to him.

"Huh." Marty exhaled in a loud and drawn-out fashion.

"Is something wrong?" I asked.

Silence.

Then Marty looked at me with wide eyes. "We've been traveling slightly off course since we set off a few days ago."

"Wait, what?" I shook my head.

Placing the map between us, Marty said, "Look, here is where we started, and when you follow the line through the dots, we are heading off course."

"But we have been following the GPS bearing that directs us to the next waypoint." I paused for a second. "Is the waypoint correct?"

"Yes, remember, we checked all waypoints in Punta Arenas with ALE," said Marty.

"And we dialed that bearing into our compass."

"And we checked our bearing each morning and afternoon. This doesn't make sense."

We looked at each other, and then Marty said, "Wait, what if our GPS and our compass aren't both set on a magnetic bearing?" Marty examined the two instruments. "That's it . . . our GPS is set to true north, and our compass is pointing toward magnetic north with zero declination."

Compass needles always point to the direction of the magnetic North Pole, which is different from the geographic (true) North Pole. The difference is called magnetic declination. Basically, we needed to make sure our GPS and compass were both pointing to the same place.

"How stupid," Marty said out loud to himself in a disappointed voice. This was a big-time rookie mistake, especially since we had competently used our GPS and compass on numerous other adventures.

"How far did we go off course?" I said.

Marty examined the map. "About five miles . . . we are slightly west of where we should be."

At our current pace, we had unintentionally added a half day of hard work to our expedition. Luckily, we'd discovered our error now.

After dinner, when I pulled out the phone to leave our blog post, I said, "I don't think I should mention our screwup in our post."

"Agreed. I don't want to worry K-man or anyone else following along. They might lose confidence in us. And it's embarrassing. We have to make sure nothing like this happens again."

Perhaps our brains were clouded by the excitement and anticipation of the journey. Whatever the cause, the incident put us into hyper-focus mode. No detail would go unnoticed—it was critical for our safety and success.

With bruised ego, I reassured myself: *We know what we are doing.*

CHAPTER 8

FIVE MORE MINUTES

I woke to the sound of wind and the tent flapping wildly. Peeking outside, I felt like I was watching the trailer for a new National Geographic series. I imagined hearing the dramatic sound of drums while video of a raging storm flashed across the screen and narrator Morgan Freeman announced, "Welcome to Wild Antarctica. Her lungs are strong, able to throw snow where she pleases and obliterate most anything in her path. She's undeniably untamable."

Drifts three feet tall consumed the windward side of our tent and buried our sleds completely. Due to the conditions, we had the bright idea of taking care of our morning "business" within the shelter of the vestibule.

Each evening when we set up camp, we dug a two-foot-by-two-foot toilet hole located about ten feet downwind from the tent that served as a partial wind block to make the open-air experience as pleasant as possible. How do you crap into a hole in the freezing cold and not get a frostbit bum? You learn to go really fast. When we departed our campsite each morning, we filled in the hole with snow, following accepted Leave No Trace standards for Antarctica. At 60 miles outside the Pole, where more concentrated traffic from scientists, tourists, and expeditions converged, we would be required to poop into special plastic bags and carry the frozen bricks with us for later disposal.

This morning in the vestibule, Marty squatted with pants down over our makeshift extreme-weather latrine. I gagged when the smell reached me inside the tent. I held my nose as I entered the vestibule for my turn. I'm sure my delicate deposit smelled much better. Given the unpleasantness of the whole scene, next time I would brave the weather and use the proper hole outside.

As we set off, the thrashing wind and swirling snow cut visibility to twenty feet and closing. It wasn't new snow falling from the sky—Antarctica was whipping the snow from the ground into the air for fun, teasing us with a bit of her wild side. The slow skiing and strong winds made for noticeably colder conditions.

I felt a draft penetrating my clothing from my left side. I hadn't completely closed my pit zipper from the day before. I zipped in my body heat and heard Morgan Freeman inside my head, saying, "As Chris braves Wild Antarctica for the first time, she strains against the mighty forces." Progress was slow.

We fought the wind all morning. At one of our breaks, when Marty took a drink from his water bottle, the insulated holder fell off the bottle and whipped across the snow out of reach. Marty quickly unclipped from his sled and set off to retrieve it. Just as he reached for the holder, a gust of wind blasted it away. He skied faster, with mounting determination and diminishing control, fighting to keep his balance, ski poles flying wildly by his side. He looked like he was chasing a wild chicken. Again, just as the holder was within reach, a gust sent it tumbling over the snow. This happened four more times before Marty triumphantly stabbed the holder with his ski pole, then raised his arms overhead in victory.

Standing about thirty feet away next to our sleds, I waved my arms in the air too, as if he'd just won a race.

As usual, we wore full face masks to protect our skin against the bitter cold and whipping wind that blew away any chance of conversation. Skiing along with my hood up and the coyote ruff dancing in the wind, I thought about how Wild Antarctica wind could instantaneously steal irreplaceable gear (a reminder to be extremely cautious) and zap energy much faster than on low-wind days. I remembered from our research that in Antarctica, the wind predominantly blows away from the Pole, which means that all roads to the Pole travel directly into headwinds. Katabatic winds, forming when cold air masses flow down the steep ice cap and spread along the ground, are notorious. With nothing to block their way, the winds pick up speed as they come down from the Polar Plateau, and their force can last for days.

At the end of this eight-hour day, we quickly set up the tent, not an easy task with wind whipping and streamers of snow shooting across the ice. Jumping inside, I was bursting to get outside my own mind and talk out loud—not about anything in particular—just debrief the day.

I began to change out of my ski clothes and into my tent clothes—usually my other pair of long underwear, long sleeve shirt, dry socks, lightweight down sweater, and down booties. "Oh my gosh, the wind today was crazy . . . right? I wonder how many pieces of gear have blown all the way across Antarctica. I can't believe how much harder it is to pull sleds against stiff wind. At least I didn't get overheated today. I can't wait to drink a hot tea to warm up. What should we have for dinner?"

Marty looked at me with wide eyes and said, "Chris, you are talking a hundred miles per hour. I'd just like to relax for a few minutes."

Feeling snubbed, I sat silent. Honestly, I'd already had enough silence from skiing in isolation for four days. *I'm trying to relax too, by talking to you.*

After fourteen years of marriage, it was no secret that I am a talkative extrovert. Clearly my download in that moment was threatening to crash his processor. Sensing this wasn't the time to push my need to talk, I gave Marty some mental space.

He turned his body toward his side of the tent and started fiddling with his boots. I imagined his ankle-rolling issue had still affected him today.

I like talking through a problem, finding different options in the course of conversation. When Marty tries to solve an issue, he retreats deep into his mind, seeking help or advice only when ready, on his own terms. Questions or suggestions that interrupt his process will bounce off his wall of focus.

Using scissors from our medical kit, Marty cut two four-by-six-inch chunks from the end of his thick blue foam sleeping mat. He inserted pieces between his outer leather shells and soft boot liners, apparently trying to make the boot liner fit more snuggly.

While he continued his project, I grabbed the orange technology bag, found the iPhone, and pecked out a short email. "Hi, Leni, Marty tells me that I'm talking one hundred miles per hour. As you can imagine, after skiing in silence all day, I was ready to chat. Marty was ready for bed. Funny. At times like this, I can see the role women, like my running friends, have in my life." With iPhone connected to sat phone, I sent the email into the ether. I hoped Leni would remember a conversation we had had while running about how friendships with women complement spousal relationships. While both provide emotional support, the perspective of a trusted friend outside a marriage, who shares similar views about life, can add great value.

As I waited for actual human conversation, I organized damp gear. On various lines across the ceiling, and inside mesh pockets, I hung an assortment of items to dry—glove liners, mittens, hats, balaclavas, long underwear, and face masks—like ornaments on a Christmas tree. We would move the wettest gear to follow the sun as it rotated in the sky throughout the evening. When I leaned forward to change my position in my Crazy Creek chair, a lightweight portable folding chair, my head knocked my long underwear onto the tent floor.

I could give Marty personal space to stare at his boots in silence, but I couldn't give him any more physical space. The inside of our tent was about the size of our king-sized bed back home. About seven months into my pregnancy with Keenan, I'd traded in a queen mattress for a king to ensure maximum comfort as I grew more uncomfortable with each passing month. The luxurious feeling of room to roam was missing from our current living situation. Our one-room stamp acted as kitchen, family room, study, bedroom—and sometimes bathroom. You better not need privacy. You better not have a problem with finding food crumbs inside your sleeping bag. You better not have an allergic reaction to smelly, unwashed clothes. And you better not be shy about squatting in the open to pee into a bottle.

Maintaining an organized tent was one way we kept our sanity under close quarters. From the front door, I slept on the left side and Marty slept on the right, the same spots as our bed at home. The tent was divided into two main sections by an imaginary line down the middle acting as our own Great Wall. We each had our individual territories to help ensure peaceful coexistence—a small slice of personal space in a sea of family-style sharing of everything. We'd devised our system after reading time and again about abundantly qualified teams capable of enduring an expedition to the Pole that failed for reasons that seemed to boil down to team dynamics, often tent dynamics. We took our tent etiquette seriously.

Our mats and sleeping bags lay next to each other, with our feet positioned by the entrance of the tent. Beside our sleeping bags, at the outside edge of the tent, we each stored a large lightweight nylon bag containing personal items; the bag made for easy transport to and from the sled. The small areas near the top of our sleeping bags contained our big down jackets. Thermoses, Nalgene bottles, boot liners, and bags of snacks for the next day all lived near the bottom of our sleeping bags. We tucked our Gore-Tex pants and anoraks over any exposed areas on the floor so we wouldn't unknowingly roll onto cold spots during the night.

Though it was below zero outside, our tent trapped the heat from the sun like a greenhouse, making it a comfortable 40 degrees that night—a welcome change from the wind and cold of the day. The temperature inside the tent would likely drop to between 15 and 20 degrees on cloudy days, and as we moved closer to the Pole.

After Marty finished his solo boot-fitting project, we completed our regular mapping and blogging process and prepared dinner.

As I took a bite of warm, creamy seafood chowder, Marty said, "My ankles still feel like they're rolling, so I tried adding foam inside my boot to make them tighter."

"Yeah," I said, "I did the same thing to one of my boots back home, and it seemed to help."

"Sorry I didn't want to talk earlier . . . this ankle thing is really bugging me."

"I sent Leni an email saying that you told me I talked one hundred miles per hour," I said with a smile.

"You were talking a lot. I just needed to decompress."

"I get that. Sometimes I need to talk, though," I said, acknowledging what he already knew—that I like to talk more than he does, even in our daily lives back in North Bend.

Marty said, "Just remember," and he pointed to the quote by Sri Ramana Maharshi scribed on the tent wall by our friend Maren, "that 'silence is also conversation.'"

We both laughed.

Marty reached for his iPod. "How about some music?" He plugged the device into a small travel speaker (one of our few luxury items) and the *Lord of the Rings* soundtrack transported me not to Middle-earth, but home. While eating the macaroni and cheese dinner, I rode the wave of music all the way back to Keenan. I saw us sitting in the family room—the three of us in our fleece pajamas with cozy blankets and bowls of popcorn on laps watching the epic tale for the first time.

After dinner, we phoned home—one of my favorite parts of every other day.

Marty and I sat close to each other so we could both hear, then I said, "Hi, Keenan, it's Mom and Dad."

"Hi."

Just the sound of his voice took me home.

"What did you do today?" I asked.

He rattled off a laundry list of his day at school, walking us through four subjects, lunch, recess, three more subjects, then back home with free time, homework, and dinner.

Listening, I realized that for the 8 to 10 hours that Keenan moved through the many activities of his day, Marty and I were doing just one thing—skiing. We were on track to average 60 to 70 hours of exercise a week, more than a full-time job. We weren't taking weekends off; our job was to keep moving forward every day with minimal breaks.

Keenan closed by saying, "Miss you, Mom and Dad."

I hung up the phone feeling both joy of connection and sadness of separation, an emotional trail mix.

BACK OUT IN the elements the next day, I looked ahead at a solid block of blue sky on top of white landscape and listened closely to the sounds of my environment—whisper of wind, crunch of skis, rhythm of breath. I thought about the sheer adventure of skiing in a unique environment that would be our playground for weeks to come. *An adventure playground.*

Then I remembered. Adventure Playground was the name of a summer camp I had attended when I was ten years old and living in the flatlands of Champaign, Illinois. With wind in our hair and the freedom of our own rides, my three friends and I had pedaled our multicolored banana-seat bikes to camp each morning, where we ran wild with hammers and nails and a huge pile of assorted scrap lumber. Under the minimal supervision of YMCA camp counselors, we built a village of unique fortresses that a stiff Midwest wind could have sent tumbling to the ground like a house of cards. Creaky bridges connected slouching forts, and the whole place looked like a temporary shantytown for victims of a natural disaster, but to me, it was paradise.

One day we arrived at camp to find that the counselors had built a huge thirty-foot-high zip line. It was like the circus had come to town overnight. Kids pushed their way to the front of the line, while I tucked in near the rear as my stomach turned with the thought of climbing up so high. "Come on, Chris, it's fun," yelled my friend Karen. I slowly began climbing up the long ladder to the small platform on top. My heart raced as I took frequent pauses along the way to secure my foot placement. There was only room for one person on top, no camp counselor to offer help. Shaking, I stepped precariously off the ladder and onto the platform. I peered down as everyone looked up at me. I wrapped my legs around the three-foot-wide wood-plank seat and held on with a death grip. There was no safety harness or safety net—no kidding—only the pulley attaching the seat to the high wire. I launched off, closed my eyes tight, and screamed, first out of fear, then out of excitement. I felt the rush of air as my speed accelerated, burst out laughing, then came to a jolting stop as the pulley crashed into a tire bumper that softened the blow of the end of the ride.

"I did it!" I exclaimed, beaming. I was part of the zip-line tribe. I had tried something new, even though trembles of fear had stirred my body.

It was that moment on the zip line that began to shape my life philosophy. Antarctica did not always have that adrenaline rush. But feeling the weight of my sled as I lunged forward, I still felt that life here was an adventure playground.

I skied for a few more hours. Hungry for a distraction from the white world, I decided to break the silence of the last five days of skiing by listening to music. I tuned in to favorite soundtracks from *Band of Brothers*, *Harry Potter*, *Avatar*, *The Hunger Games*, and more. Just like music from the night before, each song brought me closer to home, and to Keenan, motivating me to push hard and make him proud.

When Marty took the lead, I fell in behind, slowing down to match his pace. I could see by the way his boots still rolled out—causing his skis to continuously dig into the snow on the outer edges—that his foam-insert idea wasn't working. The two-inch layer of soft snow didn't help either. *Is something wrong with Marty's equipment, or is it his skiing ability?*

Toward the end of the day, I glanced at my watch and noticed we had five more minutes until we reached our agreed-upon stop time of 4:30 p.m. Given we'd already traveled about eight hours, I felt surprisingly strong and thought I could have gone an hour and five minutes longer. Just then, Marty pulled over and said, "Let's go ahead and stop for the day."

"But we have five more minutes," I snapped, surprising myself at how quickly my words shot back at him.

"Chris, we have all the time in the world, this isn't a race."

"We can stop if you want. I just want to reach our time goal," I said in an indifferent tone that meant I really didn't want to stop, and I couldn't explain at the time exactly why it was so important to continue.

Without discussion, Marty turned away from me and continued skiing forward. While we pressed on for an insignificant five more minutes, I didn't feel good about it. The sting of my snappy reply lingered in the cold air between us.

Once in the tent, I asked, "What was our mileage today?" I chomped down the remains of leftover snacks—a handful of nuts, a few chunks of bland white Chilean cheese, and a half-eaten Clif Bar.

"We covered eleven and a half miles in 8.15 hours."

"Oh," I said in a neutral tone.

I picked up my journal and quietly calculated our average daily mileage based on four full days of skiing—10.5 miles. *Not bad, but it could be better. How are we going to make it to the Pole in forty days if we don't start hitting 15 miles a day?* I didn't want to start our expedition with the weight of playing catch up—at the same time, I'm sure Marty hadn't wanted to start with the stress of his ankle-rolling issue.

As we lounged in our comfy tent clothes, sipping on warm tea, Marty said, "Since my ankles are rolling, my legs feel tired at the end of the day. And I'm mentally exhausted. It's hard staring at my feet to try to figure out what's going on and navigating at the same time."

"I didn't realize that. I'm sorry I didn't stop when you wanted to."

"I'm just trying to stay calm. Take the long view about our pace."

After dinner, I titled the day, "Five More Minutes" in my journal. As I wrote, I realized I had clung to the extra five minutes like a child embracing her teddy bear during a scary movie—those five minutes represented a jumble of unspoken emotions that had been building inside me. I had been worried about our lower-than-expected daily mileage for a few days now, and I convinced myself that sticking to our time goal would make me feel better about falling off our expected pace. I thought to myself, *We are the mighty Fagans—with strength forged from climbing in the mountains and running long on trails—and we aren't supposed to have problems this early in our expedition.* I was embarrassed to admit that, deep down in my irrational, dark place, I started believing we could make more miles if Marty just tried harder.

I looked up from my journal at Marty, who was bent over the map studying our route. In reality, I don't know anybody who works harder without complaint than Marty. He tried to put on a happy face, suck it up, push ahead, and cork any cracks forming in his confidence. While I wholeheartedly believed we would eventually figure out his issue, I wondered: *Is Marty starting to worry that Antarctica might break him?*

To the side of his head, the words scribed on the tent said, "To two of the strongest people I know, 'Life only demands from you the strength you possess' (author unknown)." I thought about what Marty had said. We were in the infancy of our journey, and we would find the strength to overcome any obstacle, including his ankle-rolling issue. No need to worry about our progress at this point.

Right now, I needed to be more patient and compassionate.

I needed to remember my tire-pulling training, when I learned to "Smile, breathe, and go slowly." Going slowly didn't mean something was wrong.

I YELLED OVER the wind to Marty, "Are you ready to go?"
He nodded.

Each morning after packing up the tent, we completed a series of actions as quickly as possible before setting off—like a pilot's preflight checklist. Ideally, we'd synchronize our movements to minimize waiting for each other and avoid setting off with frozen hands. We'd take down and stash the tent, and I'd have already finished the following: buckle and tighten sled straps; clip boots into skis; take off big down parka and store in front of sled; strap on compass and harness; stash extra pair of goggles that became foggy from the dressing process; take off heavy balaclava, put on hat and pull up buff to cover chin and ears; put on fog-free goggles and, to prevent fogging, check to make sure no piece of hat or hair were lodged inside; thread mittens into ski poles; look up and hope Marty was ready to go too. Miss any step and it would likely mean stopping while on the move to make an adjustment.

I glanced at my watch—8:00 a.m. Over the past week, we'd reduced our packing and preflight checklist time to two hours.

This day, like most days, fell into a predictable rhythm. Our bodies and minds (and sometimes moods) undulated across the frozen snow like waves moving across the open ocean. While the specific details might vary, the general outline and tempo of each day flowed to a similar melody.

Our days were usually broken into two-hour sessions; an eight-hour day consisted of four sessions. Sessions replaced hours, making our time goals more palatable and easier to digest. Every two hours, we would stop for a break.

During our morning break that day, I unzipped the front of my sled bag and pulled out my puffy blue down jacket to put on over my red anorak, and then fished around for my water bottle and bag of snacks. Sitting on the front of my sled, I gazed at the sun reflecting off shimmering snow and threaded my gloved hand up under my face mask so I could munch a handful of nuts.

Marty said, "How's it going?" as he sat on his sled next to me, sipping water by slightly pushing up his face mask to make room for the wide-mouthed bottle.

"Fine. How about you?"

"Good. Nickelback, the *Superman* movie soundtrack, and AC/DC are helping me get through the day."

With little time before cold set in, we focused on eating and drinking as quickly as possible for 10 minutes. Then I stuffed my down jacket and remaining snacks back into my sled just as my fingers began descending into cold, a constant threat even on a milder day like today.

I plunged my gloved hands into down-filled over mittens as we set off in calm weather and on relatively easy terrain. Fifteen minutes later, generating heat moving uphill, I took the over mittens off, and then opened side zips in my pants and jacket so the fresh air could balance my body temperature. *Remember to breathe in a downward motion away from your goggles to prevent the dreaded return of the fog.* Twenty minutes later, a cloud of irritation enveloped me. *Crap! What is causing my goggles to fog again? Is part of my hat, buff, or hair inadvertently stuck inside them?* Like driving with a muddy windshield, the constant battle of foggy goggles was starting to drive me crazy. Marty didn't seem to have the same frequency of goggles issues. I desperately wanted to enjoy the beautiful day without the filtering effect.

The wind picked up 10 minutes later, so I battened down the hatches, moved my buff up over my ears and head, and donned the hood of my jacket. Ten minutes after that, I felt warm again, so I pulled down my hood. Compounding my constant clothing adjustments were my unpredictable, menopause-induced hot flashes.

While hot flashes differ by person, mine felt like waves of intense heat starting in my face or chest and spreading throughout my body, often resulting in uncontrollable sweating—especially on my forehead and back. To cool off, I needed to expose skin to air—which made me worry about frostbite and sunburn at the same time. During the day, the wave might last a few minutes. The frequency, duration, and intensity increased at night—I'd sometimes wake up in a full-body pool of sweat.

By the end of our second break, despite my best efforts, I set off with one goggle lens partially fogged over. Then the wind picked up, and the temperature dropped. I had dressed a little lighter because I'd overheated the past few days, and I now wished for warmer base layers. I skied straight into a stiff wind on sand-like snow; both made for difficult pulling. My pace slowed, body chilled, and fingers had trouble working zippers.

After a while, it was time to switch leads, and I decided to take the opportunity to pee. Peeing in Antarctica into wind was a bit of a trick for me, being female. Using my sled as a wind-break, I pulled down my pants and squatted in one quick and fluid motion to expose my skin to the harsh cold for the shortest possible time. No time for toilet paper. Given the limited dexterity of gloved hands, pulling up pants and tucking all base layers in place without irritating folds and bumps was no small feat. Looking down, I noticed pee had blown onto the top of my skis and frozen into yellow patches of ice. *Next time it's really cold, I'll pull out my special pee device.*

Back when I was sourcing gear, I read an article reviewing female pee devices in *Backpacker Magazine*. The article stated, "Just unzip your fly (or move your clothing away) and place the plastic 'trough' firmly in position. Aim the spout at your target and . . . ahhhh. Caution: Don't try this on a peak without practicing at home—proper technique is critical." Some companies attempted to broaden their market by advertising, "Easy for women to stand when restroom facilities are less than sanitary (or nonexistent)" and "Great for festivals." I ordered four models for trial at home, geared up in three layers of Antarctica clothing, and drank a liter of water, then waited for the urge to test drive the devices. I'd be judging by personal fit, ease of use, and likeliness to be leakproof.

Each funnel had a slightly different shape and came with a tube to extend its reach outside layers of clothing. The Go Girl, made from medical-grade silicone, collapsed when shoved under clothing, leaving too much room for messy errors. The P-EZ Travel Urinal was made with an angle and size that didn't fit my body; the gap could result in possible leakage. The She Wee, with a small, dainty narrow design, would never contain my regular pee flow (I'd have to put my pee faucet on drip or risk backflow), and the tube on the end was too short—clearly more for festivals, less for expeditions. Finally, a device made of plastic that fit my body—the Freshette. I stood in the privacy of my backyard, shoved the Freshette into place, tube sticking outside my clothing, and let it flow. The Freshette won a trip to Antarctica.

After three skiing sessions, Marty and I huddled together so we could hear each other talk over the whipping wind.

"I'm really cold, and stopping only makes it worse," I said directly into Marty's ear to pierce the microclimate around his face created by hat, balaclava, buff, and hood.

Marty leaned in and said, "We should just push on without a break."

"Agreed."

First, we dug into sleds, then slipped vests over anoraks to provide extra protection against the bitter cold. We skied strong for another two and a half hours, sneaking handfuls of nuts and bites of frozen bars from our pockets whenever possible.

Inside the tent, Marty looked at the GPS. "We made twelve and a half miles in eight and a half hours."

"Awesome, our longest mileage yet."

"And there's more," said Marty. "The GPS shows we've been traveling in a relatively straight line, which is what we want." While we usually had the GPS turned off for most of the day, Marty left it on today to assess our line of navigation.

"Great job, Fagans!" I said, holding a piece of salami in the air.

"Yeah . . . and my legs don't feel quite so tired." The smile on his face widened.

"It felt like we were moving more in sync."

After six full days on the ice, we had covered a total of 67.8 miles, an average of 11.3 miles per day. We still had 129 miles to the waypoint of our big turn, and 478 miles to the Pole.

I hooked up the various technology devices and checked for email. I read Brett's note out loud to Marty as he rummaged around in food bags for dinner. "Lewis Clarke's blog reports he's doing well, although he has a cough, horrible blisters on his heels, and has gotten a rash between his thighs from overheating and rubbing. Considering what he's experiencing, I think you've chosen well with your slow and easy start. There is no rush here. Stay healthy and remember the tortoise and the hare."

Unlike Lewis, our bodies were holding up well. We each had experienced only one small blister that vanished after a day, and although Marty's legs were tired, his knees hadn't acted up. While Lewis was not part of our team, I worried about him, as a fellow adventurer, and as a mother.

I moved to the next email. Leni had responded to my one-hundred-mile-per-hour email from the other night: "Thanks so much for your note. Not only does it mean a lot to me, but I also had to chuckle a bit. It was just a couple of days ago that Randy fell asleep while listening to me chatter. Shortly thereafter, I eagerly accepted an invitation from Laura to have a 'hot-tub meeting' to discuss some new business ideas of hers. We chatted away for over three and a half hours (I got home at 1:00 a.m.). Of course, some of the conversation was about the two of you—how you're doing and how each of us is inspired by you. Not the same as a long, therapeutic run with you, but it'll do for now. So despite the continents that are between us right now, I believe we remain on the same wavelength."

"Marty," I said, "Leni sent over a few questions submitted by kids on our website. I'm going to read the question out loud, and let's decide our answers. Then I can leave our responses on the blog message tonight. First question: 'Do you have a grappling hook to pull yourself out of a hole if you get into one?'"

"Ha, that's cute," said Marty. "Let's say: No, but we do have a rope and other safety equipment in the unlikely event that we were to fall into a crevasse."

"Next question: 'If your son wanted to go, would you let him go with you?' I can say that you have to be at least sixteen years old to fly to Antarctica with ALE and do any excursion there with them, so Keenan isn't old enough. Right now, there is a sixteen-year-old British boy that we met who is skiing with a guide on a different route than us."

At 9:30 p.m., I finally lay still in the comfort of my down sleeping bag, staring at the bright-yellow sunlit walls. A feeling of contentment washed over me as I relaxed my weary back and basked in the satisfaction of a hard day's work. With virtually no wind outside, the quiet almost hurt my ears. I strained to hear the nothingness beyond my own breath. Here we were, lying on the ground of an otherworldly place, as the stillness gently opened the door to a remote corner of my mind. I thought about how Antarctica was a blank canvas waiting to be filled. It captivated the imagination and invited me deep inside its hidden beauty, beyond its cold, barren exterior. It dared me to look deep into the sculpted snow patterns, the eye-popping blue sky, and the vastness of it all—as if peering deep into my own soul.

Marty leaned over to kiss me good night. His week-old beard felt rough against my wind-chapped face. He gently reached over and held my hand across our sleeping bags, then handed me one of the headphones connected to his iPod. He said, "I love this song from the soundtrack of *The Pacific*. Listen with me." We pushed our bodies and heads close together until they touched, stuck in earphones, and listened to the song "Honor" for *five more minutes*. I exhaled a deep breath that released the last bit of tension from the day, and then drifted into a comfortable sleep.

CHAPTER 9:

SKI SWAP TO THE RESCUE

Gusting wind pounded the tent with fury, shaking me from my deep slumber. The weather report from ALE last night hadn't warned of what I saw outside the tent door. *Episode 2: Welcome to Wild Antarctica.* In my imagined trailer, I heard narrator Morgan Freeman announce, "They thought they had experienced wind before, but that was child's play. Will Chris and Marty brave the chaotic thirty-five-mile-per-hour force of nature, risk the threat of frostbite and being swallowed in a whiteout of swirling snow—or will they bury their heads and hide away from the day?"

Every rational fiber in my body said it was too windy and cold to set out.

Cozy in my sleeping bag, I looked at Marty and said, "What do you think?" I knew from our research and training that we would never make it to the Pole if we stayed in the tent at the first sight of bad weather. I remembered what Keith had advised: "Go out in the weather every day."

"I think it's time to get going," said Marty as he sat up.

I nodded in agreement.

Time to pull up my big-girl panties (the really warm ones) and step into the craziness, especially since I was so preoccupied with daily mileage. If the weather worsened, we could stop, set up our tent, and dive inside. As I dressed in extra layers and packed up the contents of the tent, I grew more excited about testing myself against the power of Wild Antarctica.

Before setting off, as we stood clipped into our sleds, Marty and I inspected each other to ensure that every inch of our bodies, particularly our necks and heads, were completely protected from the menacing headwind by our multiple layers of hats, buffs, face masks, and hoods. In these conditions, a small crack in our armor could result in a major battle with frostbite.

I remembered seeing famous mountaineering pictures of swollen black fingers and toes that had sustained frostbite, which occurs when skin is exposed to extreme cold for too long, and the skin and tissue just below it freezes, causing irreversible cell damage. Our faces and ears were the most susceptible. There is also a lesser-known condition that Keith told us about called polar thigh—a skin rash that can affect the thighs of people who travel in extreme cold and wind. Last time he was in Antarctica, Keith got red dots on his inner thighs that turned to purple (but luckily didn't get infected).

I also remembered what we had read in a blog post by ALE medic Robert Conway: most major issues start as small injuries that get out of hand—including blisters, sun and wind exposure, and cold injuries. He went on to say, "The best expeditions are often not only those that complete their goals, but those who do it a way that they do not also destroy themselves physically and mentally."

We skied on into the wind—likely the katabatic type—for what felt like the first time. With nothing on the landscape to block or deflect the headwinds, I took on gale-force gusts to my face, hands, and thighs while laboring to thrust my skis forward, struggling to keep my balance. I moved slowly and deliberately through bumpy snow scoured and shaped by this force of nature. The wind left divots and voids in hollowed-out areas of the snow, and a top layer of sugary stuff made it tough to maintain traction.

Taking a break from training at Snoqualmie Pass, Washington, with our son, Keenan.

Dragging two SUV tires for up to 10 hours to simulate pulling sleds in snow.

Arriving at Union Glacier Camp in Antarctica with the Ellsworth Mountains in the background. Photo © Christopher Michel.

A plane drops us at our official starting point 2 miles out on the Ronne Ice Shelf on the coast of Antarctica.

Our campsite on the first day of our expedition. Pulling 220-pound sleds is difficult in soft and sticky snow.

Navigating with a compass held by a custom piece of gear for hands-free use.

Taking a short break before dinner. Getting accustomed to twenty-four hours of daylight during the summer in Antarctica.

Tough work pulling sleds over bumpy snow features carved by the wind.

Feeling good while enjoying the expansiveness of Antarctica.

Keeping our faces completely covered at 30 below to avoid frostbite.

A quick break for a sip of water and a few bites of a bar before hands begin to freeze.

Sharp ridges of windblown snow, called sastrugi, dwarf our tent.

Marty's nemesis: low light and whiteout conditions.

Finally arriving at the South Pole.

Friends and family welcome us home at Sea-Tac airport in Seattle.

Posing with students at St. Joseph School who followed along throughout the expedition.

The wind continuously whipped the snow free from the ground, sending it swirling into the sky and all around us and creating blizzard-like conditions.

I stared at my compass as I navigated through the whiteness. The gusting headwind slammed into me from the left, pushing my sled off to the right. I leaned slightly off to my left to pull my sled forward in the desired direction. The coyote-fur ruff on my hood flapped in front of my eyes. With the toss of my head, I brushed it away and strained to see through the area that remained fog free in the corner of my right goggle.

Nothing was easy. There was no falling into a rhythm. No wandering of my mind. The tension of each moment—of holding my body upright against the pressing wind, of pulling my sled over the undulating landscape—required the strength of every muscle in my body. Every nerve on high alert. I imagined myself as a sharp sword cutting through the thick wind. Holding this position for hours felt like a new power-strength workout on steroids.

Just keep moving forward so you don't get blown backward. The blasting wind muffled everything except my heavy breathing within the shelter of my hood. *Wait, did Marty just yell my name?* Glancing back, I saw his red jacket and sled about twenty feet behind as he leaned similarly into the wind, showing no sign of distress. If Marty suddenly needed to stop to deal with a gear issue and I kept skiing forward, the swirling snow and low lighting could easily create a barrier between us within minutes. I pledged to look back more frequently. *We cannot become separated.*

At break time, Marty battled his way to pull up next to me, and we turned our backs on the wind, our first chance to catch our breath.

"Holy shit—this is crazy," I yelled.

"Hard to make any progress at all." Marty dug around in his sled and said, "Let's make it quick . . . just grab a drink and a bite and let's go."

When Marty took the lead, I struggled to see through the madness to keep his red jacket and sled in sight, but I welcomed the change from the mind-numbing white nothingness I stared at while leading.

The terrain began to slant upward. *Focus, you can do this.* I watched Marty's skis and noticed they still seemed to be rolling outward, but the strength required to battle wind while moving uphill seemed to give him an advantage as I strained to match his pace and keep him in sight. After four hours of pulling, I wanted to shout at Wild Antarctica, "Stop! Enough already!" but she wouldn't hear my cry through her fury. I desperately wanted to capture the raw scene on video—one truly worthy of my imaged *Welcome to Wild Antarctica* series—but when I removed my camera from the warmth of my pocket, the lens instantly froze shut.

By the end of the day, we knew firsthand why Antarctica was known as the windiest place on earth. We'd covered 10 hard-earned miles and now set up camp at an elevation of 2,030 feet.

In the tent, lounging in my sleeping bag, I said, "I think that was the hardest eight-hour workout I've ever experienced."

"Maybe the hardest day of our lives . . . those eight hours may have been harder than twenty-four hours of ultrarunning."

"Yeah, it felt like each minute required so much mental focus and physical determination." I munched on some Pringles. You could never take a break, let your mind wander, or go on autopilot—like we do to get through long trail races.

Marty shoved a cube of cold cheese into his mouth. "We were in survival mode . . . there was no room for errors. The stress was huge. Ultrarunning hasn't felt life-threatening."

"Still I think our ultrarunning experience, the tough mental side of it, really helped today . . . to keep going even though it would have been easier to stop."

"For sure."

While I started dinner, Marty sent a short email to Brett: "Temperature 0 degrees with wind chill likely −40 degrees. Winds 25 to 35 miles per hour all day. Traveled almost directly into icy wind, made the sleds slide sideways all day and feel twice as heavy. Tough, bumpy terrain. Only took three ten-minute breaks—easier to just push through."

I collapsed into bed feeling satisfied for passing our first big test. We were becoming Polar Chris and Polar Marty, the Polar Couple from North Bend. Before closing my eyes, I wondered how Lewis had faired today, and how his mother would react when she learned of today's serious conditions.

IN THE MORNING, Antarctica was kind to us; the wind had diminished to between 5 and 10 miles per hour, the temperature hovered around five below, and the sky was welcoming, sunny, and crystal clear. It reminded me of Montana, nicknamed Big Sky Country because the state is sparsely populated and free of many tall structures. The sky reaches endlessly across the landscape, like the Antarctic sky that I gazed upon. Today, the cold whiteness was dominated by the warmth of aqua blue. I felt I might be swallowed up by the blueness, like a scuba diver exploring the depths of the Caribbean Sea.

After 30 minutes of skiing, the terrain gradually changed from the kind of ripples seen on sand dunes to more jumbled and bumpy ridges; it seemed we'd hit our first patch of sastrugi—frozen wavelike ridges and grooves formed by wind eroding the surface of hard snow. Imagine looking out onto an ocean of waves that flash freeze in place—that is sastrugi. Like an artist gone wild, the wind sculpted the landscape with sharp lines and unlikely curves. I'd read about it, seen pictures, and now, I finally stood upon it. But I never found out why sastrugi only forms in some places in Antarctica.

As I picked my way through the waves, each about a foot high, I felt the terrain taunting me with each push of my ski. I was back on the Trail from Hell—the rocky, rooty trail of my first 100-mile race a decade earlier. My ski bridged the gap between two waves, flexing slightly in search of stable ground. My sled announced its presence as it crested each bump with a sharp jerk of my harness or attempted to slam into my legs when I struggled to ski out of its way. I worked to find a rhythm and flow while skiing through this splendid mess. It was actually a bit exhilarating to encounter a more dramatic change of terrain, another new challenge to figure out. Based on all I'd read, I guessed I'd probably learn to despise sastrugi, but for now it felt like another Antarctic rite of passage—like braving the forces of blasting wind—one I shared with polar explorers who had struggled across this continent almost a century before us and likely cursed the same frozen waves.

At break, after two hours of pulling, Marty skied up next to me. "How do you like the sastrugi?"

"I'm starting to get the hang of moving through it. At first, I was excited. Now, not so much. What an energy zapper."

"It's cool to see actual sastrugi, though. But it's going to get much bigger." Marty pulled out a bar from his snack bag and held it up. "Want a bite?"

"No, thanks." I shoved a piece of cheese into my mouth. "How are your ankles handling all the bumps?"

"Okay, I guess. The firmer snow yesterday was better than this soft stuff." A mushy layer of two to three inches of snow blanketed the surface.

As we prepared to set off again, I said, "I'm going to plug into an audiobook—I need a little boost."

"Me too . . . sounds like a nice distraction."

We had packed audiobooks instead of real books in order to save weight. I started listening to *Where'd You Go, Bernadette?* a tale set in Seattle with an unexpected plot twist that lands the main characters in Antarctica. Marty tuned into *Mirage*, a Clive Cussler adventure novel set on the high seas. While skiing along, I felt a little disconnected from the environment. The soothing woman's voice reading to me provided a welcome distraction. The fatigue of the last ten days—particularly from struggling in the wind yesterday and pulling hard through sastrugi today—had begun to settle into my bones.

I remembered Keith saying, "Some expeditions schedule rest days every ten days." We planned to rest only when our bodies demanded or if the weather was deemed too dangerous. For now, there were no rest days on the icy horizon as we focused on pushing out more miles.

We stopped after nine hours of skiing—still in a field of small sastrugi—and searched for a flat area to set up the tent. Luckily, between the wind-scooped grooves in the snow, there were level areas big enough for our tent. Inside, the GPS showed we'd covered 13 miles, a new record, but still short of the 15-mile average we needed.

Between spoonfuls of my chicken fried rice dinner, I said, "I feel completely exhausted. The sleds need to get lighter for us to make any real progress in this kind of stuff."

"It's usually at six hours into the day that I feel spent. I think because of my ankle-rolling problem. That is mentally my toughest time, when I know we still have two to three hours to go."

"We're probably both feeling the fatigue of the last ten days without a break to recover."

After I cleaned our mugs from dinner, there was still some hot water left in the pot. I looked up at Marty. "Let's take an Antarctic bath to reward ourselves for all our hard work."

I dug out our mini pack towels and small bar of soap, and we took off our clothes. I dipped my light-blue towel into the pot on the stove, then rubbed warm water over my skin.

"Oh man. The warm water feels so awesome . . . makes my skin tingle." Marty sat naked next to me, smiling while waiting his turn.

Lathering up, I gently wiped away the buildup of oil, stress, and fatigue. Then a quick rinse. I grinned at Marty and handed him the soap and towel.

He followed a similar process, then poured the remaining warm water out of the pot and onto the snow inside the vestibule.

We sat on the cool tent floor air-drying our naked bodies, gazing at each other with mischievous grins. While in normal life such a scene might turn sexual, that part of our brain seemed to be turned off. For the next few hours, the smell of soap lingered in the tent like fresh-cut flowers on a spring day.

OVER THE NEXT few days, we held on to pleasant weather and started settling into our new normal. My goggles stopped fogging over all the time (or I got better at managing them), I could eat all of my daily rations (or I was burning more calories), and I felt comfortable navigating and moving over sastrugi (at least for now). But we still hadn't resolved Marty's ankle-rolling issue. He continued to brainstorm new solutions, like clipping his boots into my shorter skis, which were equipped with the exact same binding (which didn't seem to help), and remounting his bindings, which may have been mounted incorrectly. Though we had brought the tools to do this at Keith's advice, Marty decided against the idea since it might cause other problems. Each morning, he set out with renewed hope, and by late afternoon, his optimism would disappear as his overly fatigued legs told him something still wasn't right.

Back when we chose our ski-boot-binding system, we had learned that many systems had been tried in Antarctica, and they all had potential issues due to the unforgiving terrain and harsh cold. We picked a proven Norwegian-made leather backcountry ski boot with a removable liner, and a traditional three-pin backcountry ski binding. The more modern clip-in binding had been known to fail in extreme cold. Our backcountry skis had full metal edges for better control on the ice, and heavy-duty skins screwed onto the underside (the sticky adhesive on skins fails in extreme cold, which is why they are screwed in) to provide traction while we pulled heavy sleds uphill.

During our tests in the Cascade Mountains and at Mount Rainier, we hadn't detected any ankle-rolling issues, although we hadn't been in extreme cold conditions, and our sleds had weighed 170 pounds each instead of 220. After suffering from blisters during our Rainier trip, we'd traded out our stiff boot liners for a less rigid option recommended by another polar guide—but we hadn't had time to test the new liners before departure. Now I wondered if they were contributing to Marty's issue.

Although days earlier I'd pledged to myself that I'd be more patient and drop the "five more minutes" mentality, our continued slower-than-expected pace was still eating at me. The calculations scribbled in the margins of my journal told me so. At the end of each day, I felt we came up short, while Marty remained optimistic that we would speed up when our sleds got lighter. We were always short of our expected 15 miles—and simple math told me that unless we started hitting that mark, we wouldn't reach the Pole in forty days. Somehow, I believed that hitting that average would make me feel on track—in our expedition, and in becoming Polar Fagans. Funny, Marty was usually the data and numbers guy, as evidenced by his yearly fitness calendar, where he logged stats for every workout. He could look up his average running miles from any week since I'd met him. And he was usually the physically stronger one. But now, in Antarctica, our roles had reversed.

Tonight, I decided not to burden Marty with my hamster-brain spinning about daily progress because I thought it would only make him feel bad. Instead, I grabbed my journal and wrote:

Day 12: Today we covered a strong 12.5 miles in 9 hours of work. Marty continues to have ankle-rolling issues caused by his boots, bindings, or skiing form. Whatever it is, it feels like he usually can't keep up with me when I'm leading and navigating, which seems to frustrate him. During the first two sessions, Marty had a good pace, but by the afternoon, he noticeably slowed. I estimate we could cover about one additional mile per day if we didn't slow down each afternoon. Doesn't sound like much until you consider that in forty days we will lose 40 miles—which equals about three days of skiing.

I closed my journal, looked up at Marty with his scruffy face and gentle demeanor as he prepared dinner, and thought: *Oh my gosh, come on, Chris . . . you know Marty is doing his best. Where is your positive attitude? Don't become like past polar explorers who placed blame on their teammates. Remember to focus on one day, one hour, one mile at a time—that's what has got you through ultrarunning and climbing adventures before.*

Between bites of creamy beef Stroganoff, I said, "Marty, how are things going?"

"Okay, I guess," he said in a way that didn't invite additional inquiry, especially about his ankle-rolling issue and exhausted legs.

I decided to change our focus to something outside the tent. "Hey, it's our night to call Keenan."

Keenan was now on his fourth group of caregivers—Uncle Mike, Aunt Mel, and their son Marcus had flown in from Ohio a few days earlier. Uncle Mike, with his infectious smile and helpful demeanor, is five years younger and five inches taller than Marty. Aunt Mel has fiery red curly hair and a matching personality, and a natural motherly way about her. Marcus, who's two years older than Keenan, is always up for fun and games.

Keenan answered the phone and launched in. "Yesterday we stopped for a giant donut at George's Bakery, and for dinner we ate greasy burgers at Herfy's." Keenan was talking with a fast, excited pace. "We also took our picture holding a wad of money in front of the Snoqualmie Casino sign. Then we watched *Call of the Wildman* with a crazy guy named Turtleman. Uncle Mike loves that show."

When Mike got on the line, Marty chuckled and said, "Mike, don't teach Keenan any tricks from our childhood."

I laughed, remembering all the stories I'd heard. One time when their parents were gone, Marty and Mike pulled their cow, Bulregard, through the front door, around the family room, and out the back door. Luckily no cow pies were left behind as evidence of their mischief. Another time, Marty jumped on the John Deere tractor and chased Mike around in the snow, swerving this way and that, pretending to try to run him over. When Mike slipped, Marty swerved but the back wheels ran over Mike's legs. Luckily, he stood up, laughing as he stared at the impression of his legs in the snow.

After hanging up, I thought about how well Keenan sounded. It didn't seem like he missed us as much as we missed him—probably because he was busy being entertained every minute by his different surrogate parents.

I connected our technology gadgets and waited. A few emails popped into our inbox, and I read Brett's email out loud to Marty. "Lewis's blog reported he's still dealing with blisters on heels, has an annoying cough and cold that began on Day 5, and has polar thigh that resulted from the extreme wind a few days ago. To combat the problem, he's wearing three layers of trousers but now he's sweating too much."

"Getting polar thigh would suck," said Marty with raised eyebrows.

"Yeah, I hope his issues clear up soon."

"At least he's not having irritating ankle-rolling ski issues like me."

IT WAS DECEMBER 14, our thirteenth day of skiing in Antarctica. We had covered 116 miles and still had over 450 miles to go. Today the landscape was broken into three horizontal stripes, with a layer of fluffy white sunlit clouds on top, a band of dark-blue sky in the middle, and a swath of white snow on the bottom. It was a giant blue-sky sandwich. As I moved along in front, the terrain beneath my skis still felt rippled and bumpy, with a light coating of sugary snow on top.

After an hour, in the mood for music, I chose a Christmas mix that Marty had created before we left. If I were back home, I'd be playing holiday music during the few weeks leading up to Christmas—so why not bring Christmas cheer to my day of skiing? While I listened to "Rockin' Around the Christmas

Tree," I noticed my body responding to the beat as I picked up the pace, working harder than when I listened to audiobooks. *I am a human metronome, keeping time with my skis.*

Fully in the holiday mood, I thought, *Yes, I love this song,* when a version of "People Get Ready" by Jim Brickman boomed through my headphones. I sang out loud to the lyrics that first became popular by singer-songwriter Curtis Mayfield back in 1964.

The music hypnotized me and my body moved effortlessly—like the time I came down from the summit of Denali and spontaneously began singing "Amazing Grace." I fell into a rhythm, flowing over frozen waves of snow, picking my path to the Pole, one sastrugi field at a time. I hit the back button and replayed the song, transported by the sound of piano and soulful voices. Completely engrossed in the moment, my body glided with ease uphill. Like in moving meditation, I felt alive. A huge smile formed behind my face mask.

I played the song two more times. *I believe in our ability to ski to the South Pole, to stay united as a team,* I thought. My heart swelled with faith, pushing out worries about pace, weather, the unknown. I trusted that skiing across Antarctica was exactly where we were supposed to be in our lives. We would figure a way past Marty's ankle-rolling issue, because that was what Polar Fagans did. In that overpowering moment, I felt light, full of energy, and at peace. Tears pooled inside my goggles.

No judgment. No worries. Only now.

Wondering how Marty was doing, and wishing he could be in this very moment with me, I looked behind me and saw him staring down at his skis as he pushed his feet forward and planted his poles in a lackluster fashion. I could almost hear him thinking, *WTF!*

I looked down at my watch—break time. I stopped, turned off my music, and unclipped from my sled. Sitting next to Marty on his sled, I asked in a soft voice, "Would you like me to take some weight from your sled to help you out?"

"Thanks, but it's not really a weight issue that I'm having. It's all about my ankles rolling on the soft snow."

I decided not to mention my euphoria of the morning. It was dawning on me that while we traveled through the same days under the same sky and over the same snow, we often had different experiences, based on what I could tell at this point. Like in life, we were united, but separate in our strength and struggle.

About two hours later as we made our way uphill, Marty waved his arms overhead to get my attention and shouted, "I'm stopping to take off my skis." Luckily, I could hear him yelling on this low-wind day. He bent over, unclipped from his sled, and stepped out of both skis, then hastily strapped them on top of his sled. *Odd*, I thought, but I didn't say anything as he was obviously inside his own overpowering moment. As I stood waiting, I looked off at the horizon, where the clouds from earlier had dissipated, revealing a magnificent powder blue. Behind me, Marty clipped back into his sled and stomped ahead on foot. Slipping backward with each step in the soft snow, he shook his head and looked like he might explode with frustration. I skied forward, until about 10 minutes later, I heard him yell, "I'm stopping!"

I looked back in silence, wishing I could help him through his struggle.

Marty unclipped from his sled, grabbed his skis, threw them onto the ground, and snapped back in.

At our four-hour break, as I tossed a handful of nuts into my mouth, Marty said, "Maybe if I put my skis on opposite feet, my boots will sit more squarely on them."

He hefted his left ski over his right one and clicked his boots into place. He pushed off on a test run and then circled back to me.

"Chris, this might work."

"Really?" I grabbed his arm with my free hand and half shook him. "How in the world did you think to switch your skis?"

"Desperation." Marty turned to lead out and said, "Hopefully I can learn to control the ski tips. They want to flow into each other instead of glide straight past each other."

It took 20 minutes of testing this new system for Marty's ankles to stop rolling outward. As he learned to control the glide, the thick cloud that had enveloped him for almost two weeks began to disappear. He stopped looking down at his feet and held his head high, moved with ease, and even kept a faster pace. At our next break, Marty seemed more like himself—more talkative, more full of energy, more engaged in the surroundings, and more connected to me.

By the end of our day, I had led for eight of the nine hours, allowing Marty maximum time to learn to master his improvised ski system.

Inside the tent, he pulled out the GPS. "We pushed out another thirteen miles."

I let out a gasp of excitement. "Yes!"

"Bring on the Pringles," said Marty. These chips were not typically found in our diet, but in Antarctica they satisfied our craving for fat, salt, and crunch, and traveled well in handy crush-proof containers.

"Here's your seventeen chips . . . actually . . . today you get a few extra," I said with a smirk as I handed Marty his well-earned reward.

Munching his chips, he said, "I've been worrying that I'd have to call ALE to airdrop new boots and skis. My legs are so exhausted. I didn't think I'd be able to go on like this much longer."

"Really? You thought you'd need to call ALE?" I asked in an accusatory tone.

"Yeah. At the end of each day, my legs were dead weight. Like fifty-mile-race dead."

"Why didn't you say you were *that* tired or concerned?" I thought about how Marty's inability to quickly solve his gear issue and control the situation had put him in a vulnerable position right from the start.

"There was really nothing you could do about it . . . and I didn't want to dwell on it."

While that might have been true—that I might not have

had a solution—knowing how he felt might have helped me be more supportive. It seemed Marty and I were trying to figure out how to balance independence with intimacy in Antarctica.

"Were you thinking that if you called ALE for an airdrop, you would end our chance to travel to the Pole completely unsupported?" I said.

"Yes. I was trying to avoid calling by just pushing on each day. I would have been pissed if we'd had to call for help. We worked so hard to be completely self-sufficient."

"Would calling ALE have ruined the expedition for you?" I ate my last chip and licked the salt off my fingers.

"No. After a while, I'd have gotten over it," he said, then paused and looked inside the Pringles can for crumbs. "Just like when we run hundred-mile races, we have an ideal race plan. If things start to fall apart, we trash our time goal and focus on just finishing. That is still an amazing accomplishment. I will be ecstatic if we reach the Pole—even if we have to get an airdrop."

"Me too," I said. "I'd still feel the accomplishment of being self-guided and carrying all our own supplies."

Marty started cooking and I checked email. In popped two questions from school kids that Leni had forwarded. I wrote them down in my journal, then called in our voice blog for the day. Toward the end, I said, "We've got a few questions tonight. Our first one comes from Mrs. Piper's third-grade class from Opstad Elementary School, who ask, 'What do you do with your clothes that get sweaty? We know you can't wash them, so how do they stay clean?' Well, we have about two pairs of clothing each, and basically, we just keep wearing them over and over. So they smell . . . yep, they sure do . . . and they will be that way until we get home. The next question comes from Dr. Matsumoto (our periodontist), who asks, 'How are you maintaining your weight so far?' It's hard to tell. We've probably lost a little, but so far we aren't feeling hungry after we've eaten all our food each day, so that is good."

After I organized my sleep area, I peeked out of the top slice of the back door that was open for ventilation. "Oh my gosh, I can see a range of mountains off in the distance."

"Really, let me see," Marty said as he squeezed his head next to mine. "Yeah, looks about fifty plus miles away."

"I can't believe we didn't see them earlier today . . . they must have been hidden behind the low-hanging clouds."

"I wonder what range it is."

Marty grabbed the map, and we decided it was the Patuxent Range, which rose 6,400 feet from the area near the Foundation Ice Stream. From our vantage point, a strip of hazy clouds cast a blue hue on the snowcapped mountains, almost camouflaging them from view.

I was reminded of Mount Rainier popping out in its brilliance after months of hibernating in the clouds, always a delightful surprise.

I wondered: *What else is out there hidden from our view—ready to surprise?*

CHAPTER 10:

THE TURN

The snow looked like the surface of the moon as gray contours and shadows reflected off the cloudy sky. Skiing here was probably the closest I'd get to being on another planet, where I imagined the lack of gravity would make for quick, easy miles. The moonlike landscape morphed into White Sands National Monument, with great wavy dunes of gypsum sand rising from a dry, barren New Mexico landscape. I could see the footprints I had made twenty years earlier. Then I noticed animal prints from a bear, a herd of deer, and a couple rabbits. But there were no animals in the interior of Antarctica—wind had whipped them up overnight. Hours drifted.

I listened to the sound of skis scraping over the snow and ice, leg muscles acting as natural shock absorbers, my body now instinctually adjusting to the choppy landscape. My mind was free to wander. I designed my ideal home office perched in a special cedar tree in my backyard. Composed short stories and repeated poignant lines over and over to try to save them permanently on my hard drive for future export. I remembered a sleepover I had at Grandma's apartment with Pat, eating Swanson chicken dinner, and playing a mean game of Pokeno (a combination of bingo and poker). I heard her say, "God love ya," like a punctuation mark at the end of a sentence as I drifted back to Antarctica.

I looked up at Marty skiing in the lead, wondering if his ankle-rolling issue was truly over. I was thankful for our new pace—and for other things too. Compared to my decade-plus of winters in the cloudy gloom of Seattle—where I forced myself to run through months of downpours—the nearly 24/7 intense sun in Antarctica invited me outside into the cold, infusing me with energy. Besides the sun, I was falling in love with the purity of this experience. The untouched land as if from another time. The unblemished blue sky, void of pollution. The fresh drinking water made from crystal-clean snow and ice. I reveled in the purity of our singular focus each day. Lack of distractions. Self-sufficiency. Carrying only what we needed to exist. I loved the cold beauty of moving through nature with Marty—the adventure bonded us, even if our experiences were different.

Continuing to move through the cold, I breathed the words *Thanks, Antarctica* into the warmth of my face mask. The Patuxent Range kept us company and grew bigger all day in the distance to our left. Soon, nine and a half hours had passed—it had been a busy day of thinking. While I melted snow, Marty pulled out the technical gear to call in our voice blog, having reluctantly agreed to provide a guest post once a week. Our followers clamored for Marty's firsthand accounts in addition to mine—at least that is what Leni told us.

Marty cleared his voice, then reported:

We had our best day yet, covering 13.5 miles, and crossed south of the eighty-four-degree mark. We will stay on this bearing for another 44 miles and then make our turn to the south. Today, I thought about how our expedition compares to epic journeys portrayed in Lord of the Rings *and* The Hobbit. *I'm intimately familiar with these tales since Keenan loves the books and movies. In my comparison, Chris is like*

Frodo, because she seems to feel the pull of the ring a little more powerfully than me at the moment. And since Frodo looks a bit like a girl and has nice blue eyes, Frodo fits better with Chris. I am like Sam, happy right now to be out here following along. Instead of pots clanging together on my backpack, it's my ski tips that knock together because I am not as proficient of a skier.

Also, coincidentally, my fingers have swollen, so I put my wedding ring on a string around my neck. And our tent is like a little home in the Shire with an oval shape and door, and the inside feels like a wonderful little homey place. Finally, our feet are sort of hobbit-like. They've become callused and hard over the last thirteen years of ultrarunning, so we haven't experienced blisters or problems with them.

Resting in our hobbit home, embraced by the clear sky and sun that never sets, we were finally in sync and poised to make real progress.

After dinner, I decided to place a call.

"Hi, Mom!"

"Oh my, Chris! Let me get your father." She yelled, "Jim, pick up the phone, Chris is calling from Antarctica."

Her familiar excitement at the first sound of my voice brought me home. I thought back to 1998, when I'd used Marty's brick of a satellite phone—it weighed three pounds—to call them from Camp 4 on Denali. There hadn't been social media or an easy way to keep loved ones informed of our status.

Dad got on the line and said, "We are so proud of you. I've got a bunch of folks from Hot Springs Village following along."

"I hear Mac is playing our daily update for you over the phone," I said.

Mac, my brother-in-law, had been pulling up the voice blog on his computer, hitting play, and then holding the phone next to the speakers while my parents listened because they didn't own a computer.

"Yes, they're great," said Dad.

After a little more conversation, I said, "I love you both."

"We love you too," they said in unison. And then Dad said, "Bye for now."

As I lay in bed after saying goodbye, I thought that maybe our South Pole expedition was the best medicine for Dad—something to look forward to each day to keep his mind off his failing health.

At his eightieth birthday party back in April, Dad had looked tired. Tired from the months of an open wound on his ankle that his body was too weak to heal, and the weekly doctor appointments to scrape it clean. Tired of stents to open arteries in his heart, and hospital stays and physical therapy. Tired of keeping track of the twelve different pills to take every day, a delicate balance of potions meant to keep his heart beating, to keep his quality of life intact.

On a warm spring day, we had gathered in my parents' garage with tables set in a circle so that all twenty-two family members could see each other (a formation that didn't fit inside the house). My parents sat next to each other like newlyweds at a wedding reception, their heads framed by a rack of weathered golf hats, a collection of found golf balls stored in egg cartons, and well-used garden tools. After dinner, we presented Dad with a large photo of everyone in the family, and below the photo was a list of eighty things that we loved about him. Going around the room, we each read items from the list: "Garage sale king," "Can make friends with anyone," and "A laugh that makes you want to smile for the rest of the day." Afterward, sunlight broke through the clouds, casting a soft, divine glow over the room, and one by one we each stood and shared heartfelt words honoring Dad. I had thought, *This family is rare and precious.*

I missed my family, and more, my connection to other people—the feeling of their energy, support, and love pulsing through my body.

IT WAS DECEMBER 16, our fifteenth day of skiing. I strained to see forward through low visibility. The cloudy white sky and snowy landscape merged into one, making the horizon disappear. A whiteout. There was no up or down, only white. Imagine skiing in complete darkness and feeling totally blind—now turn darkness to whiteness, and that is a whiteout. I squinted through foggy goggles to find a reference point—a faint shadow on the snow or a micro piece of snow—to take a bearing. There was nothing but white. In the lead position, I skied with my head down, relentlessly staring at my compass. I remembered seeing a *MythBusters* episode that showed how humans don't instinctually travel in a straight line when blindfolded, and indeed, when I looked up from the compass, I began veering right or left. I didn't feel like I was veering off course—I only knew because Marty told me so, and because I saw him do it when he led. I moved along in a fog at a plodding pace, feeling my way forward over the undulating terrain, barely able to keep the tips of my skis in sight. When my ski took a sudden drop, I stabbed my pole into the whiteness and caught myself. I stared down at my compass to check my bearing again while fighting the queasy feeling associated with vertigo. An hour dragged on as I repeatedly lost my balance and rechecked my compass until it was finally time to change leads.

I slipped in behind Marty and exhaled deeply as the stress of leading in a whiteout drained from my body, leaving me feeling tired and depleted. With Marty working to find the way, I looked ahead at the nothingness of endless white and thought about the sound of silence. Being enveloped in a cloud of white made the silence even more pronounced. Back home, my day filled with the whistling of the morning tea kettle, ringing of the office phone, revving of the car engine, clicking of keys on the keyboard, barking of Kiya and her neighborhood friends, chopping and sizzling of stir-fried vegetables, clanging of dirty dishes. Here, beyond man-made sounds—skis scraping against snow, poles stabbing ice, breath hissing inside my face mask—was a silence that I had never known. For much of the morning, I tried to make sense of it.

I remembered hearing a TED Talk describing a man who stopped speaking for seventeen years. He didn't set out to stop talking for that long, it just happened that way. After fifteen days on the expedition, I still wasn't used to the lack of talking. I wasn't sure why this felt so new. After all, I spent hours running on trails by myself, and that didn't make me ponder the meaning of silence. Ultrarunning Chris took pleasure in running in silence. But I also delighted in chatting with a good friend while moving through the wild. In Antarctica—for eight plus hours a day—silence was my constant companion. Sometimes I filled it with music or audiobooks or drifting thoughts. Sometimes I simply endured it. Sometimes the profound silence made me lonely.

Loneliness made me uncomfortable, so I emptied my mind and focused on skiing faster. After six hours of whiteout, the sky changed to low visibility and I could just make out the horizon. Thirty minutes later, the haze burned off to reveal a clear blue sky. Sun reflected off snow, making it come alive with movement and energy, a welcome change that lasted the rest of the day. My loneliness disappeared with the clouds. Before long, we had covered 13.4 miles in nine and a half hours, a good day that was about to get even better.

Inside the tent, Marty and I quickly changed and got ready. "I can't wait." I said. At the agreed-upon time, I dialed up Keenan's school, Saint Joseph School, and Leni answered the phone.

"Hi, Leni, this is Chris."

"Hi, Chris, I hear you loud and clear."

We were testing the equipment before the official call with the entire school that would take place in an hour. The speakerphone would be amplified into the gymnasium, where all of the students from the school would gather; each class had prepared a question to ask. A photo of us would be projected onto the big screen in front of the room. Joining Leni from our support team were Sue and Frank and my other sister Jean, who had recently arrived from Birmingham to help care for Keenan.

I hung up the phone after our successful test, and Marty and I wolfed down our teriyaki chicken dinner. At 5:00 p.m. in our tent—2:00 p.m. at home—I dialed. I held the phone a few inches away from my ear as Marty and I huddled together to listen.

After two rings, Leni answered and said, "Hello. We have a few people here that are excited to talk to you." An eruption of delightful screams blasted all the way from Washington to Antarctica. Leni had told me that kids would stand in a line that led to the speakerphone. Then the question and answer session began:

"Hi, I'm Jennifer. My question is: What do you miss the most?"

"Besides Keenan, I miss sleeping in a warm, comfortable bed, fresh fruits, and being able to sit in a comfortable chair," I said.

"This is Jack. Have you seen any animals?"

Marty replied to this one. "A lot of people think we'll see polar bears or arctic foxes, but those animals are found in the Arctic, up north. We would love to see penguins or Elephant Seals, but those animals live on the Antarctic coast. So we haven't seen any animals and probably won't see any because they don't live in the interior of the continent. Although we did get an email that said one other person skiing here saw a bird that must have lost its way."

The next kid to ask a question was Tom. "How does Chris keep her contacts from freezing when she takes them out at night?" he said.

"I keep them in a little pocket that I sewed into the inside of my sleeping bag before we left Washington. That way the heat from my body will keep the contact solution from freezing."

"I'm Sara, and I'm wondering: How long do you sleep at night?"

"We try to lie down for at least eight to nine hours to give our bodies enough time to recover," said Marty. "We don't always sleep that whole time as we roll around trying to get comfortable, and sometimes we actually get too hot in our really warm sleeping bags."

The satellite phone dropped our call three times during our 35-minute conversation with the kids. Each time we called back, the kids greeted us with unrestrained enthusiasm from 9,500 miles away.

The last question came from Nathan, a member of the cross-country team that Marty and I coached. "Have you stretched your *hammmmies* lately?" I could hear the smile in his voice. This was an inside joke with the team—the kids referred to hamstrings as *hammies* and said the word in an exaggerated, drawn-out fashion for fun during practice.

"No, but that is a great idea, though," said Marty.

To close, I said, "Thanks for all of your wonderful questions. We love hearing your excitement, and we'll carry it with us for the rest of our journey. Have a wonderful Christmas, keep following along, and thanks for all of your support. Bye from Antarctica."

As I turned off the satellite phone, I said, "That was awesome. I loved hearing all of their questions . . . and they sounded so excited to hear from us."

"I know, they totally pumped me up. I knew they would."

A FEW DAYS later, on Day 18, we continued skirting the Patuxent Range to the east. I was still feeling excited that we'd hit 14 miles on the previous day, our best day, and that we'd left Marty's ankle-rolling issue behind for good. In front of the snow-drenched range, about a half mile from where we stood, were giant gaping cracks and fractures on the surface of the ice, black voids in an otherwise white landscape, the telling signs of massive crevasses.

Because of my mountaineering experience, I was accustomed to carrying rescue gear—ropes, pulleys, harnesses—while moving near crevasses on glacier-covered mountains like Mount Rainier or Denali. Before we departed, we had asked Keith what he thought about bringing this specialized gear to Antarctica. He told us, "When I guide there, I don't carry crevasse rescue equipment, because the dangers are minimal since big crevasses had been mapped. It's common practice not to bring it." Our route gave us wide berth around the Foundation Ice Stream and Patuxent Range, avoiding the dangers of major crevasses nearby. Still, we'd heard from an ALE guide about a woman solo skier, Meagan McGrath, a Canadian Air Force Major and experienced mountaineer who in 2010 had wandered off route on the second day of her expedition, plunged into a crevasse, and found herself trapped on a snow bridge above a gaping abyss with no way out. She had called ALE from the sat phone stashed in her pocket, and luckily, they mounted a considerable rescue effort to save her life before hypothermia took hold.

Whether due to experience or an undeniable gut feeling, I couldn't accept the idea that it was safe to travel without crevasse rescue gear in Antarctica. Watching my husband freeze to death forty feet down in a crevasse was not an option—and I promised Keenan that we would be safe.

I turned my gaze away from the gaping crevasses I saw to my left, and thought of the rescue gear we had stashed in my sled. It gave me peace of mind.

About two hours later, and a few miles past the massive cracks, Marty stopped and turned on the GPS to verify our exact location. We stood less than a half mile from The Turn—the one major change in course on our route to the Pole. After about 15 more minutes of skiing, Marty stopped and checked the GPS again. We had arrived at our designated waypoint. With sunny skies and gentle weather, we stopped for a short break.

I pulled out the camera, pressed my goggle-clad face close to Marty's, and clicked a few celebratory photos. Then I snapped one of Marty's face next to the GPS screen showing the waypoint numbers. Marty was our team's GPS guy. On Day 1, he'd turned on the GPS to check our first bearing, and after that, he never asked to share the role, and I never volunteered to trade off—guessing he enjoyed it.

"Hey, do you see something flapping in the wind over there?" I pointed as I dug into my front pocket for a quick handful of nuts.

"I think those are marker flags where ALE would have dropped a resupply for us if we weren't carrying all of our own supplies."

I pondered the idea of pulling a sled half the weight of mine. *What does it feel like to carry less of a daily burden?* Besides the physical weight of pulling heavier sleds, I felt the mental weight of having no guide. My mind and body were on constant alert. If I was outside, I was on duty—watching weather, terrain, sled, and gear. Don't get too cold. Don't lose focus on navigation. Don't let my sled hit me. Don't lose a piece of gear to the wind. Don't get too far away from Marty. Don't make a mistake. Don't screw up. Don't endanger our lives.

The weight of those don'ts was beginning to wear on me, but seeing the flags boosted my confidence. We could do this on our own.

Now safely west of the disturbed ice area, we dialed in a new compass bearing of 230 degrees—changing our course by 50 degrees so that we were heading directly south. After skiing in a southwesterly direction for 209 miles over eighteen days, we would be heading on a more direct route to the Pole, and into the headwind. I turned and pointed my skis toward our distant goal, still 360 long miles away—miles that would likely take us through much worse weather and sastrugi as we moved deeper into the interior. As I skied forward, I strained against the wind and instantly felt colder—a reminder that my tired body had much more to endure.

In the tent that night, Marty started his blog post by saying, "I was listening to the *Band of Brothers* soundtrack while I skied throughout the day to channel one of my heroes, Major Richard Winters."

Winters led the Easy Company, 506th Regiment, 101st Airborne, as described in the book by Stephen Ambrose. I knew Marty deeply admired the courage, honor, and humility displayed by Major Winters in World War II.

Hanging wet clothes to dry, I listened as Marty went on. "Besides Winters, another hero that I thought about today was my wife, Chris."

I glanced up and caught his eye as he continued talking into the phone while looking at me.

"She embodies many of those same characteristics, and I wish everybody could see her out here, and how strong she is, and how she motivates me to keep going. I am so lucky to be with her. And my son, Keenan, is also one of my heroes. I always feel like I hit the jackpot with the K-man. He's showing such strength and confidence at home. And I'm so proud of him. I can't wait to get home and sit in our man-chairs together and watch *Andy Griffith* and *Leave It to Beaver* reruns."

After Marty hung up the phone, I said, "That was a beautiful blog." I leaned over and kissed him. Then, as Marty rummaged through the food bag to choose our dinner, I connected wires to gadgets to download emails. I read a message out loud to him from a parent from Keenan's school: "I just wanted to let you know that the Christmas concert for Saint Joe's was awesome last night. Keenan did such an amazing job in advanced band. All smiles, he was beaming from the stage. My favorite part was watching him play "Hedwig's Theme" from *Harry Potter.* You have a wonderful son—a testament to wonderful parents. Keep on plugging guys. We are pulling for you here in the Snoqualmie Valley."

The positive news from our virtual dinner guest provided a welcome boost.

After the rest of our nightly routine, I lay down for the night and thought back to what Marty had said, that he believed I was strong. But by this point I felt like I'd run a daily marathon while dragging an overweight friend along for a free ride for eighteen days straight. I was starting to push my mind and body into uncharted territory, and worried I might drain my strength and stamina dry.

MY CLAWLIKE HANDS throbbed with fatigue, as if frozen stiff while holding imaginary poles. This wasn't the first time. As I slowly sat up, it was harder than usual to shake the sleep out of my eyes. The pull of my bed was strong, but it was my turn to cook, so I forced myself out of my sleeping bag and started boiling water. I sat staring into the rising steam, thinking about how my emotions seemed to rise in the heat of the moment, then cool down and vanish into thin air. Sometimes I felt so alive, every sense firing on all cylinders, astounded to be in Antarctica; other times I struggled to keep pushing as the daily grind overpowered my mind and body. For each of the last ten days, we'd pushed out nine and a half hours of hard work that left my body hungry for more rest.

After swallowing a bite of oatmeal, I said, "I'm tired. Maybe we should dial our time back a little today."

It was Day 19, and we were both starting to show wear from all our hard work. It wasn't any particular day that had done the damage. It was the cumulative effect—like adding an imperceptible amount of weight to your backpack each day until one day, you can hardly lift it onto your back and your knees feel they might buckle. Something had to give.

Marty said, "Let's go eight hours to give our bodies a little break."

"A Fagan rest day."

Absurd as it may sound, ending an hour and a half earlier sounded heavenly. I was motivated to make those eight hours count.

We stepped out into a cloudy day, and the absence of sun meant colder temperatures. Because of our new bearing, the wind slammed against my body head-on instead of coming from slightly left over my shoulder. Skiing in the lead felt harder. I pushed directly into its full force while pulling my sled over the very bumpy and hilly terrain. At home, even when I'm traveling directly into wind, its path is broken by trees, boulders, mountains, or buildings. In Antarctica, wind roams wild—the average wind speed at the South Pole between November and January is 11.5 miles per hour, while the average for February through October is 16.5 miles per hour.

When Marty took the lead, my thoughts drifted like the shifting snow blowing in front of me. By now we should have had all of our systems wired and be marching on autopilot, but the constantly changing environment required endless adaptations. Hood up. Hood down. Pit zipper up. Pit zipper down. Down mittens on. Down mittens off. All while simultaneously trying to focus on skiing on a designated bearing. The simple act of taking thousands of breaths each day in extreme cold caused condensation to wreak havoc on gear—goggles fogged up, zippers flash froze in place, and face masks became brittle with massive blocks of ice formed inside or hanging like daggers from chins.

Compared to skiing on Day 1, today each movement felt labored. While each of our sleds probably weighed about thirty-five pounds less than when we started since we each consumed our daily food rations, we didn't seem to be going much faster.

After eight hours, we jumped inside the tent to get warm. Marty gently pried his half-inch-long beard from the frozen mass that hung from inside his face mask, then hung the mask to dry. I noticed how much gray his beard had versus the receding hair on his head.

"Nice to be done a little earlier." I began taking off my boots.

"Yeah . . . the afternoon didn't drag on and on."

"I'm not sure it was much of a physical break, but at least it was a mental break."

I grabbed two seafood chowder soups out of our dinner bag—one of our favorite meals because it tasted like the thick, creamy award-winning soup Marty and I had shared at Ivar's in Seattle when he first moved there. I lit the stove and began the snow-melting process, then dumped the powdered soup into our two mugs. As I waited for the water to boil, I started changing into dry clothes and noticed a white powdery substance on them. *Did I spill the soup mix or electrolyte powder on myself?* Investigating further, I noticed it seemed to be coming from the inside of my clothes. Then it dawned on me. *Gross!* It was my flaking, shedding skin that had been pulverized inside them.

Skin will completely regenerate itself about every twenty-seven days, and we had proof of this phenomenon all over our tent, in our clothes, and inside our sleeping bags. Humans shed a little over a half pound of dead skin each month. Usually, microscopic dust mites that live in our homes eat old dead skin for dinner. Without dust mites here, we would be living with these flakes for the duration.

Seeing the dead skin inspired me to leave this voice blog:

An expedition to Antarctica is one of the best kept secrets in adventure travel. You wear the same clothes every day with the side benefit of not having to do laundry. You can create any number of South Pole hairstyles using your natural buildup of oil 'product.' You pack up your house every single morning, so you're treated to a different view every night. You never have to wonder, 'What's for dinner?' because it is always a just-add-hot-water dehydrated meal. Your hole-in-the-ground alfresco bathroom keeps unpleasant odors at bay. And you eat as much as is humanly possible and still lose weight. Yes, an expedition in Antarctica is the ultimate couples' getaway with endless undisturbed time together.

I wondered how Keenan might describe the glamorous side of spending weeks without his parents. We'd heard about the fun he'd had with Aunt Jean over the last six days: decorating Christmas cookies cut in the shape of stars, snowmen, and Santa; holding a gingerbread house design contest; singing Christmas carols; attending the new movie *The Hobbit: The Desolation of Smaug;* and hosting a taco dinner with a houseful of our local family and friends. Aunt Jean—a five-foot-three-inch spark plug of pure energy and enthusiasm for life—loves holidays and traditions. Traditions are a touchstone of her life.

I dialed home, and Keenan said, "Mom, it snowed today and school was optional, so since Aunt Jean didn't want to drive in snow, I stayed home and we made a snowman!"

"Wow, sounds awesome."

"I hope it snows more so I don't have to go to school tomorrow!"

When Jean got on the line I asked, "How's Keenan doing?"

"When I first arrived, he seemed a bit tired," she said. "So, on Monday, I let him skip his basketball practice—he seemed to need some down time. But we've been having tons of fun, and I still have four more days of activities planned."

As I lay down to sleep, I noticed the tent felt considerably colder than usual—probably because the cloudy sky meant no greenhouse effect tonight. I couldn't imagine how cold it would feel with no sun in the sky. At the South Pole, the sun is always above the horizon in the summer and below the horizon in the winter. This means that starting September 21, the region experiences up to 24 hours of sunlight, then starting on March 21, it falls into 24 hours of cold darkness. Still, I sometimes longed for a clear closing of the day. For twilight, the moon, stars. For a blanket of darkness to tuck me in at night, protect me from the never-ending expansiveness of this exposed world.

"WANNA GO NINE and a half hours again to try to make up some miles?" Marty asked the next morning.

"Okay," I said, though I didn't feel very rested from our shorter day.

Pushing my ski forward, I noticed the surface of the snow looked like the texture of driftwood and felt less bumpy than yesterday. Despite the sun burning bright, it still felt cold as wind continued to blast us head-on—likely our new normal after our turn. An hour into the day, the condensation from my breath flash froze inside my goggles rendering them useless. Frozen goggles left a thin icy film on the inside—different than foggy goggles that can sometimes self-clear. Feeling irritated, I stopped to change into my backup pair. My chest and the front of my thighs felt much colder than normal, reminding me of Lewis and his polar-thigh issue. *Maybe I should reinforce the front of my clothing against the more extreme cold.*

Like usual, the sun traveled in a slow and continuous circle overhead. I skied as if on an endless treadmill; my changing shadow indicated time was actually passing. At the start of the day, the sun hit the left side of my body; by midday, it was on my back, and by late afternoon, my right side. Today, at midday, the back of my body began to sweat from the intense rays, while the front of my thighs felt frozen from the blasting wind and cold ambient temperature.

Off in the distance to the right, about 70 miles away, a portion of the Thiel Mountains came into view. This isolated snowcapped range rose 6,500 feet against the blue sky like a cluster of islands rising from the frozen ocean. Stretching 45 miles long, the range framed the western strip of my view. The night before, I had seen on the map that our route threaded through an opening about 100 miles wide between the Patuxent Range to our east (already out of view) and the Thiel Mountains to our west (likely in view for a few days). An aircraft fuel cache is located near the Thiel Mountains, where planes traveling between the Union Glacier base camp and the Amundsen-Scott South Pole Station stop to refuel.

It was about an hour before our stop time. As I skied along, I strained through partially frozen-over goggles to see if my jacket was zipped all the way up. *Yes, zipped up. Why is my chest cold?* I kept skiing. *Has the cold found a crack in my clothing? Has ice formed inside my jacket?* For the next 30 minutes, skiing behind Marty, I obsessed about the cold spot on the left side of my chest, wondering if my flesh was freezing. The temperature with wind chill hovered around −20 degrees, and I'd read that exposed flesh freezes instantly at −40 degrees.

When we stopped for the day, I suddenly thought, *My iPod . . . maybe it's my iPod.* Located inside a small pocket above my left breast, the cold metal surface felt like it might have frozen to my chest—and at that moment, I wasn't sure.

Just then, Marty unclipped from his skis, walked up to me,

and said, "Hey, hon, should we take a few photos of the two of us with the mountains in the background?"

I blurted out, "My chest is freezing."

"What are you talking about?"

"I . . . um . . . it feels like . . . something . . . maybe my zipper was open . . . I mean . . . sure, let's take a photo."

As we took the photos, my teary eyes hid behind goggles.

With the tent up, I jumped inside while Marty shoveled snow onto the flaps. I sat down by myself, took off my goggles, and began crying. I tried to stop. I feared I would open an emotional floodgate that I wouldn't be able to close. And I didn't want to appear weak to Marty, who wanted us to keep our emotions in check. I wasn't sure why I was crying—but surely it was for reasons beyond being scared by the possibility of my iPod freezing my skin.

While listening to Marty work outside, I felt like a tangled mess of stress and emotion—the kind of intense hormone-induced feelings that sometimes accompanied my period.

When Marty came in from shoveling snow, he looked at me with eyebrows furrowed. "Chris, are you okay?"

"Not really. I think I just need to cry."

"What can I do?" Marty sat down next to me.

"Nothing."

Wanting to hide, I crawled into my sleeping bag, closed my eyes, and drifted away from it all—the cold, the isolation, the exhaustion. After being strong for twenty days straight, perhaps I just needed to release pent up stress.

I heard Marty say, "Hi. Marty and Chris here, team 3 Below Zero, and I'm doing the voice blog tonight. Chris is lying down. We're officially both exhausted today, but we hit a couple of good milestones. Milestone one was that we crossed eighty-five degrees south. Also, we went nine and a half hours again today, and made 15.1 miles—our biggest day yet."

He continued talking into the satellite phone, but I stopped listening.

Twenty minutes later, when I heard Marty light the stove, I sat up and began changing clothes. I saw a pink mark on my chest, but no visible skin damage from the frozen iPod, which hadn't actually frozen to my chest. When I pulled off my long underwear to put on my other ones for lounging, I noticed a few pink dots on my left inner thigh. I wondered if they were the start of polar thigh. If the weather-related skin rash became irritated, the spots could fill with puss or turn to purple-and-black frostbite.

Marty said, "Here, this might make you feel better," and handed me a warm ramen noodle appetizer.

I let the steam linger on my face as I glanced down, avoiding eye contact with him. Then I looked up and said, "I'm not sure what is wrong with me. I feel completely wiped out."

"I'm tired too."

As Marty prepared our main meal, I wrote a few notes in my journal and calculated our stats.

Soon he handed me my cup of fettuccine alfredo and then raised his cup into the air and said, "Here's to crossing eighty-five degrees south." We clinked them like champagne glasses.

Each time we crossed a degree, we celebrated our progress toward our final destination of 90 degrees south. Only this time, despite Marty's best effort, I wasn't in the celebration mood.

I swallowed a bite of noodles. "Well, it's day twenty, and I wish we were halfway to the Pole like we'd originally thought. We've gone 236 miles, and we still have 334 to go."

"I still think we'll go faster as our sleds get even lighter."

I glanced at my journal notes. "Even if we pick up the pace to fifteen miles a day, it will take us twenty-seven more days to the Pole," I said with a blank expression on my face. "It will take a week more than we had hoped."

"Well, we planned for forty to forty-five days. We're doing great. I'm not worried." Marty's voice was soft and smooth like the bite of noodle in his mouth.

After dinner, as I lay in bed, I still felt I might burst into tears at any moment.

CHAPTER 11:

REST DAY AND HALFWAY

Really? How can it be 6:00 a.m. already?
I rolled over, cracked open my eyes, turned off my alarm, and moaned. While still cozy in his sleeping bag, Marty said, "I think we should take a rest day."

I looked into his bloodshot eyes, paused, and in a raspy morning voice whispered, "That sounds great."

I pulled my hat back over my eyes to block the perpetual sunlight and instantly fell back asleep.

When I woke, I checked my watch. It read 9:00 a.m.—in a blink, we'd slept three more luxurious hours. After logging 12 hours of rest, I felt giddy with anticipation for a day of relaxation in the tent. I looked over at Marty, who had just removed his hat from his eyes. "It's December twenty-second," I said. "Let's celebrate Christmas early."

We ate a relaxing breakfast, then boiled extra water for another Antarctic bath, only this time I planned to wash my hair for the first time. Sitting inside the tent, I bent my head over the pan of water resting in the vestibule and poured cups of warm liquid over my head. I lathered up the soap, massaged it into my oily hair, and rinsed the suds away. The feeling instantly breathed new life into me. Shaking my hair like a wet dog, I broke free from the numbness of exhaustion; I felt more awake than I had in weeks.

After Marty bathed, we used the leftover hot water to wash our underwear. For the past twenty-one days, we'd each been wearing the same two pairs. Nestled back in my warm sleeping bag, wet underwear hung overhead.

"Now what should we do?" I said with the excitement Keenan had expressed on the phone a few days earlier when school was canceled due to a snowstorm. Only instead of going outside to play in the snow, I wanted to play inside the cozy tent.

"Let's listen to a *This American Life* podcast." Marty plugged the iPod into our mini speaker. I always love their original stories of people in surprising situations. Back home, we often tuned in while working out in the garage or cooking dinner together. Keenan loved the stories too.

The first story opened with a man driving his father to familiar places, like the home where he grew up. As they drove around, the father—who was suffering from Alzheimer's—had no memory of the various destinations and kept forgetting if the man in the driver's seat was his son or a nice taxi driver showing him the sights. Marty's eyes misted over as the emotions of this father-son heartbreak appeared to wash over him. I wondered: *What is life if not a collection of our experiences? Isn't that why we are here, in Antarctica, not paying off a mountain cabin or luxury car, but creating a once-in-a-lifetime experience together?*

While another story played in the background, Marty threw on his boots and jacket and went outside to retrieve our skis. Back inside, he said, "I'm gonna cut down our skins, hopefully give us more glide and speed."

At this point in our expedition, our sleds were getting lighter (even though it didn't feel like it), so traction wasn't as critical.

"I'm going to make a mini sleeping bag for my iPod."

Marty looked up as he peeled back a few inches of the skin from the bottom of his ski and said, "Huh?"

"I'm recycling my worn-out sock to make a little holder for my iPod so I don't freeze my chest again. Do you want one?"

"No, thanks," he said with a smile, then he went back to his project.

Back home, I'd hand-sewn fleece face masks onto the bottom of four pairs of goggles (two for each of us) so there would be no gaps between goggles and face mask, to ensure complete facial protection and prevent frostbite. Today, after completing my mini iPod bag, I sewed Windstopper fleece material, harvested from extra mitten liners, onto the front thighs of my thermal underwear. The extra protection would hopefully keep bitter cold from turning my suspicious pink dots into nasty polar thigh.

For fun, I read through my journal from the last few days and started connecting the dots. Shedding skin. Frozen skin. *What is going on with skin? Am I trying to shed something and become somehow new?*

Marty interrupted my deep thinking when he asked, "Want to dig out our Christmas treats?"

I instantly shut my journal.

He rummaged through food bags and laid out our special penguin gummies (similar to gummy bears) and chocolate chip cookies. I ripped open the bag and shoved a handful of gummies in my mouth, then put the rest of them within arm's reach—like Keenan does when he mindlessly munches while watching a movie.

"Save some for me," said Marty.

"Better grab some before they all jump into my mouth!"

We huddled close to watch a series of short videos that family and friends had created before our departure. Marty held the small two-by-three-inch screen on our iPod nano a few inches from our faces. First, members from the Fagan family in Ohio came into view. We laughed until our partially digested penguin gummies nearly migrated north. At the end, Marty's brother, Mike, came on screen and said, "Be strong and courageous. I look at your life like a big puzzle. Each piece is filled with so much life. That is what

I admire so much about you both, and this journey is only one piece of the amazing puzzle that is your life."

My brother Pat made a video entitled "From the North Pole to the South Pole." His video showed close-ups of mounds of barbequed chicken, prime rib, fresh salad, chocolate cake, and apple pies that he had prepared for three hundred people. I could smell the scent of beef wafting through the kitchen and taste the flaky crust and hint of cinnamon in the pie. He shared a few Alaskan-style bar jokes and then said, "I admire you for going after your dream." Pat had come full circle since he had expressed his earlier reservations about the risk of our adventure.

"Are there any cookies left?" asked Marty.

"Yes." I put the package in front of us, and we each inhaled four more along with the crumbs at the bottom.

Then we promptly consumed the rest of the videos that we had planned to save for another day. Like we were eating a favorite type of ice cream, we couldn't stop ourselves from indulging in all of the goodness. Friends shared special poems, played the piano and saxophone, and performed a hilarious rendition of the Harlem Shake. There were even a few videos created by classrooms of kids from schools following along. (I later learned Leni had contacted schools to make the videos.) One person after another told us, "I love you guys," "I know you'll make it," "You can do it," "I am praying for you," "I am proud of you," "Have fun," and "I can't wait to have you safely home."

Then Keenan came into view. "Hi, Mom and Dad. I hope you're doing well. I know you are going to make it. I love you. I guess I'm doing well too."

"Oh my gosh, I was keeping it together pretty well until Keenan's video," I said.

"I know, me too."

I took a deep breath. "All that video watching made me hungry."

"Lounging around burns a lot of calories." Marty grinned at me. "Let's make dinner."

Marty rummaged through bags in search of our special Christmas meal. When I was growing up, Christmas meant the smell of prime rib roasting in the oven. In Antarctica, I smelled a less appetizing Spam like product—a Chilean brand of canned meat sizzling in our pan.

I grabbed a cooked piece, smelled it, then took a bite. "Yuck, it tastes like soap." Not quite the signature salty, fatty taste of Spam that I had expected.

This Spam-like product was the closest thing we'd be eating that resembled pemmican, a calorie-dense block of dried ground meat, fat, and cranberries that early Antarctic explorers ate on a daily basis. Pemmican was eaten alone or dropped into a pot of boiling water to make stew or "hoosh," and served with hardtack or sledging biscuits on the side.

To our cups, I added the dried stuffing and the mashed-potato-and-gravy concoction that I first tried on Denali, poured in boiling water, and covered them. While they rehydrated, I lit the cinnamon-spice scented candle that I brought as a gift for Marty, and hung a stuffed penguin ornament from the ceiling of the tent.

Smells of our nontraditional Christmas lofted through the air. At last, we munched our feast.

"Hey, we should break out the port," I said with lifted eyebrows and a grin.

Marty poured an inch of the strong red wine into each of our cups, raised his up, and said, "Merry Christmas, baby."

"I love you," I said as I clinked my glass with his.

"I love you too."

"I love this day," I said, looking into Marty's eyes as we leaned together and kissed.

After dinner, I said, "Let's watch part of *The Blind Side*." I didn't want the day to end.

With bulging stomachs, we lay down and huddled close. We gazed at our small screen until we couldn't keep our peepers open any longer.

Life was good.

"WOW, I FEEL awesome," said Marty, popping up in his sleeping bag.

"Me too."

The morning after our rest day, we were on our way in 90 minutes, a record time. The Thiel Mountains stood off in the distance, our skiing companion for the day. The bright sun, light wind, and soft snow created perfect conditions for sleds and skis to stick, making pulling difficult. One hour into the day, struggling to find a comfortable temperature, I changed from my warmer hat to my lighter one and replaced my anorak with my vest.

Skiing along, I felt something bunch up below my knees. The custom thigh warmers that I had painstakingly sewn into my thermal underwear had already torn free from the movement of skiing. I stomped my skis into the snow like a toddler, holding back a full tantrum of frustration. *Why am I overreacting like this?* It wasn't that big a deal; I should still be riding the high of a superb rest day. Without the stiff, cold winds of the previous few days, at least I wasn't worried about polar-thigh problems.

During our first morning break, I removed the bunched-up material from my pants and squatted to pee. As I peed, I noticed red dots dripping into the snow. *Ah—another early Christmas present—my period.* That explained the waves of emotion flooding my body over the past two days. In addition to feeling fatigued, I was hormonal.

"Hold on. I started my period." I dug around in my sled for my period paraphernalia. This wasn't something I typically announced to Marty, who probably didn't want to hear about it.

The previous day, we had listened to another *This American Life* story about seven things not to talk about because nobody cares. One of the off-limits topics: a woman's period. I wasn't planning to voice blog about this tonight.

Because I was forty-eight years old, my period had a split personality. Sometimes it paid a quick visit, like a distant relative passing through town. Other times it erupted with the force of a volcano flowing wild. According to research, this is fairly common among women my age as our bodies get close to menopause. At home, I would never attempt to exercise for nine hours straight with a volcano period erupting between my legs. I planned to contain any gushing in Antarctica with a silicone cuplike contraption called The DivaCup. The website said it would be reliable for up to 12 hours without leaks.

I'd read every line of information on the website in preparation for Diva to arrive in the mail, and one of the tips was to practice. When Diva arrived, I took her out for a spin, first on a two-hour run, then on a ten-hour tire-pull. Wow, they were right: no leaking, and no problems. The DivaCup was my new best friend. I ordered another for backup purposes in case the first one failed in the bitter cold of Antarctica.

Another tip listed on the website had caught my eye. "If The DivaCup does move up in the vaginal canal and you are experiencing difficulty removing it, please refer to Section B of the User Guide for assistance. In the rare case that you are still unable to remove The DivaCup after more than twelve hours, seek medical advice." While this sounded a little concerning, it didn't prove to be a problem during my test period (pun intended), so I wasn't worried. My backup plan: Marty was a trained EMT, so he would know what to do if I had a problem. Yeah, right.

After digging around in my sled for Diva, I triumphantly held it up and said, "I found it!" Marty nodded and continued eating a chunk of cheese. Showtime. As we began moving again, I felt confident in Diva and fell back into my skiing rhythm. I skied with ease for the rest of the day.

In the tent, Marty said, "Nine and a half hours, and we traveled 15.3 miles!"

"Fifteen again. Awesome!" And Diva and I were leakproof. With Marty on cook duty, I relaxed and wrote in my journal while chomping on leftover cheese and salami from my snack bag.

After dinner, I went outside to our hole-in-the-ground bathroom to remove and empty Diva. I took off my liner glove, a rare occurrence as I almost always wore these gloves, even when going to the bathroom. I needed to move quickly to avoid frostbite on my bare hand. I reached up to pull out Diva, just like I had practiced multiple times at home, but it seemed to be just out of reach. I tried again, and this time I was just able to touch the tip. I tried again. No luck.

Cold was closing fast. Panic rising. I yelled, "Fuuuck!" into the bitter breeze. My hand was freezing. I tried one more time. "Fuck, fuck, fuck!" Abort mission. I yanked up my pants and dove into the vestibule of the tent like a baby kangaroo seeking shelter in her mother's warm pouch. My hand tingled with searing heat as blood started coming back into my frigid fingers.

I needed to try again. Since the vestibule wasn't tall enough for me to squat, I knelt on one leg. Suddenly the warning from the website appeared in my mind like a disaster-news-flash ticker tape, *If the Diva gets stuck, "seek medical advice." Shit.* Marty looked on in silence from inside the tent, his face turning Antarctic white. *Think, Chris. What is the problem?* According to the website, it was critical to get a good seal with the cup to prevent leakage. *Okay, so the seal needs to be broken in order to remove it.* But I was also having trouble getting ahold of Diva. I took a deep breath, then inserted my partially thawed finger as far up as possible and broke the cup's seal. My elation turned to dread as the cup, as if in a slow-motion movie sequence, tipped sideways before I could pull it out. The dam breached; gushing blood from the Diva reservoir spoiled the surrounding snow. The snow looked like a Jackson Pollock painting, or a scene from a documentary of an African lion kill.

"Fuuuuuuuck," I yelled, piercing the silence.

I tried to process what had gone so terribly wrong with my well-tested plan.

I turned to Marty, who was sitting frozen in place, and asked, "Can you grab me a paper towel?"

Still kneeling inside the vestibule, I grabbed my backup friend from my toiletries bag, then tried to cover the scene of the crime with fresh snow.

Inside my sleeping bag, I hoped I wouldn't have to relive this nightmare again, and I sensed Marty felt the same way. I thought again about how—despite sharing each other's company and living quarters—our experiences, at times, were worlds apart.

THE NEXT MORNING, I woke with a revised technique in mind to remove and empty the cup. Back outside in our open-air bathroom, I squatted and, bearing down like I was giving birth to a little Diva, I removed it with ease. Problem solved.

As we set off, I remembered it was Christmas Eve. I glanced down and read the words that Keenan had written with black permanent marker on the side of the pogies attached to my ski poles. "I love you, I know you will make it." A perfect holiday message.

As I looked away from the Thiel Mountains, I noticed a haze of white off in the distance in the Thiel basin in front of me. A storm was coming our way. Straining to make sense of it, I soon realized it wasn't a storm but a giant wall of snow that looked like a supersized ocean swell from the movie *The Perfect Storm*. Luckily this swell was frozen solid and didn't threaten to sweep us into the depths of the sea. I skied with renewed vigor, anxious to reach the base of the wall to get a closer look, and strangely excited to tackle this new obstacle in our predominately featureless terrain. I estimated we'd begin climbing in 20 minutes. When I next looked at my watch, an hour had passed and still we hadn't reached the base of the mighty wall. Inside an Antarctic optical illusion, I couldn't accurately judge the scale of this feature. It was two hours later that we arrived at the base of the climb.

As soon as I moved onto the 25- to 30-degree slope and felt the full weight of the sled pulling against my harness, I knew I was in for a struggle. I studied this new piece of Wild Antarctica's anatomy, her giant bicep flexing in my face. It looked to be about 1,000 feet of elevation, but I wasn't sure since I couldn't see the top from my vantage point. I could run this distance uphill at this pitch in about 30 minutes. But I had no idea how long it would take to climb while dragging a sled.

My harness dug into my shoulders and waist as I held my core tight against the downward pull of my sled. I slowly lunged my leg forward, jammed my poles into the snow, and leaned into them to lever my body and sled forward. Then I lunged again, holding my form and balance by engaging every muscle in my body—especially my abs, back, shoulders, and butt. I noticed that I held my breath at the point of maximum effort—like when bench-pressing a difficult weight—then exhaled during the space between lunges. Soon I felt I'd completed a full lunge workout back in my garage, only when I gazed up, I could see I'd tackled only about half of this uphill beast.

When we stopped for a short break to change leads, I glanced back to bid the Thiel Mountains farewell and looked down over the vast terrain that we'd covered. With all of the hard uphill work, I hadn't noticed that the wind had seemed to increase to about 15–20 miles per hour, and the temperature felt like it had dropped to 25 below zero.

After Marty pulled up next to me, I said, "Holy shit, this is so hard."

"Yeah . . . I didn't know we had such a steep climb on our route."

As I sliced through the stiff wind behind Marty, my legs endured the slow burn of maximum effort. This felt different than those times during 100-mile races, when I pushed to the edge of endurance. There were aid stations and support and a way out. Right now, I was pushing to the edge of my strength with no choice but to keep inching my way up, use my mind to ask more of my body. I tightened my hood, trying to hide inside my warm cocoon from the elements and my growing fatigue.

The giant wall stretched on endlessly. As the icy pitch grew steeper, to about 30-35 degrees, I struggled to keep from slipping backward. I felt dangerously exposed on the open slope since my sled weighed more than me. I risked being dragged downhill like a rag doll and ending up in a battered and broken heap. When I started to slip, I wondered if we'd prematurely shortened the skins on our skis. I thought of the lightweight crampons buried in my sled, but in this committed position, it seemed too steep to stop, with no easy way to anchor our sleds. Moving slowly and methodically, I lifted my ski and pushed it forward only when I could feel the other one hold my position. With a death grip, I stabbed poles in ice to stabilize myself.

TWO CHRISTMAS EVES ago, I was in the middle of a different challenging climb on Mount Kilimanjaro in Tanzania, the highest mountain in Africa. But at that time, we were together as a family with ten-year-old Keenan by our side—not separated by 9,200 miles. At midnight, the three of us headed out of high camp into the cold and prepared to hike the final 4,000 feet to the summit at 19,341 feet. We were with our group of guides from Summit Expeditions and Nomadic Experience, a top-notch adventure company owned by our ultrarunning friend and native Tanzanian, Simon Mtuy.

To get to that point on the mountain, we'd spent the last six days hiking four to eight hours a day. Right before we set off with headlamps into the darkness, Keenan said, "My stomach kind of hurts." I thought his discomfort could have been due to a number of factors: the fatigue from getting only a few hours of sleep and the stress of waking in the middle of the night, or a tired body from four days of mountain biking before hiking up Kilimanjaro. Since we'd been tracking the oxygen levels in our blood with a pulse oximeter, we knew it was highly unlikely Keenan had altitude sickness. Thirty minutes into our hike, Keenan stopped, bent over on the trail, and vomited. As he lifted his head, he said, "I'm not stopping. I want to keep going." Marty and I knowingly glanced at each other. *Keenan's likely not going to make it to the top of Kilimanjaro*, I thought. On average, it takes six to eight hours to reach the summit from high camp, and vomiting this early didn't bode well for his chances. We continued up into the darkness, allowing Keenan to push himself within safe limits.

In less than an hour, Keenan's pace slowed dramatically, making it difficult to generate enough heat for any of us to stay warm. We opened our backpacks and put on every stitch of clothing we had carried, including a down wrap-around hat that I'd thrown in as an afterthought and put on Keenan. By now, the rest of the group was well ahead of us, leaving us alone with our guide, Wilson. A retired schoolteacher, Wilson had climbed Kilimanjaro dozens of times and had become Keenan's mentor on the mountain. Over the next three hours, Keenan stopped to vomit two more times, but each time insisted that he wanted to push forward.

Finally, when he couldn't eat or drink without gagging, I knew Keenan was physically and mentally at his limits.

Through tears, standing slumped over in the darkness, he said, "I don't want to let my friends down. What will they say? I don't want to let you down."

"Keenan, you are not letting us down." I stretched my arm around his shoulder and pulled him close. "We are so proud of your determination."

"K-man, you did awesome," said Marty, his eyes locked with Keenan's.

At 2:47 a.m., perched on a cold, windy ridge at 17,100 feet, we made the call.

"You two are strong. You go on," said Wilson. "I will take Keenan back to high camp."

"No," I said with arms crossed and a wide protective stance. "I will go down with Keenan." Mama bear was staying with her cub. We would not attempt to summit with the rest of the group. "Marty, we don't both need to go down. You should go for to the summit to represent our family," I said.

"Are you sure? I can go down with you guys."

"You should go to the top."

Keenan looked one last time into the darkness, where the summit would appear at dawn in a few hours, then hung his head, softly crying into his coat, and visibly shaken from the entire ordeal. As we began hiking down the mountain, Keenan wobbled along and said, "I'm so tired." Since he looked like he might fall over, I locked my arm around his to stabilize his body for the two-hour trip. A cloud of sadness followed us back to high camp. I couldn't shake the feeling that Marty and I had caused Keenan undue suffering—after all, we were the ones who had hatched the idea for this adventure.

As soon as we were safely in our tent, Keenan yelled into the air as if possessed, "Why did we turn back? We shouldn't have turned back. I'll never be able to face my friends. I don't care if I almost made it. I didn't make it! I failed!"

"Keenan, your friends will be amazed that you worked so hard for seven days straight and made it to 17,100 feet. They'll say, 'Keenan, you are awesome.' You went higher than the top of Mount Rainier at 14,411 feet."

Reasoning with his raw emotions was like trying to stop a river from flowing. Luckily, within minutes, Keenan surrendered to exhaustion and collapsed onto his sleeping bag and into a deep sleep. Instead of relief, an unexpected tidal wave of emotion rushed over me as I became short of breath. *What is happening? Is it oxygen deprivation? Fatigue? Adrenaline wearing off?* A mix of love, guilt, and vulnerability hijacked my body. I lay down in the tent, listening to the heaviness of Keenan's breathing, and cried.

I closed my eyes and relived each frame from our summit bid and retreat, trying to splice together a different ending, one that would take away Keenan's obvious pain. *Keenan is safe. I am not a bad mom. We made a good decision.*

Then Keenan rolled over and yelled in his sleep, "No, no, I don't want to go back." While he slept, I picked up my journal and wrote this letter:

Dear Keenan,

You are a truly amazing ten-year-old. I'm thankful that you're always ready to take on any adventure that your dad and I dream up. While other kids were building snowmen or playing Legos during their Christmas break, you were biking and hiking in Tanzania. You tackled a tough mountain bike route, well beyond your biking experience, with confidence, flexibility and at times, covered in mud. I was in awe the first day, when you biked thirty-six miles of tough trails.

On Mount Kilimanjaro, you endured long miles and tough days without complaint. In fact, everyone said that you were a joy to be around. This trip provided me with a unique window into the depths of who you are—and who you will become. Your determination, confidence, and humility are traits that will take you far. At the tender age of ten, you've gained wisdom and experience that will shape who you are. You've learned that goals, like summiting a mountain, are great to strive for, but not at any cost. Your life and health are more important. Your character is formed through all of those hard days leading up to summit day. You'll carry those experiences with you forever.

If you never take a chance at pursuing a hard goal, like climbing Kilimanjaro, you'd never know the depths of your strength and determination. I see who you are, Keenan Fagan. You are a strong and powerful ten-year-old who is bound to summit all kinds of mountains.

I love you and I'm so proud of you,
Mom

AS I EASED my skis and sled up the icy Antarctic slope, I told myself: *You can do this. Just keep moving.* Back stiffening, harness digging further into my shoulders and waist, and leg muscles burning, my body threatened to buckle under the pain of pulling uphill. Compared to flatter terrain, this hill required triple the effort. I glanced down and watched my ski glide over a boot-sized crack in the ice. Ahead, Marty appeared to move with more ease up the relentless mountain of ice; his body looked less strained. We didn't stop for any breaks. Instead, I shoved a few nuts in my mouth on the fly and kept moving. When we finally crested the wall, I glanced at my watch—it had taken three and a half hours of hard work to scale the gigantic frozen wave.

As the terrain leveled out, I noticed that the adrenaline that had pushed me up had worn off, leaving me feeling I'd dipped deep into my reserves. We took a quick standing break to grab a sip of water and a bite of a bar, and then we were off again.

A few hours later, I needed to empty Diva, as I could feel that she was on the verge of leaking. "Marty!" I yelled as loud as I could into the harsh wind. Marty was skiing ahead of me with his hood tightened around his face for extra warmth, so he didn't hear me. I desperately wanted to avoid a calamity inside my clothes, especially in these conditions. Since Marty and I were unlikely to get separated on a clear day, I decided to stop and hoped he wouldn't get too far ahead. As if we were connected telepathically, 30 seconds later, Marty glanced back and started skiing in my direction.

After eight and a half hours, we had covered 13 miles—a respectable Christmas Eve outing—so we stopped and set up camp. We both devoured our beef Stroganoff with vigor, then called Keenan.

He said, "I'm going to church with Sue and Frank, Lindsey and Ben, and the Nunns." Talking fast and excited, he continued, "Then we'll open Christmas presents."

Brett, Becky, Emillia, and Isabella, who had stayed with Keenan during Thanksgiving, had returned to North Bend from their home in Port Townsend, Washington, to spend Christmas with him. The Nunns would follow our tradition of opening presents on Christmas Eve, and then open Santa Claus presents in the morning. Keenan still liked the tradition of Santa Claus despite knowing the truth, while the Nunn girls were still believers.

I could smell the noble fir, see it decorated with a string of memories—the golden star that I purchased at an art show the year Marty and I got engaged, the hand-carved wooden fish from our honeymoon in Zimbabwe, the "Baby's first Christmas" ornament from Grandma, and the mini cow bell from our family trip to Switzerland.

Feeling a sudden wave of emptiness, I said, "Keenan, I'm sad that I'm not there with you for Christmas." I choked back tears as the words left my mouth. "Are you sad too?"

"Yes," he said in a soft voice.

Marty chimed in, "I really miss you too, buddy. I can't wait to see you. I love you so much."

As our Christmas Eve came to a close, I realized that during this holiday season, just two years after Kilimanjaro, Keenan was climbing a different mountain—the one where he had to live without his parents for two months. The one where loved ones filled the void. While he outwardly appeared to have acclimatized to his new situation, I couldn't help but wonder how he was really doing. And how long he could keep it together.

THE NEXT DAY, skiing across the barren snowpack, I imagined Keenan lounging around in his pajamas on Christmas morning while building his new mega Lego set and playing with his coveted Mindstorm robot that I'd purchased and wrapped before departing. I saw him sipping on hot chocolate and fighting off hugs from his two surrogate sisters, Emillia and Isabella.

Then my mind flipped like a Rolodex through Christmases past when I was growing up—the tinsel glistening on the tree, Dad wearing the Santa hat, family gathering in the living room ready to rip open gifts. After all those years, Mom and Dad were still married. My siblings and I still loved to get together. Our spouses, children, and grandchildren had added vibrant colors and textures to the fabric of our family. Despite being scattered across the country—Alaska, Washington, Illinois, Alabama, and Arkansas—we remain connected, unbroken, and united in the belief that family, and our place in it, still mattered.

As I looked out across the frozen landscape, I thought: *There is no greater Christmas gift than knowing I will always find a home in this family. It's like finding a lifelong winning lottery ticket under the tree.*

After our third session of the day, Marty pulled out the satellite phone and said, "Let's call in a Christmas blog right from the trail instead of inside the tent." We huddled together, turning our backs on the 15- to 20-mile-per-hour wind that blasted us with white grains of sand-like snow.

Marty started out by saying, "It's sort of an emotional day for us, Christmas Day, because we are not home with Keenan. And we had a call with him last night that brought Chris and I to tears at the same time—not that we haven't had tears separately. And we really miss him and hope he's having a great Christmas." Then he handed me the phone.

"I've been thinking a lot about our family and friends while skiing today, and of all the fun they are having," I said. "I'm sad not to be home, but also, actually happy and joyous to be in Antarctica. And all the love . . . that you guys are giving us . . . fills me up."

Since my voice became paralyzed with emotion, I handed the phone back to Marty and he closed with, "We haven't given you much emotion or drama in our blogs, but it's a little different calling you right in the middle of a tough day. Merry Christmas, everyone."

In the tent that night, I realized that being in Antarctica while staying connected with loved ones back home was a tough balancing act. Some days I teetered toward strength and perseverance, while others I tottered toward struggle and longing to end the isolation. Besides the emotional strain, the physical fatigue wore me thin.

I glanced at our stats written in the pages of my journal. Over the past four days, we'd made good progress, averaging 14.3 miles a day. We'd covered a total of 280 miles in twenty-four days.

We were halfway to the Pole.

CHAPTER 12:

COLD HARD DAYS

Over the next three days, it felt like we were in the movie *Groundhog Day*—reliving the same day over and over again. I was trapped inside a repeating loop of low visibility, tough sastrugi, sticky sand-like snow, harsh winds, and menopausal hot flashes. Having been immersed in a never-ending palette of white, I missed the color green. Grass under foot. Lush ferns mixed with dense brush. Evergreens stretched overhead.

On the positive side, we hit 14 miles each day, but I was pushing my body into overdrive to keep up with Marty when he was leading. The refreshing feeling from our rest day had disappeared. While Marty felt similarly fatigued, his tired pace was now faster than mine. When I led, I could feel him right on my heels, chomping to go faster.

On top of the physical and mental strain, my period dragged on—now on day six. At night, Diva had started leaking, so I switched to using my small supply of regular tampons to contain the chaos. Sleep had been restless as spontaneous hot flashes made me feel like I might suffocate in my sleeping bag. I'd frequently squirm out as fast as I could, only to find myself freezing a few minutes later. Lack of restorative sleep added to my growing bone-deep fatigue.

On Day 27, after settling into the tent, I opened our email and found Leni had forwarded a question left on our blog. I read it out loud. "After following along for weeks, I'm wondering, where do you get the courage to do this?"

While preparing to start the stove and melt snow, Marty said, "Hmm . . . I'm not sure how to answer that."

"Me neither."

I pondered for a few moments, then said, "Knowledge from past adventures and intense planning and training built my confidence to go." After taking a bite of cheese, I continued, "But is courage a skill you learn or a reaction to a situation? Doesn't fear bring out courage?"

"I think it has to do with applying your knowledge to a scary situation and then trusting that you'll make the right decisions," Marty said as he plopped another chunk of snow into the pot. "I know when I was a police officer, I sometimes felt reckless courage by walking into dangerous situations feeling invincible. I probably wasn't showing courage; I was lucky to walk away unharmed."

As Marty filled thermoses with boiling water and prepared to rehydrate our macaroni and cheese dinner, I thought about the time on Denali when I'd called upon courage to descend an icy wind-blasted ridge.

The morning after we had summited, I woke at 17,200 feet to the sound of the tent whipping wildly in the wind. I didn't have to look out the tent door to know we weren't going anywhere in those conditions. An extreme windstorm, like I'd never experienced, thrashed through high camp, threatening to pin us there for days.

Midway through the day, I said, "Susan, how much food do we have left?"

She took inventory of our dwindling stock. "About two days if we stretch it. Remember we've got more cached below at 14,000 feet."

The tent thrashed around all day, at times forcing me to lie down to avoid a repeated head-bashing. I thought about how blasting wind combined with sub-freezing temperatures increased the chances of damaging gear, getting frostbite, and losing footing on steep, icy rock. When I heard muffled talking outside, I poked my head out of the tent and saw two Rainier Mountaineering Institute (RMI) guides and their four clients struggling against the wind to break down tents and stuff gear into packs.

"Wow, RMI is leaving in these conditions. Seems too dangerous to me," I said.

Thirty minutes after the RMI team set off toward the knife-sharp ridge, I heard them return. Struggling through high winds, the team reset camp in worsening conditions.

Inside our tent, we huddled together around our radio in anticipation of the nightly weather report. The park ranger started out by saying, "We are predicting one-hundred-mile per hour winds at high camp for the next four days."

Susan, Alyson, and I stared back and forth at each other as if we'd heard that someone we loved had been diagnosed with a terminal illness.

The ranger continued reporting the forecasted weather for different parts of the mountain, and then it became difficult to hear him as his voice crackled in and out.

Alyson said, "I think he said it will be devastating at 17,200. Do you think our tent can take the wind?"

"Yes," I said confidently, even though I wasn't sure. We had to believe that our tent would be strong, that we would be strong, because we had no choice but to stay put until the wind died down.

I thought back to the night I had been nestled in my sleeping bag at 11,000 feet, listening to the search plane flying overhead. Back and forth it went, six times. And in the morning, teams emerged from their tents like hibernating bears from dens—we had been pinned in stormy weather for six days. A guy from Colorado came over and told us, "I heard on the radio that a Canadian solo climber was blown off the ridge at 16,900 feet toward the Peters Glacier, and that a Park Service volunteer tried to help but fell to his death too."

That ridge—one of the most exposed places on the route—was just four hundred feet below where we now sat at high camp.

While I was intimately aware of the dangers of the mountain, those two lives the ridge had taken reminded me that summiting was only half the climb. There was still a long way to safety.

That night, we set watch alarms to ring every two hours throughout the night so we could monitor the weather. If the wind died down, we'd pack up and leave, even if that meant traveling in the dark with headlamps. Worried about the weather, I couldn't sleep. Finally, at 6:00 a.m., a lull in wind signaled it was time to go.

Marty yelled over from his tent, "Chris, we are getting ready to go. How about you guys?"

"Yes, we are too."

We packed quickly in order to take advantage of the weather window as it could suddenly snap shut. As we departed, we noticed the RMI group preparing to leave.

Our team set off with Team Hawaii as we'd agreed to move as one unit in case anyone encountered a problem on the ridge. Safety in numbers. Marty, Kevin, and Brian made up the first rope team while Alyson, Susan, and I followed. In conditions that varied from low visibility to whiteout, we began descending the 40-degree slope of solid blue ice and rock. The wind picked up, blowing 60- to 70-mile-per-hour gusts from left to right across our bodies. Inside my tightened hood, I heard my labored breathing, and just beyond, the crunching of ice axe and crampons against snow. My heart raced as I tried to remain calm. *Nobody is going to die today.*

The world shrank to a small bubble around my body as I placed each step deliberately, ensuring the rope between Susan and me was tight enough to avoid tripping on it, but loose enough that I didn't get pulled off balance. I crouched low to the ground, making myself small and powerful against the wind. *Focus. Chris. Focus.* As a gust hit my left side, I leaned hard into it to counter the blast, then, as it eased, I shifted my weight back to the center of the trail, like a tree branch flexing in the wind. I exhaled deeply as I prepared for the next gust to strike. I pushed all negative thoughts of what could happen to us out of my mind.

I briefly looked up to see Susan and Alyson looking strong against the blasting wind—and felt grateful for this team, my lifeline.

As we descended the final stretch of the ridge, I could see the rocky gulley below. Once we'd scrambled into the safety of the gulley, I felt relief rush through my veins.

I looked up from my daydream about Denali, and Marty handed me my cup of steaming chicken fried rice. I took a bite, then said, "What about that day our teams made our way down from high camp on Denali—did you have courage that day?"

"For sure. I remember looking over at the RMI guides who were packing to leave at night and thought about leaving too. It took courage not to follow them down, to wait until the morning. My gut told me not to go, and I convinced Brian and Kevin to stay put."

"That's interesting . . . that it took courage not to do something." I watched Marty stir his noodles. "So where do we find the courage to do this?"

"It's part experience and part faith in yourself when put into unknown situations."

While I'd found courage on those days when Antarctica first threw me into the unknown, I was starting to feel I needed something more to keep from cracking under the mounting physical and mental pressure.

I GAZED OUT the tent's front door. "It's snowing." This was a rare sight in the frozen desert that is Antarctica, since snow was usually whipped up from the ground, not falling from the sky.

By now, Day 28, we'd covered 335 miles and were at an elevation of 6,088 feet. While unsure about how much weight we'd lost, we knew we were hungry. Our bodies were on overdrive, burning more energy to push out tougher miles and combat the increasingly cold days. To beef up the calories in our morning oatmeal, I tried dropping in chunks of chocolate bar from my daily ration of snacks. I swallowed a bite of my chocolate-swirled oatmeal surprise. "Oh my gosh—yum!"

As we set off, the low clouds soon collapsed onto the horizon, leaving nothing but a view of white. I was inside a giant eggshell, and my head felt scrambled. Stripped of my depth perception and without any discernible clumps of snow to ski toward, I constantly stared down at my compass to avoid straying off course. For the next three hours, I slowly pushed my skis forward, feeling the contours of the snow, my ankles bending to meet changes in the terrain as we made slow progress across the endless up-and-down bumps and rough crusty snow in a field of sastrugi. The wonder of sastrugi had long worn off; now it was simply a feature of the terrain to endure. After four hours, the thick clouds lifted, replaced by a hazy sky that released us from the prison of white.

With a change in the sky came a change in the terrain— rough crusty sastrugi was replaced with flat sticky snow. I'd already come to learn that flat terrain, at least this year, usually meant soft sticky snow. No glide. As I skied forward, with my lower back tight and leg muscles tense, I felt like I was pulling through small sand dunes. Instead of skiing in a more upright position, I leaned forward as I lunged over the surface in an exaggerated fashion for added pulling power. I felt like a prisoner chained to a huge heavy rock. Back when I was training with tires, pulling on blacktop took a similar effort, while pulling on the gravel surface of the Iron Horse Trail felt more like pulling on regular Antarctic snow.

When Marty led, I struggled to keep up and realized for the first time how he must have felt at the beginning of our expedition, when he had asked me to slow down. Now it seemed I was the slow one, and I didn't have equipment to blame, other than a body that wasn't as strong as Marty's in these conditions.

Feeling spent at the end of the day, I was looking forward to dinner and the distraction of email. I hooked up the various wires and gadgets and turned on the iPhone. An email came in from Brett that I read out loud to Marty. "Lewis broke a ski on sastrugi despite the fact that Carl"—his guide—"famously assured him that his skis were unbreakable. Steve from ALE said Lewis has joined a very select group of polar expeditioners who have broken skis. ALE will drop a new pair of skis to him when they reach the Thiel Mountains, likely today. In the meantime, Lewis has been skiing on it despite the crack. At least his blisters have healed, his chafing is gone, and his polar thigh continues to improve."

"I'm glad that wasn't you who needed new skis," I said.

"Me too."

"I wish there was something I could do to my skis to make them glide on the sticky crap we were on today." Then, through misty eyes, I confessed to Marty, "I felt weak not being able to keep up with you on the sticky snow. I hate it."

"The sticky snow is hard. Just like I hate low visibility and whiteout days, you seem to hate sticky snow."

I turned my head away from Marty because I felt I might cry like I had a few days earlier, when I hadn't been able to keep my emotions in check. Just saying the word *weak* out loud made my confidence shrink a bit, and felt like a blow to my Polar Chris ego. I cut off further conversation because I didn't want to focus on my frustrations from the day, or make Marty relive them with me.

AFTER NUMEROUS LOW-visibility days in a row, I opened the tent door to the chill of a bitter −30 degrees, and the sky above was an unbroken sea of blue, without even a wisp of white. The vastness stretched out above me, clear and full of life. Out on the horizon, I saw flat terrain changing to bumpy sastrugi. *At least I'll be able to see my way to negotiate through it,* I thought.

About an hour into the day, we were skiing through much bigger and bumpier frozen waves of snow than before—some rising three to four feet high. While pulling my sled up a sizeable wave took tremendous effort, maneuvering it down the other side became dangerous. Each time I labored up the sastrugi, I'd stand at the crest and plot my path down—traversing sideways to keep the sled from ramming into me on its downward path. I repeated this scenario over and over: dodging my sled, celebrating near misses, balancing on one ski in hopes of staying upright, and sometimes falling hard on the ice. The constant jarring caused by the tension and slack of my sled moving over small bumps exhausted my already weakened body. When I first traveled through smaller sastrugi, I'd sometimes marveled at the unique, natural beauty of this wind-carved landscape. Today—not so much.

As the day wore on, our friend low visibility joined the relentless sastrugi party—a one-two punch that guaranteed hours of fun.

Finally, break time.

"How are you doing?" said Marty.

"Fine." I pulled out my bottle of water from the sled. "Want some?"

"Sure."

Real conversation took too much effort, so we drank, ate, and got moving.

Pulling through the never-ending maze of jumbled snow and ice, I grunted and heaved, yanked my sled back into alignment, tripped when my ski tip got hung up on a piece of ice jutting out sideways, and cursed into my face mask. Finally, break time again.

"That was tough," said Marty.

"I have to pee." I pulled out my Freshette from the front pocket of my anorak, where I stored it for easy use, and shoved it inside my pants, then watched as pee shot out the tube extension and into the snow.

"I'm getting cold," Marty said.

I finished storing the device in my pocket. "Just a minute. I can't get my iPod to turn on."

"Let's go," said Marty as he turned and pushed off with his ski. He led us back out into the jumble.

Visibility continued to diminish as clouds pressed down on us. Soon we were enveloped in a complete whiteout, again, and could no longer see the frozen waves under foot. As I gingerly pushed my ski forward, I felt the front tip dangling in midair. *I must be perched on top of a large frozen wave.* Alarms blared in my mind—the conditions could easily break skis (an image of Lewis popped into my mind) or poles or limbs. Moving off my precarious position, I felt my way around the icy wave. I continued on, catching myself from falling over multiple times.

Marty stopped short at eight hours, and when I skied up next to him, he said, "I know we planned to go nine hours, but I think we should stop, it's getting dangerous."

"I agree." I pointed to a flat trough between frozen waves. "Let's squeeze the tent in there."

Inside, it seemed that Marty and I spent less time debriefing the day and instead focused on completing our evening chores. I snuggled into my sleeping bag and called Leni. It was Christmas break back home, and for the next week, Keenan was staying with her family, which included his best friend, Ryo.

"How do you think Keenan is doing . . . I mean, emotionally?" I asked. Given that it was the holiday season and we'd been gone for six weeks, I had braced myself for him to have had an emotional meltdown.

"He seems to be holding up really well," said Leni.

"When I talk to him, he sounds good . . . but I still worry."

"I'll do anything to make sure that Keenan feels comfortable, even if you think we should stay at your house instead of mine."

The sincerity of her words caught me off guard and caused my eyes to well with tears. Holding back my own emotional meltdown, I handed the phone to Marty.

He said, "Leni, we are trying not to have drama, but this is so hard. Every day feels like a quote I read once from a mountaineer that said, 'Yesterday was easy.' Each day seems harder than yesterday . . . we are being crushed by the cumulative effect of so many days without rest. I keep thinking we may go further tomorrow and build a little cushion to justify a rest day. But so far, that hasn't been the case."

Leni must have said something encouraging to Marty, because he replied, "Thanks, Leni. And thanks so much for helping with K-man too."

After we said goodbye to Leni, our emotional lid was shut again. As if we'd silently agreed to change the subject, Marty and I stared at the map together while we ate dinner.

He said, "I think we've started the 150-mile patch of sastrugi that ALE told us about before we left."

I choked down the bite of chicken fried rice in my mouth. "That means we've got about eleven to twelve more days of the stuff."

While we finished dinner, I thought about how surprised I had been to hear Marty explain the difficulty of our journey to Leni. While I agreed with what he'd said, he'd never explained the depth of the struggle out loud to me, nor had I to him. We'd defaulted to an expedition communication style that was different from our regular way of interacting as husband and wife. Maybe he thought talking about the cold hard days would cause it all to seep into our psyche, crack our defenses, and steal our confidence. As he'd said earlier during his ankle-rolling issue, maybe we didn't talk about it because dwelling on it wouldn't change the situation. There was no way out. Just like when you're in the middle of a mountain climb or 100-mile race—you just keep moving to outrun anything that might stop you from finishing. Maybe Marty had talked about it with Leni because she was a safe outlet, outside of our tent, for releasing emotions.

Still, whether we spoke it aloud or not, we couldn't hide our mental and physical decline.

DAY 30. NEW Year's Eve. The last day of the hardest year of my life.

At the end of the day, inside the tent, there was no fanfare, no party, no celebrating, and no half-hearted resolutions. Instead, we took stock of the here and now. We had twenty-five paper towels (twelve and a half each), twenty days of fuel, fifteen days of food, and one remaining wet wipe. No more tampons.

"We should keep a close eye on food so we don't run out," I said.

"Okay . . . and we better start rationing paper towels."

I thought, *Which is worse, running out of food or paper towels?*

In our best-case scenario we would arrive at the Pole in fifteen days by averaging 14 miles per day—a target that we found difficult to consistently hit. Honestly, I didn't see how we would ever be done in fifteen days.

Marty had already inhaled his dinner and was staring at mine like a vulture waiting to swoop in and devour dead prey. He knew that sometimes I couldn't stuff in all of my nighttime calories, despite a day of intense work. I tossed Marty the remaining scraps of my teriyaki chicken. Based on his thinning face and shrinking chest and legs, he looked about fifteen pounds lighter, and with little remaining body fat, his system was turning to muscle for energy. When I looked at my stomach and legs, I guessed I had lost about ten pounds of muscle and strength.

For the second night in a row, I reached across the airwaves and called Leni.

As if picking up where Marty had left off the night before, I said, "Hi, Leni. Man, what a tough day, tough conditions. All day, we had low visibility turning to whiteout and really difficult sastrugi . . . oh, and crappy sticky snow that really slowed me down." I glanced up and noticed Marty looking at me, appearing to be listening as he brushed his teeth. "We never got a break . . . and it's starting to feel really cold all the time . . . it was thirteen below . . . that makes me worry about polar thigh. I'm really starting to feel the stress of it all."

"Chris, you are right where you are supposed to be, feeling low," Leni said, "just like when you hit a low spot during a hundred-mile race. Things will get better. You just need a good day to boost your confidence. We love you guys. You are like family to us. Keenan is like family to us."

"We love you too." I hung up the phone, grateful to have released some of my growing stress and grateful to know that Keenan was in such good hands.

We went to bed early in hopes of grabbing a little extra sleep. After settling in, Marty reached over and held my hand, our arms entangled across sleeping bags for a few silent minutes. I never knew holding hands with Marty could feel so intimate; I never knew how much the silence could communicate.

MORE. RELENTLESS. SASTRUGI. Ugh! As I skied along, thinking about all those miles of tough-it-out sastrugi still to go, I imagined myself in a children's book. The sastrugi was a scary dark forest or field of flowing lava. The castle on the other side was the Pole, and it appeared Sastrugiland was the journey we had to bear.

Within a few hours of skiing with a temperature of −17 degrees and 20- to 25-mile-per-hour winds blowing sideways, my goggles froze into a mess, my face mask turned into an icy cluster, and I couldn't make out the needle on my compass to navigate. Meanwhile, the sastrugi conspired against me, trying to break me. It took all of my strength and focus to move through the maze of ice. No music or audiobook. *No matter what, stay with Marty.* Today, he was stronger on sastrugi, and pulling through it was wearing me thin.

Zapped by two big uphills, drained from the cold, now running on fumes, I pulled up next to him at break time after three two-hour sessions.

Marty said, "I'm really cold. I think we should just push through without a break."

My own frigid fingers and body were fighting to stay warm. I said okay, though I'd felt a mind-numbing emptiness in my stomach for the last few hours.

I grabbed a glove full of nuts from my pocket and shoved them up under my frozen face mask and into my mouth. Then I turned back into the wind. Another sentence of uphill marching, more jagged ridges of sastrugi, and blasting cold wind. I willed my legs forward to keep up with Marty while on the verge of tears.

After setting up our tent, I collapsed inside. Marty collected snow to melt for water. I sat with my legs dangling in the vestibule, blankly staring into space, unable to think clearly or change clothes or get on with the night. I began to cry. Alone in the tent, I didn't want to fight it this time like I had a few nights before on the phone with Leni—I let it rush in and envelop me completely. I wept harder and deeper.

Marty jumped into the tent. "I'm ready to warm up." He stared into my distressed eyes and said, "What's wrong?" and then looked away as if trying not to put me on the spot.

Looking down, I said, "Nothing . . . I mean . . . I can't explain it . . . it was a tough day for me." I didn't really know what was happening to me, and to be completely honest, I knew Marty didn't really want to discuss it. All he wanted was to get inside the tent, change clothes, and get on with nightly duties. He wasn't being inconsiderate; he was being practical. Self-preservation came before communication. All I wanted was to snack on my cheese and salami, but they were frozen. I sat in silence, eating my nuts, and I couldn't even wash them down with water because it was frozen too.

We both changed clothes, and I tried to pull myself together.

I found strength to connect gadgets to download email, and I read a message from our good friend and neighbor, Laura. "Yesterday, Keen, Ryo, Jack, TJ, Ian, and John were running amuck outside like chickens loose with no coop. Laser guns, soccer balls, dog frolicking, and video camera. Lots of chatter, strategy, shouting, and laughter. The occasional Izze drink break. We had to send them all outside to run it off because they were bouncing off the walls downstairs. Plus, the stench from a pack of sweaty boys in the playroom was fierce. Out ya get! Too funny."

Laura had recently been sending us regular updates and cheer, like she had appointed herself our pen pal. I found that her bubbly emails filled me with energy and connected me to home. In one of her emails, she mentioned that Leni had forwarded our private address to her.

Then there was an email from Leni.

As you mentioned before, this is uncharted territory for you physically and mentally. Of course, it's going to be the hardest thing you've ever done. The difference this time is there's an emotional pull on your heartstrings in addition to the mental fortitude and psychological determination demanded of any extreme endurance challenge.

I do hope you embrace this as a part of the journey. It's stretching you in a way for which you couldn't have trained.

As for Keenan (who is currently in a vicious Nerf gun war with Ryo and Randy), the worst thing that could happen to him is that he will deeply miss you and worry. Keenan has been remarkable; Becky and I were talking about how he's kept it together incredibly well. Perhaps he is able to compartmentalize, or perhaps we may see emotions seep or flood out in the next few weeks. Whatever happens, he'll grow because of it. It may not seem like it now, but you are giving him a gift in so many ways—many of which may emerge at different phases of his life. He is experiencing a village surrounding and embracing him. The village is stronger for it and so is he. I believe one's heart is like a muscle. It may be stretched and strained through discomfort or pain, but over time, it grows larger and stronger. It's that strength that will undoubtedly get you to the ends of the earth and back.

Today, my heart definitely felt stretched and strained, but Leni's email gave me reassurance that we were on track, that I was being shaped and molded in ways that would not only get me to the Pole, but impact life beyond the Pole.

I stored the tech gadgets and Marty looked at our GPS. "We covered thirteen miles in nine hours."

Not bad for a full day of sastrugi, but we still had about 125 more miles of the stuff—at least ten days of pulling over body-exhausting and mind-numbing bumps—and 80 miles beyond that to the Pole. I feared the toll the fields of sastrugi would take on me. Unlike 100-mile races, where exhaustion builds and dissipates in a 24-hour race window, here, exhaustion was like a slow-drip drug, and I hoped I wouldn't overdose.

WE WOKE TO the sound of wind, and as we prepared to depart, the wind meter read 20 miles per hour and −20 degrees. With more intense cold and wind ahead of us, and my overheating days seemingly behind me, I dressed in warmer under layers of clothing and switched to a new combination of hat and balaclava for better protection against the elements. We also improvised a soup to carry in our thermoses—created with our dehydrated chicken fat and electrolyte salt tablets—intended as a quick pick-me-up to warm our bodies during breaks.

As the morning progressed, the winds picked up to 25 miles per hour, gusting to 30. Temperatures likely hovered around −30 to −35 degrees. Bracing myself against the elements, I thought, *Here comes episode 3: Welcome to Wild Antarctica.* Narrator Morgan Freeman was back. "Zip your hoods tight, because today, Wild Antarctica may just blow your mind. She's whipped into a fury to test Chris and Marty with her full katabatic force. Can their battered bodies stand strong against her blasting, knock-you-over, bitter cold wind, or will this be the time she breaks them?"

After hours of leaning hard into the chilling wind and pulling over brutal bumps, we began ascending a hill—at least it wasn't a scary steep climb like the one near the Thiel Mountains. I muscled my heavy sled directly into her wild temper, hunching over to break through the gusts and stabbing the ice with my poles for added leverage. I made impossibly slow progress despite my extreme effort. I tightly cinched the hood of my anorak around my head, polar-style, leaving a small hole. The coyote ruff obscured my vision as it danced in the wind. At times, I found it difficult to breathe, as if trying to take in air through a straw. With a lack of calm and grace, every breath, every movement, felt labored.

I could barely make out Marty's silhouette about fifteen feet ahead through blasting bits of ice and snow. Despite my slow movement, the gap between Marty and I remained constant. *He must be experiencing similar challenges with the conditions.* I wished for freeze-proof headsets that would allow us to communicate while on the move. Finally, Marty pulled over so we could consult on the deteriorating conditions.

"We should stop, these conditions are getting dangerous," said Marty.

"I totally agree. But we can't stop on this slope."

"Right," he said. "Let's stop as soon as we reach some flatter terrain. Okay?"

"Yes, let's go." Pushing off with my ski, I thought: *It's going to be tough setting up our tent without it ripping or blowing away.*

Continuing on, my body stiffened against the cold. I tried to move faster, generate heat, but instead moved uphill in slow motion, unable to stop cold's steady progress inward. *Where is a hot flash when you need one?* I felt coated in cold. There was no way out as cold closed in on me.

We crested a hill and found a relatively flat area to stop, three hours earlier than planned. At least we'd scratched out 9 miles. We threw on our puffy down jackets and turned our attention to setting up the tent, our lifeline against the wind. We relied on the setup process that we had down cold. In these conditions, one mistake could lead to tragedy—misplaced poles could tear holes in the tent, or the tent strap could break free from a safety line or rip out of our hands and the tent could tumble across Antarctica, leaving us frozen in disbelief.

There was no room for error.

We meticulously clipped, staked, and secured the tent, fighting off the cold a little longer until we could jump inside and thaw out. Inside, my body took a long time to calm down from the cold—to stop shivering, slow my heart rate, release stiffened shoulders, relax clenched fists. As the wind shook the tent like mad, we hung gear to dry and changed clothes. Then, when I rested my head in my hands, I noticed an absence of feeling on part of my chin. Thinking my face wasn't completely thawed out from the day, I deliberately touched my chin again—it felt a little numb, like when you get a shot at the dentist.

"Marty, do you see anything on my chin?"

"It just looks a little red," he said as he ate a piece of salami.

Looking at my face in the mirrored lens of my goggles, I thought it might have become irritated from the ice buildup inside my face mask, or perhaps wind had found a way in through my new hat system. I was ravaged with hunger from our day, so gave it little further thought and focused my attention on snacking and preparing our dinner of chicken and noodles.

When I went to brush my teeth, I noticed an item resting next to my toothpaste inside my toiletries bag: the Saint Christopher medal that Mom had sent me a week before departure. I had worn it on a necklace in Punta Arenas, but now kept it here so the metal—when frozen—wouldn't damage my skin. Marty kept his medal inside his coat pocket. When I'd called Mom and said, "Thanks, they are awesome, just perfect," she had burst into tears. "Honey, I know this may sound silly," she'd said, "but I feel so much better knowing you and Marty have those medals with you to protect you."

I didn't think it was silly—and at that moment in the tent, I felt a direct connection to Mom's love.

The unsettling noise of wind gusting and tent flapping continued well into the night—at one point shaking me awake.

When I flopped over in my sleeping bag, I felt my face and discovered that a sore had developed on my chin. I shot up like I would when I heard baby Keenan crying in his sleep, and pulled my hat off my eyes. Breathing heavy, Marty was asleep facing the other side of the tent. He could sleep through anything, especially alarms going off in *my* head in the middle of the night. I reached for the medical kit and pondered my options.

While assembling the kit back home, we had chosen each item with extreme care and endlessly debated worth versus weight. Exclude the wrong item and you could end your expedition. The entire exercise was more art than science. Polar experts recommended some necessities, while other items were labeled personal preference. At the last minute, on the advice of an ALE medical specialist, we had added a small tube of aloe vera gel.

As I sifted through the kit at 1:00 a.m., I remembered that aloe vera gel was the best defense against a cold injury that seemed more like frostnip than frostbite. I slathered on the gel. I repeated the process two more times in the night when tent flapping woke me up.

Please, don't let this turn into frostbite.

A FEW DAYS LATER, as I layered up with clothing, I noticed my chin hadn't worsened but was still tender and raw to the touch. I double-checked that my headgear had no gaps before heading back into the intense wind. Given the vulnerable state of my chin, I was hyper-focused on ensuring that I didn't brush too closely against cold. Life in Antarctica was colder, windier, and harder now.

About 40 minutes into our morning, Marty waved me forward and said, "I can't lead any more in this whiteout crap. I can't concentrate or focus. If you can lead, I will follow." With a jolt of adrenaline, my mind and body found a new gear. *Marty needs me, and I will not let him down.* Now in the lead, I deliberately moved across the ice with renewed strength. I said the word *strong* as I exhaled my breath. On the next breath, I exhaled the word *powerful*. For hours, I repeated the mantra—*strong, powerful*—over and over as I cheered myself on.

The whiteout changed to low clouds and low contrast lighting after a few hours; conditions that hindered sight and erased contours in the snow were Marty's nemesis. I could only imagine the curse words piercing the cold behind me. Navigation became more difficult for me, requiring energy-zapping focus and constant staring at the compass. During a quick break at four hours, I noticed Marty had his head down and body leaned over his ski poles, a posture I hadn't seen since his ankle-rolling days the first two weeks of the expedition.

Unclipping from my sled, I swished over the snow to him, gave him a big hug, and said, "I love you."

"I suck," said Marty, his head still hanging low.

"You don't suck. If you're out here long enough, you are bound to have a tough day."

"I just have no strength or energy."

"You're doing great . . . just keep following me, and we'll get through the day."

I imagined he was butting up against his own humanness, expecting more from himself and coming up short.

Gazing through the dissipating haze at a complex labyrinth that was our route, I tried to map a path in my mind. Wild Antarctica began to talk to me, showing me the way one section at a time: veer left, pull a little harder, forget your burning muscles. I began to move with decisiveness and ease and find a rhythm to my motions. I knew with certainty that I had the strength to lead us through this day. Hours melted away as Antarctica continued whispering in my ear. Music played in my mind, yet my iPod remained off all day. The space between my thoughts lengthened. I felt a sense of harmony and connection to everything. And suddenly, nine hours had passed.

Immediately after we got inside the tent, Marty sat down without changing his clothes, pulled out the satellite phone, and called in our voice blog:

Today represents why Chris and I make such a good team. Every day or so, I have a bad hour or two where I am tired, but today I had a bad day . . . I had no energy, down to my very core. I just couldn't lead or concentrate. I thought at some point I would rally. I didn't. I just put my head down and followed Chris for the entire day.

At one point Chris hugged me, and for the first time I cried on the trail. We know we'll get through this together, and that is why it's great to have my spouse out here as a teammate. If I was here with another guy, he probably would have looked at me and told me to man up or punched me in the arm; and I probably would have done the same to him. But with Chris and me, it's different.

Chris has had bad times, and I've been able to step up, but I don't think she had a bad day. *But I certainly did. Great job leading today, Chris.*

After Marty hung up the phone, I caught his eye, reached over, and touched his scruffy bearded cheek with my hand, then leaned in, closed my eyes, and rested my forehead against his for a few quiet moments.

As we went through the motions of our nightly duties, I thought about the value of this day—of being with Marty as he struggled through a vulnerable moment, of letting him know we were in this together and no matter what his condition, I would love him.

And I pondered: *Is this the good day that Leni mentioned I needed to boost my confidence for the duration?*

We were halfway through Sastrugiland and closing in on the castle.

CHAPTER 13:

LETTING GO

A few days later, on Day 36, I woke to the warmth of the sun penetrating our tent and a wisp of a breeze outside—a welcome change from the tough conditions we'd slogged through for the last ten days, and the last six in rough sastrugi. The whole landscape was bathed in the warm glow of the sun. The unending bright sky was a glorious luminous blue. On days like this, it was sometimes hard to remember that it was still freezing outside—today a blustery –10 degrees on our temperature gauge.

An hour into the day while leading, I realized that when Antarctica wasn't trying to break me with blasting windstorms, mind-numbing whiteouts, sticky snow, and choppy sastrugi—it was actually a stunningly beautiful place. The network of ripples and ridges of snow glistening beneath the striking blue sky welcomed me into a new day. Fresh air filled my lungs and I felt refreshed and exhilarated. There were no more mountains on our route, only the undulating icy terrain. My goggles were fog free. My body temperature was in balance. I pushed out worries of weather, fatigue, and my chin injury, which had remained a bit raw the last few days (but luckily hadn't gotten worse), and got high on the scenery of Antarctica, a sight few people will ever experience up close.

Despite the mental high, I still wasn't at full strength physically.

After I floated through the first session, at break, Marty asked, "Can I see your compass to check that you're on the right bearing?"

What a strange request, I thought.

He leaned over and checked my compass. "It's right," he said, mostly to himself in a questioning tone.

A few hours later, at another break after I had been leading, Marty asked, "What were you navigating toward? I couldn't tell what line you were following. You know you can use the shadow of the sun to help you stay on course."

I stood in silence with lips pursed, looking out at the white sastrugi field that tumbled into the distance, heat rising inside my jacket. *Does he think I'm navigating off course?*

By the third time Marty interrogated me about my navigational skills, providing me with unsolicited tips after thirty-five days of navigating just fine, thank you, I thought I might explode. "Marty, what is your problem today? I know how to navigate. I just might not navigate exactly the same as you."

He didn't reply. We both quickly finished eating our snacks in silence and set off with Marty in the lead.

I skied along through a thick cloud of doubt. Marty's incessant questions replayed in my head and conspired to crack my confidence. It didn't help that the physical challenge of the day was on the rise as I worked through endless bumps and frozen ridges of sastrugi that had grown to two to three feet tall.

Suddenly, a sound off in the distance pierced the silence that was growing between us. I looked around in disbelief, trying to determine if it was actually coming from outside my head sealed tightly within my hood. I scanned the sky and saw the outline of a plane—our first sign of civilization in over five weeks. A few weeks ago, the man-made sound would have annoyed me, but now, the buzz of its engine filled me with excitement and anticipation. Marty must have heard it too, because he stopped and looked up. Standing side by side, gazing up, we followed the red dot against the blue sky as it moved south.

"A plane. I can't believe it," I said.

"They must be flying a group to the Pole."

"Probably some of those penguin people."

Marty looked over at me. "I wonder if they can see us . . . two red dots on the white landscape."

"If they can, I bet they're taking our picture right now."

We stood there until the sound of the engines faded and the dot disappeared. For the next hour, I skied with lifted spirits. It felt like those times when hikers would say, "You're amazing," as I flew past, running down mountain trails.

When we stopped for the day, the GPS told us we'd covered a solid 14 miles.

Marty and I sat on sleeping bags chomping Pringles topped with leftover cheese. "I still can't get over seeing that plane," I said. "It made me feel less isolated."

"Yeah . . . it was awesome," Marty said while fiddling with the stove. He reached into the repair kit. "I think it's time to replace the fuel pump." After he pulled off the old pump, Marty sheepishly looked at me and said, "Today I shouldn't have questioned you about navigation. I'm sorry. Can I have a pass on the day?"

I took a few seconds to process what he said, wondering why he did it. Then said, "Yes, you can . . . thanks."

Enough said.

Marty wasn't one who typically analyzed the why of his actions; he just moved on. But I had a hunch. Maybe this was Marty's version of trying to push our pace and squeeze every mile out of each day—the role I had played during our first two weeks. Maybe Marty had directed his attention to fixing my unbroken navigation skills because he wanted to control an uncontrollable situation, force our growing stress into submission, and put us on a fast track to the Pole.

With the new pump in place, Marty fired up the stove and I could instantly hear how much stronger it sounded. Funny, I hadn't noticed the slow decline in performance—it still boiled our water but took longer than usual to get the job done.

While Marty pulled out dehydrated macaroni and cheese dinners from our food bag, I inspected the cold injury on my chin. No longer raw, it had finally scabbed over, just like my feelings from earlier in the day.

Wanting to ensure that our food lasted us to the Pole, I grabbed my journal and did a quick calculation. If we skied 12 miles per day for the remaining 146 miles, we would arrive in 12 days.

"Marty, I'm going to pull a little food from each day of rations and create a few more days of food—okay?"

"How many more days?"

"We have nine days of food left, but likely have twelve more days of skiing. So I'll make three more days of food." This would drop our daily intake of calories from about 5,400 to 4,000 each.

After finishing my food-redistribution project, I called home to talk to Keenan and discovered that my two brothers had arrived—it was the start of a boys' week in North Bend. Pat had flown in from working near the Arctic Circle, and Jim had left home in Wheaton, Illinois, just outside Chicago, just when subzero temperatures blasted in from the north.

Keenan said, "Mom, today was our first day back to school after break. Lots of kids were excited to see how you and Dad are doing. When I walked in, they were updating the bulletin board that shows where you are."

"Keenan, that's awesome," I said. "Tell everyone at school we're doing well, and we're excited for them to keep following along."

Marty continued, "K-man, does the map look like we've covered a lot of ground?"

"Yes, you're about three-fourths of the way there."

"About a hundred and fifty miles to go," said Marty.

After dinner, I took stock of paper towels. I estimated one and a half towels to share per day instead of two. Hopefully that would cover us.

THE NEXT MORNING, I woke with a tickly feeling in the back of my throat, sat up in my sleeping bag, and started coughing madly. After taking a sip of water, I held my throbbing head in my hands and stared at the yellow tent walls. I'd likely picked up a head cold and a minor case of polar cough from the dry air, wind, and altitude.

Following Marty out of camp, I started out slow; my legs felt like dead weights strapped to skis. With labored breathing, I struggled to match his pace. *What is wrong with me? Is it the thinner air at 8,500 feet? Am I breaking under the weight of thirty-six days of hard work with only one rest day? Do I need a new pump like our stove?*

At our two-hour break, Marty asked, "Do we need to stop . . . for the day?"

"No," I said, stiffening. "I just can't go any faster."

I led out at a plodding pace.

Thirty minutes later, I gazed in disbelief at a jungle of waves of snow so high that we could lose sight of each other behind them. As I moved forward, I struggled to pull my sled over a nasty patch of the devils. Despite pulling harder and harder, I failed to dislodge the sled from the jaws of jagged ice. One last pull, and my sled crashed on its side. I unclipped from the sled and, in a huff, knelt beside it. I summoned every ounce of strength to right my sled, as if flipping over a beached seal. I clipped back in, lunged forward. A few yards later, as I yanked over a mighty bump, my sled crashed over again. I unclipped from it. Pushing and tugging repeatedly, I lacked the strength to turn it over. "Fuck!" I yelled into the wind.

Marty skied up beside me and unclipped from his sled. Together we heaved with what remained of our strength and righted my rogue sled. A few minutes later, it tipped over again. "Seriously, what the fuck!" I shouted. The load in the sled had become unbalanced, like a sailboat without sufficient ballast. I crouched next to Marty as we pushed it back over again. As he gazed over at me, his silence couldn't hide the look of frustration that, I was sure, hid behind his face mask.

In my head, we had a lively conversation:

Marty: Chris, what is wrong with you?
Me: I'm trying my hardest.
Marty: No way. You are barely moving.
Me: I'm not going that slowly!
Marty: Yes, you are. I'm sick of it. You need to suck it up!

I looked over at Marty, and then stared uphill at the relentless terrain, and hung my head low. I relinquished the lead to him. It was Marty's turn to lead me through a bad day. I stared at the back of his sled in a trancelike state, my legs heavy and arms weak. I felt misunderstood, like a child whose parents didn't believe she was sick enough to stay home from school. With body breaking and mind failing, I lumbered on as best I could.

At our break at nine hours, I turned to Marty and said, "I feel light-headed, like I could faint. I don't think it's worth going another hour as we'd planned."

"We can stop if you need to . . . I'm tired too, but I could keep going."

We stopped and set up the tent. Marty stayed outside with the shovel and whacked chunks of ice off the frozen waves to melt into water. It sounded like he was beating the ice into submission, slaying a sastrugi dragon. Inside, I had the overwhelming feeling that we could have covered more miles if I hadn't been moving so slowly. I felt so weak. I wondered if leading all day when Marty had felt bad had depleted my physical reserves. And emotionally, I was cracking from the continuous isolation of so many hours in my own head. I craved connection, to feel understood, to be reminded that I was not alone.

Marty entered the vestibule of the tent looking triumphant and holding up a bag full of dead sastrugi.

He started changing clothes and asked, "Chris, how are you doing?" His curious eyes turned worried when he saw my face.

"Okay," I said, tears pooling in my eyes. I felt a flicker of the familiar compassion and open communication of our marriage.

Yet as tears trickled down my face, I quickly wiped them away, sick of crying. I tried stuffing my lingering feelings back into hiding—I was afraid of completely breaking apart from the weight of it all. I couldn't bear to be strong anymore, afraid of crushing my soul, because today I couldn't remember what it felt like to be full of passion. I was in survival mode, protecting myself from feeling too exposed.

"You're doing your best," said Marty as he slipped into his down booties.

"Yeah," I said. I still felt inadequate.

I burrowed into my sleeping bag and pulled out the satellite phone, then held it without dialing for a while as I collected my thoughts. As I labored through an uninspiring blog, unable to sound upbeat, I said, "So what we really need is a rest day, but unfortunately, we can't afford to take one given the time we have left to the Pole and our limited food supply. No question, we're ready to be done, ready to be there."

I hung up. Marty pointed at the map and said, "We crossed eighty-eight degrees today, only two more degrees and we'll be standing at the Pole." His forced enthusiasm couldn't hide the fact that two degrees equaled over 130 miles and about ten more days of hard work. After dinner, to celebrate 88 degrees and to lighten the mood, Marty whipped up a dehydrated cheesecake for dessert. I stuffed in a spoonful of raspberries mixed with a creamy-textured filling, then burrowed into my sleeping bag, trying to hide away from my feelings. I closed my eyes, and a few minutes later, I saw Keenan's face.

I reached for the iPhone and flipped through photos of him from our trip to Japan a few months before we departed. *There* was happy Chris and happy Marty and our happy family standing on top of Mount Fuji. I stared into Keenan's smiling eyes for a long time, letting the feeling of home seep deep into my heart, holding the phone next to my chest as I drifted off to sleep.

THE NEXT MORNING, as I was packing up to depart, Marty said, "I'm going to grab some weight from your sled to lighten your load. Hopefully even our pace."

Reluctantly, I nodded in agreement. It was tough watching as he stashed fifteen to twenty pounds of my food in his sled—because I'm a woman who likes to pull her own weight. But I knew it made sense for the good of our team. As I skied out of camp, I instantly felt the difference from a lighter sled, and from Marty's kindness.

Our new "evening the pace" strategy seemed to help me, but I could see the burden the extra weight was placing on Marty. Skiing behind him, I noticed he regularly repositioned his harness, as if trying to find a comfortable location for it.

After a morning filled with more energy-sucking sastrugi and whiteout conditions, the clouds that had been pressing down on us lifted and the terrain eased to smaller bumps. My mood followed the changing terrain. The day moved along without incident. I was grateful to lean on Marty as my teammate—we were only as strong as our weakest person, which had seemed to be me for the past few days. With our new strategy, we pushed out 10 hours and 14.3 miles and almost reached the Polar Plateau, an area that promised gentler terrain on our final leg.

Inside the tent, as we settled into eating snacks and relaxing, I said, "Marty, today I noticed you were messing with your harness. What's up? Is it uncomfortable?"

"Oh, well . . . my harness seems to be pinching something. Probably my femoral nerve. I sometimes get shooting pain down my leg."

"What? How long has this been going on?"

"I'm not sure, maybe a week or so."

"A week? How often does it happen each day?" I stared at Marty with my serious motherly face and pursed lips.

"A few times. I don't always get a shooting pain. Sometimes it's just really uncomfortable when the harness pulls tight on my hips. I think it's because I've lost so much weight."

As I cooked dinner, Marty wrapped his extra fleece mitten liners around his waist belt for added cushioning, trying to compensate for the natural padding that had long since fallen off his body. Back in the early 1900s, polar explorers who were hauling giant sleds of gear likely suffered from the same problem.

Before bed, Marty left the voice blog:

> *The last ten days have been a battle for every mile for both Chris and me, mentally and physically. I've seen enough sastrugi in the last ten days to last a lifetime. But today we were strong, and I let the thought of actually reaching the Pole enter my mind. I've always believed we would make it. So many things—planning, training, the financial investment, quitting my job, all of the sacrifices along the way, and the amazing support from friends, family, and our son—all drive us forward. Chris and I have never talked about stopping. We've always known we will keep driving on. Still, with a big expedition like this, I worry about things that could go wrong. At this point, I'm confident we are going to make the last 120 miles with our remaining nine days of food.*

While I had no doubt we would make it to the Pole, I feared I was nearing the end of my physical and mental reserves and wondered what would fuel me to the finish.

AS I PULLED through another mind-numbing whiteout, my pace slowed to a crawl. *We're probably not making good miles today like we did yesterday.* As I pushed one ski, then the other, into the white nothingness, my mind wandered back to Day 21 (eighteen days earlier)—the day I slept long into the morning in my warm sleeping bag, watched videos while munching on gummy penguins, and breathed in the flowery smell of my freshly washed body. The day I felt renewed. That day had long faded. Instead I felt the extremes of Antarctica embedded in my body.

As I heaved my sled forward, I thought: *How long can I keep this up?* I wished for a clear path back to the energy and happiness that usually surged through me.

At break time, I stopped and pulled out my salami and cheese. Marty pulled up next to me, leaned in to be heard over the wind, and said, "What can I do to help you?"

Strange question, I thought, because it wasn't like I was trying to open my water bottle or find a piece of gear in my sled.

Wait, maybe he's talking about my pace.

Suddenly on the defensive, I shot back, "I feel like you think I'm not trying hard enough, that something is wrong with me."

"Sorry," he said, as if trying to wrap up the discussion as quickly as possible, cutting off any additional debate. In normal life when we had a misunderstanding, we talked it through to clear the air. But the air was too cold and windy.

After our quick break, Marty led out and I fell in behind. Just 10 minutes later, he waved me forward to where he had stopped. Leaning against his poles, head down, sounding like he might burst into tears, he said, "Chris, you are doing awesome. You are such a strong woman. I'm sorry if I made you feel otherwise."

"Thanks," I yelled to be heard over the wind, feeling a boost from his words.

That night after we had settled into our tent, Marty studied the GPS. "We hit 10.7 miles . . . a bit shorter than yesterday."

"Hmm," I said with a hint of concern. "I have an idea I've been thinking about all day. Wanna hear it?"

"O-kay," said Marty, sounding a bit skeptical.

I took a deep breath, then slowly exhaled until my shoulders fell from my ears. "I wonder if it might make sense to"—I paused, then blurted out—"take another rest day."

Marty looked me in the eye like an injured animal backed into a corner with no escape route. Before I could say anything more, he said, "If we take a rest day we will *not* make it. If that is what you need to do, then I'll do it. But we will *not* make it to the Pole."

"Taking a day off could revive us. And we could carve out extra days of food from what we have."

Marty added chunks of snow into our pot of boiling water. "Yeah, but we can't afford to burn a day in the tent. Would you actually rest if it were sunny and clear and low wind? What if bad weather strikes later and we can't move? We'll regret taking a day off." Before I could respond, he steamed on. "I will do *anything* to get us to the Pole. What do you need me to do? *What?* I will do it. I will zip you up into my sled and pull two sleds if that is what it takes. That is how motivated I am to get us to the Pole."

Marty's intense reaction—so completely out of character—shocked me silent. Maybe he just wanted our expedition to be over, and the thought of adding days to our journey made him crazy.

"We're assuming we have to make it to the Pole in eight days before food runs out. Why not redistribute the food to last more days, like before?"

At this point, fewer calories per day meant more days of food.

My idea would give us the option to take a rest day or embrace our current plodding pace without rising pressure to go faster. Yes, we might suffer through hunger, but this seemed like a viable path. I looked at Marty, who sat in silence, and wondered: *Is my desperately tired brain missing something?*

I continued, "Let's at least look through the remaining food bags and see how much we have."

Marty didn't say anything, looked away from me, then reached into the vestibule to fiddle with some of the food bags stashed there.

Does Marty think I can't tough it out? That I am surrendering to the cold and isolation? It was true that being isolated in the middle of a continent larger than the continental United States—with nobody else around—made me feel dreadfully alone, even though I shared a tent with the person I loved most in the world.

I wanted Marty to know that my vision of us standing at

the Pole still burned strong. But what I saw flaming in Marty's eyes scared me. I had never seen such a look of fear—not fear for his life, but fear of letting himself down, fear of three years of planning and training disappearing into the abyss of one bad decision. Backed into the corner of the tent, he wrapped his arms tightly around his chest, as if protecting himself from me so that I couldn't hurt our chances of making the Pole. I was a threat. I was a problem that he couldn't solve. Maybe this was the time he wouldn't be able to succeed by sheer will and determination. I saw a man fighting to keep his image of success from shattering to pieces.

Alone on the other side of the tent, I wanted only to end the isolation and exhaustion. And there we sat, stranded on separate islands inside the same tent. Shackled to our own fears, unable to help each other break free, our bond of marriage stretched to its limit.

"What are we going to do?" I demanded.

My words hung in the silent tent.

After an extended pause, Marty said, "Why don't you call Leni. We should tell someone what we are thinking and get their opinion."

Just the mention of the idea stopped the rattling inside our tent and took the pressure off of making a decision.

Leni said, "Oh, hey, Chris, I didn't expect to hear from you today."

From the instant I heard her voice, I felt emotions swell in my throat.

As I attempted to explain our situation, she said, "Chris, I think we have a bad connection—there was a long pause while you were talking."

It wasn't a bad connection. I had paused because an earthquake of emotion, exhaustion, and depletion had caused my dam of control to break. I could no longer hold it back. Out burst a flood of tears. I completely surrendered as it *all* washed over me.

I gasped for air. "Leni, I am right on the edge of my physical and emotional limits." I struggled to go on. "I have never been in this place before. I need rest, but we need to keep moving." I stopped. I was desperately afraid of going over some unseen physical or emotional cliff that would prevent me from reaching the Pole. As an ultrarunner, I'd never come to a place like this. Then another long pause before I choked out, "I feel so weak."

Leni replied, "You, weak?"

"Yes. I'm just . . . so . . . right in the middle of it," I said as my voice pitched high and constricted like it does when I get really emotional.

I couldn't articulate all that was happening: the events from the last few days replaying in my mind, the toxic cocktail of emotions that swirled within me, the way feeling weak stirred me up because I identified so much with being strong. Struggling wasn't who I was—feeling like this was like breaking some unwritten contract with myself, and Marty. I hoped Leni would intuitively understand what I couldn't say. After all, she'd been with us on this expedition since the beginning of our planning three years ago. She'd seen me at my lowest while pacing me on 100-mile trail races. We understood each other with an uncommon ease.

"Chris, I know you have the strength to do this."

"I just can't feel it," I said, straining to hold back more tears.

"But it's there. If you don't feel it now, it will come back. It always has in the past when you've pushed yourself."

Breathless, I said, "I'm just . . . not so sure this time."

I got so emotionally tangled that I handed the phone to Marty. He said, "Leni, this is the hardest thing that we've ever done. We are struggling, but we will make it through. Thanks for all your help."

Having calmed down a little, I got back on the phone. "Thanks, Leni . . . for being there."

After hanging up, I noticed that the timer on the front of the phone said we'd spent 17 precious minutes talking to Leni. Our connection had not dropped once. She had given me a way back to feeling human, and not just like a robot slogging across the ice. A way back to accepting myself as is, in a moment of complete struggle. I eased away from my emotional cliff—stopped crying and began talking in my normal pitched voice.

"I'm glad we called Leni," I said.

"Me too. So what do you think . . . about taking a rest day?" said Marty. His arms now hung relaxed on his legs that were crossed in front of him, but his tone still sounded a bit guarded.

"I guess we can keep going . . . at least for now. I just don't want to feel like a rest day is completely off the table, though."

"Okay, that's fine."

"And I want both of us to be okay with a slower pace . . . I don't want to feel pressure to go faster. I really can't go any faster. I may even get slower." I still believed that we would make it.

"Okay."

After looking over our remaining food supplies, we extended eight days of rations into nine days—the second redistribution of our food, which now lowered each of our calories per day from about 4,000 to 3,600.

DAY 40 (JANUARY 10), the day we had originally imagined standing at the Pole. But we still had 100 miles to go. I had run 100 miles on tough mountain trails in less than a day, but these 100 miles would likely take another agonizing week or so to complete. These 100 miles would require focus like never before—one long frigid hour at a time. These 100 miles would demand strong minds to overcome bodies desperate to stop.

We started the day by instigating a few strategies to help combat exhaustion: wake up 30 minutes later and end our day at eight and a half hours instead of nine and a half to ten hours. To help focus, we decided to ditch audiobooks and music. I started using a breathing mantra like I had when I led during Marty's bad day, only this time I replaced the words *strong, powerful* with *be strong.*

I forced my dragging body through another frozen day of whiteout conditions and energy-draining sastrugi. I breathed out and said *be*, and on the next breath out I said *strong*, putting myself into a state of moving meditation. Throughout the day, each time fatigue or frustration rushed in, I tried pushing it out with *be strong*. It worked, for the most part, but when I hit patches of sand-like snow that turned my already slow pace into a crawl, the power of my mantra faded, and my nemesis drained me of energy, like Superman's kryptonite. And by the end of the day, *be strong* couldn't help change the fact that I felt exhausted.

Inside the tent that night, I dialed home and Keenan answered. "Mom, oh my gosh, you'll never believe it."

"What?"

"A few days ago, Uncle Jim had to leave because a pipe froze and burst at his house. Aunt Diane asked him to come home." I had heard from Brett that arctic weather had turned the Midwest into a frozen cluster. Keenan continued, "So Pat drove him to the airport at six o'clock at night. I stayed home by myself."

"You stayed home . . . by yourself?" I blinked. We'd left Keenan home alone for an hour or so when we'd gone out for a run, but never at night. I hadn't thought to cover this with Pat, a bachelor without our built-in parent radar.

"Yes, Pat told me to work on my homework and that he'd be back in a few hours . . . but when it was nine o'clock and time for bed, he still wasn't home."

"Oh my gosh . . . so what did you do?"

"I tried calling Uncle Pat's cell phone, but he didn't answer. I think it was dead. I didn't know what to do. I called Aunt Sue. I didn't want to go to bed alone in the house." Keenan sounded certain that he should have had an adult in the home with him at bedtime.

"Then what happened?"

"Aunt Sue came over and stayed with me so that I could go to bed. The next day, Uncle Pat was there, so I guess he got home sometime while I was sleeping."

"Wow, Keenan, that's quite a story. Great work. I'm proud of how you handled it."

While Keenan's surrogate team had done a fabulous job caring for him, I was ready to be a full-on *mom* and take care of Keenan in ways I simply couldn't from Antarctica.

After I hung up the phone, I checked email. The first one, from Leni, said: *Chris, Please Read.* In her note, she told me that right after our phone conversation the night before, she had taken her daughter, Simone, to her horse-riding lesson. The instructor had told the students that the best you can do is be aware of and control yourself and not worry about trying to control the horse or the environment.

She wrote, "Chris, I've always been amazed at your total self-awareness. I have never seen you not be in complete tune with your own mind and body. It's second nature to you and is a gift. Even as you spoke with me yesterday—even at a low moment—you were keenly aware what your mind and body need. It never ceases to impress me how, like a bloodhound, you can smell what you and those around you think and feel. Even when Antarctica is trying to beat you up. Even in the thick of it, you know."

As I read her email, tears ran down my face for the second night in a row. But this time they were tears of truth for something brewing below the surface of my consciousness. *What am I trying to tell myself—and do I have the courage to see it?*

"I'M FEELING PRETTY good," I told Marty the next morning. We were packing up the sleds. "So I'm going to take back the weight you took the other day . . . it could help your pinched nerve."

"Okay, if you're sure," said Marty. He pulled a few bags out of his sled and dropped them into mine.

While skiing along through the bright sun and low winds, I admitted to myself that I simply could not push this hard any longer.

At that point, pushing hard risked physical and emotional breakdown, ending our expedition, or worse, injuring our marriage. As much as I thought Antarctica was trying to break me, I could not beat her into submission. I had to change the way I thought about moving through her harsh, beautiful landscape.

After a few hours of skiing, the waves of snow and ice turned to smaller and smaller bumps. I gazed out on a horizon that looked almost flat. *We've left the land of giant sastrugi!* We'd finally reached the Polar Plateau, a mythical place that promised flat snow and fast skiing. We were leaving the eye of a storm on the open ocean and entering the calm of a sheltered harbor. Within minutes of my celebration, I noticed that the soft, sticky snow of my fantasy safe harbor was not conducive to fast skiing. And while there were no frozen ocean swells to ski over, I braced for the days of more powerful wind and extreme cold that I knew would come with the Polar Plateau.

I shuffled along in the soft snow at a painfully slow pace, thinking about how I wanted to move through my last week in Antarctica. *I have pulled my heavy sled for forty days. What if I let myself be pulled? Maybe this is the way.* I wasn't talking about literally having Marty pull me, like he had mentioned in our heated discussion. I wanted to find a way to work *with* myself instead of *against* myself. No more of the "me against Antarctica" mentality—I'd try to accept and work with the weather and terrain. Surrender.

For the next hour, as I pushed one ski in front of the other, I focused on being happy for what I could accomplish instead of wishing I could go faster. I let go of pushing myself so hard and judging myself when I came up short. When a negative thought came into my head—*I am so slow*—I forcefully turned it inside out. *I am still moving. I am getting there.* The thought *Marty and I should talk about our feelings* turned into *It's okay if we don't confide in each other right now.* Positive energy began to seep back into my tired bones. I stopped wishing for different terrain. *I hate sticky snow* turned into *I can pull through soft snow.* My skis, sled, and mood felt lighter. I believed that every step forward was success. I focused on being pulled by the positive energy and love of others— my family and friends, and all the kids at schools following along. My mind softened and heart opened as I thought of the videos we had watched on Day 21 and Keenan's words, "I know you are going to make it." I thought of the roar of excitement blasting through the satellite phone when we'd started the Q and A with the kids at Saint Joseph School. I thought of our circle of friends at our send-off party, the feeling of their energy pulsing through me, of being united as one. I visualized the Pole as a magnet, its force pulling me into its welcoming arms.

After a day of slogging in sticky contemplation, we set up the tent.

Marty jumped inside. I stayed outside to go to the bathroom. Surprised there was only a wisp of wind in the air, I stood motionless, taking in the expanse of Antarctica, the profound stillness. I closed my eyes and floated inside the infinite silence— unable to distinguish where my body ended and where the ice and sky began, all connected as one by the silence.

While dinner was cooking, I grabbed my journal to capture the feeling of silence, but instead, a striking truth broke through the stillness, and I wrote: "I'm afraid of feeling weak, exposed and vulnerable; I'm afraid of letting go of thinking of myself as strong and powerful." More, I was afraid of being swallowed into the abyss of struggle and weakness without a way back to Strong Chris.

Do I dare let go of being so damn strong?

I looked up and stared into space. In my mind, instead of seeing the usual picture of myself thriving behind my shield of strength, I saw my heart constricted inside a protective hard shell. In that moment, I thought: *You must shatter the shell of protection and make room for your heart to stretch and breathe. Let yourself be vulnerable. Let go of the illusion of control. Accept the outstretched hands of others.* Antarctica was trying to show me how to love a little deeper—the idea I'd first pondered back at Peg's memorial service.

After dinner, we saved hot water for our third bath. Time to remove the buildup of stinky sweat, dried urine, shedding skin, and bodily oils. As I soaped up, I looked past my hairy armpits and legs and saw more muscular limbs. After drying off, I felt christened anew.

I snuggled up with my journal once again and, feeling the 24 hours of Antarctic light shining on my heart, I wrote, "Today I Am Grateful: I am grateful for the sunshine and low winds. I am grateful for a warm tent. I am grateful for my amazing twelve-year-old son, Keenan. I am grateful for love, faith, and hope. I am grateful for the strength to complete thirteen miles. I am grateful to be here, experiencing all of Antarctica."

Before going to bed, I called in the blog and ended by saying, "A few days ago, Marty stepped up and took extra weight for me. Helping each other is just what you do for a teammate to balance out the ups and downs while working toward a common goal to get to the Pole. So my shout-out goes to Marty tonight, because I want to thank him for his patience and kindness and strength and for being an awesome teammate, husband, and father. I love him so much."

CHAPTER 14:

END IN SIGHT

A few days later, at the start of Day 44, we were perched at 9,091 feet on the plateau, still 59 miles to go—our final push. Relentless low clouds and whiteout conditions made me feel nauseated, causing my stomach and brain to threaten rebellion. I tried to hang on to the positive mindset I'd pledged my allegiance to a few days ago, though it was difficult as we staggered like drunken fools through another whiteout. I tried framing the day as a whiteout party to lighten my mental mood. All white, all day. White sky. White snow. White frozen goggles. I strained to make out my compass to find my way through the white nothingness. If only our clothes were white, we'd be invisible against the canvas.

At our break after six hours, Marty turned on the GPS to double-check our position since we tended to veer slightly off course in a whiteout. He wanted to correct our path by a degree or two, if necessary, to avoid skiing additional miles.

Staring at the GPS, Marty said "What?" in his urgent cop voice. "Why does it say to make a sharp turn left?" Our route required a *slight* turn left as we approached the Pole, but the turn shown on the GPS was too extreme and too soon. Throwing his arms into the air, Marty yelled "It doesn't make sense!" as if the

GPS were a criminal providing false information. Before I could respond to his outburst, Marty continued, "Something is wrong! Did we just waste six hours of skiing off course? Wait, we aren't wrong. We have to be right. This doesn't make any sense."

With no pause to interject my thoughts into his one-sided conversation, I stood in silence, holding on to a positive, Zen-like mindset. Marty takes pride in his command of facts and data—and I knew that in the past he'd felt embarrassed and out of control when facts didn't add up. If I could balance out our team energy, I could make it appear we were in control even though one of us was teetering on the edge.

Marty continued to process the situation, staring at the GPS for a long time, pushing buttons, cursing at it as if trying to obtain a criminal's confession. He repeated questions to himself for a few more minutes, and then cursed at the imaginary criminal some more.

I wanted to chime in with my opinion, but I knew it wouldn't help because Marty was looking for facts, not opinions.

While waiting, my hands starting to feel the familiar stiffness of cold.

Finally, Marty looked at me, and instead of asking my opinion as I thought he might, he said, "You know, sometimes I just wish that you would take a more active role in the GPS."

Caught off guard, as it sounded like he'd been simmering about this for a while, I said, "Sorry, Marty. What can I do to help now?"

"The GPS wants us to turn thirty degrees, but it makes no sense," said Marty. He'd been saying that all along.

"I agree, it doesn't make sense," I said, still trying to remain calm. "Seems like the GPS has gone rogue. Let's just follow our current compass bearing for a few more miles. We can try to figure out what happened when we are in the tent tonight." I trusted that our low-tech compasses were still working fine.

Marty exhaled. "Okay." Then he stuffed the GPS back into his pocket.

We followed our earlier bearing, not the one shown on the GPS. For the next three hours, I imagined Marty was continuing to puzzle over the GPS data as we made our way through a cloud of white.

Inside the tent, I boiled water for hot drinks and doled out Pringles. Marty was all business as he pulled out the GPS, examined the map, and stared off into space.

He finally reasoned, "As we get closer to the Pole, the lines of longitude get closer and closer to each other, and satellite data relayed to the GPS must have gotten distorted."

"Sounds plausible," I said.

Marty pulled out the satellite phone and dialed Keith's number. To his surprise, Keith answered after one ring. Marty explained the GPS issue and Keith told him he'd never heard of that happening before.

"We are considering two options," Marty said. "To avoid going through the off-limits Dark Sector, we could either make a slight turn at about sixty miles out from the Pole or a sharper turn from only a few miles away."

While Dark Sector may sound like a faraway galaxy in a *Star Wars* movie, it was the name for a specific scientific area near the Pole. We were told to avoid this area because it houses highly sensitive telescopes used to study objects in space that are millions of light years away. According to the National Science Foundation, "The area is kept clear of sources of interference with electromagnetic signals that could hamper radio telescopes."

Keith thought either of the options to avoid this area would be fine. Because we were worried the GPS might intermittently show incorrect information as we continued on, we chose to do the latter. From a few miles outside the Pole, we'd be able to visually verify the buildings and markings of sensitive scientific equipment buried in the snow as we made our turn.

During our check-in call with ALE, Marty confirmed that we were on track if we continued following our current bearing. While the ALE staff hadn't heard of such a GPS problem either, wc later learned we weren't the only ones who experienced this phenomenon.

Afterward, I said, "Marty, do you want me to take a more active role with the GPS?"

"No, that's okay. I know we are on track now."

As I wrote in my journal, Marty sent an email to our team back home: "Hi, Team. Horribly hard work just staring at the compass all day long. I also came this close to having my biggest breakdown when late in the day I did a GPS check to make sure our longitude looked good and it told me to alter course 30 degrees left. Made no sense but still freaked me out. Love you all."

Despite Marty's GPS freak-out, we had crossed 89 degrees and now had less than 1 degree to go. As a reward for making it this far, we would now poop in special bags and carry our frozen bricks with us until the end.

Over the last few days, we'd averaged 13 miles in about eight and a half hours. At this pace, we'd likely be at the Pole in four days.

AS I PEELED open my eyes for another day, I felt something was missing. The positive energy pulling me forward had faded to gray. It lingered just beyond reach, like water at the bottom of a deep well. If only I could sleep away the day, maybe then I could extinguish my exhaustion and remember why I was braving this cold land in the first place.

I forced myself out of bed and started the stove. I put on additional layers of down as defense against the chill of the plateau—the wind meter said it was −35 degrees, a dangerously bitter and windy day. I poured boiling water into our cups to make our morning mochas. If I had thrown the water up into the air outside, it would have instantly evaporated.

Marty raised his glass and said, "Here's to my last cup of joe." It was Day 45, and while we'd rationed food to stretch three more days, we had packed only forty-five days of coffee. Marty savored every last drop.

After skiing for a few hours, with positive energy still beyond my grasp, my body no longer felt solid—I was like particles of snow shifting on the icy surface. I wondered where the wind would blow me, and where I would land when it was all done. We stopped for a break. Marty asked, "How are you doing?"—words he'd uttered hundreds of times by this point in our trip.

Usually I just said "Fine," but this time I said, "The sticky snow is killing me and I can't breathe."

What I meant, but couldn't fully articulate through my frozen face mask and tired brain, was that my sled felt extra heavy as I pulled it through sticky sand-like snow, causing me to work harder and struggle to get deep, oxygen-rich breaths, especially with wind blasting against my face mask. Adding to my frustration, my heavy breathing had fogged my goggles. I felt like a prisoner doing time on the ice. My mantra, *I can pull through sticky snow*, was overpowered by the voice in my head shouting, *I am SO DONE with sticky snow.*

Marty looked at me, then quickly looked away, as if there were something better on the horizon, with none of the sympathy I'd expected my answer to elicit. He ate a piece of his chocolate bar, momentarily glanced down, and said nothing. I was pretty sure he expelled air in a dramatic fashion, but I couldn't be sure with his mouth hidden behind his face mask.

"What is your problem?" I said. "Seems like you don't care about what I just said."

"Unless you're having a *real* problem, I don't need to hear about it," he replied. "For days, I've been dealing with a shooting pain down my leg from my harness pressing on my nerve. You just need to push through."

His words demanded a response, counterpoints, more counterpoints, a full-on discussion before we could reach resolution and both feel like we had been heard and understood.

That's what married couples do to maintain a healthy relationship. That's what they do when they care and want to grow and learn from each other. That's what they do in the civilized world where there are warm beds and time to pause and reflect and say you're sorry without fear of hands becoming useless frozen claws. Here, frozen face masks and constant wind obscured tone of voice and facial cues, making our conversation feel broken.

Three, two, one. Discussion over. Time to move or the panic of cold would surely rise.

I stuffed my down mittens back into the straps of my ski poles and pulled on, following Marty's lead. A one-sided conversation continued in my head.

What does he mean, real problems? Maybe he thinks my problems are minor compared to his?

Why doesn't he understand what I mean when I say I can't breathe? I'm not literally going to fall on the ground and have a heart attack; I'm just having trouble getting full breaths and I feel like I'm slowing us down.

Why does he keep discounting how I feel?

And why is he trying to hide how he feels?

The steam from my stress filled the cold air, my mind stuck in its own whiteout as we moved in single file along the ice. After about 15 minutes, Marty waved me forward to pull up next to him. He said, "I'm sorry if I got frustrated. I'm really stressed and I need you to be strong."

"So when I tell you how I feel, you don't think I'm being strong?" I said sarcastically. Then I asked myself: *Do I have to be strong to earn Marty's approval?*

Marty turned his head away from me. A few seconds later, he skied off. I followed. I felt unable to stomach an apology that seemed contingent on my future behavior.

Why won't he accept that feeling frustrated or weak is okay?

Why doesn't he love me when I feel weak?

Wait.

What was that?

My mind paused to take in a thought that rocked me—a belief that was hiding in plain sight behind my frustration, like Mount Patuxent coming out of the haze.

I tried to make sense of it. Rationally, I knew Marty loved me, no matter my state of mind or body. I thought about how throughout my life, being strong—in school, in sports, in problem-solving—resulted in praise and approval. Somewhere along the line, I must have developed a deep-seeded belief that being strong means being worthy of love and belonging; and being weak doesn't. Thus, the thought that *Marty doesn't love me when I feel weak* emerged from my cold, tired brain.

It was too much to take in, standing there in the cold. I pushed out further thoughts on this matter, turned, and dropped in behind Marty's sled.

At six hours into the day, on the edge of extreme cold, I skied up next to Marty and said, "I need to put on my vest for extra warmth." Cold was penetrating my body at an alarming rate, starting with my hands and moving up my limbs, trying to freeze me from the outside in. Cold thickened my blood, stirred my heart, made my contacts feel like they might freeze to my eyeballs or pop right out.

"You just need to keep moving. We'll get too cold if we stop."

While that philosophy often worked for us while running in the mountains, this day was different. I knew I wasn't moving fast enough to generate heat to warm my body. I stopped, zipped open my sled, threaded my arms through my vest, and cinched my hood tight. After skiing for 10 minutes, I could hardly feel my hands. The harsh wind sent a panic through me. Finally, 15 minutes later, as the terrain slanted uphill, I felt the hot, prickly sensation in my hands as blood surged through them.

Later, in the tent, as Marty boiled water, he said, "Chris, I am mentally and physically stressed. I'm at my edge. I don't want you to talk to me in exaggerations. Just give me the facts."

To Marty, facts were as critical as my fleece face mask. Yet there appeared to be no way not to exaggerate at a time when everything felt exaggerated—the cold, the exhaustion, the loneliness.

It seemed easier not to discuss our difference in opinion and to save our limited energy. So I nodded and said, "Okay."

Then I remembered Marty had said we'd need to keep our emotions in check. *But I'm not capable of being emotionless,* I thought. My emotions still felt raw from my earlier realization. And now, a new thought came rushing in: *If I do believe that being strong means being worthy of love, then there are other implications beyond Marty. Do I love myself when I feel strong, and disappoint myself when I don't? How can I love others unconditionally if I can't love myself completely?*

We sat in silence, absorbed in our own thoughts and nightly chores. Our love was still there but inaccessible at that moment, like a locked refrigerator stuffed with a smorgasbord of our favorite foods. I stuffed myself full of fettuccine alfredo and swallowed my unresolved feelings, but they made my stomach turn with concern.

I was frustrated, not so much at Marty, but at the situation we found ourselves in. My perpetual optimism and positive energy were in hiding. Marty wasn't privy to my desire to be pulled by positive energy, or to my wish that some of that positive energy and love would come from him, or to my tangled ideas about feeling strong and weak. He simply didn't have that energy to give right now. And the truth was, I didn't either. I had lost the battle to keep control of my thoughts and emotions, and I could no longer beat them into submission. I'd thought I had a mental edge from my ultrarunning experience, but now I was deep in uncharted frozen waters and struggling to stay afloat. Only a thin line separated happiness and struggle, a line that was becoming too hard to hold, too easy to cross.

I slithered into my sleeping bag even though it wasn't time for bed, pulled the fluffy down around my face, turned my head away from Marty. Warm tears rolled down my face.

After a few minutes, I remembered. *I should check email.* I connected the various wires and devices, and then a flood of messages popped in—more than we had ever received at one time.

"Oh my gosh, Marty, there are over twenty messages here . . . from all kinds of people."

With wide eyes, Marty looked up and said, "Really? That's crazy. I wonder how they got this email address."

I read the first one out loud. "Sending energy that I hope you can feel. The depth of your commitment and determination is humbling and inspiring in the same breath. May the ice be smooth and the air clear for your last three days."

I continued, reading another. "Three days left! Antarctica is unrelenting—demanding every ounce of willpower and concentration. The Fagans are meeting the challenge, mining for reserves few of us will ever need to draw upon. Push on!"

I looked over at Marty and smiled. He smiled back. The mood in the tent shifted as I continued reading the rest to myself while Marty started melting snow.

There was one from Ms. Castle, Keenan's teacher. "Keenan wrote an excellent creative-writing piece about segregation in the south in 1950s. Good news: he's been selected to share the writing with the school in our MLK Day assembly next week. I'm really proud of the work Keenan's done, especially in your absence. It's a testament to your parenting that his endurance is so strong. Beat out this weather and those last miles nice and steady and get home to us safely. You are in our hearts and prayers."

Keith ended his note with a quote from Ernest Shackleton that said, "We had seen God in His splendors, heard the text that nature renders. We had reached the naked soul of man."

I nodded to myself. When I looked into my fear of feeling weak—and the way it made me feel inadequate—I felt like a naked child standing in the bitter cold.

After I finished, I handed the phone to Marty so he could read the rest of the messages.

While tending to the boiling water, Marty said in a humble voice, "Wow, these are all amazing."

"Inspiring, right?" I said, then leaned over and kissed Marty.

Love had radiated from the emails and filled the tent with the much-needed warmth we could not generate ourselves. The power of words from friends connected us to a world beyond this treadmill of challenges. They delivered a jolt of adrenaline, a jump-start to our failing batteries, redirecting our attention to our shared purpose of reaching the Pole.

Unbeknownst to us, Leni had told an extended circle of friends about our physical and mental states (something we hadn't fully disclosed on our blog to avoid worrying Keenan) and suggested they reach out to us at our private email address.

We had 34 miles left to the Pole.

BREATHE IN AND out *calmly. Be Zen-like.*

I was trying to leave behind my *be strong* mantra and just be. It didn't work. For nine and a half hours and 13.2 miles, my breath, coupled with freezing wind, wreaked havoc on my goggles. Pair that with sticky snow, and that summed up my day.

That night, Marty left the blog post. "Almost 8:00 p.m. now, and we are still melting snow, eating, and calculating food. You go through periods of complete exhaustion followed by short bursts of energy. I honestly have never done anything so physically, mentally, or emotionally difficult. The ups and downs are major. But we are so close. We're not excited yet. We might be excited when we see the Pole."

By now, we were calling Keenan every night instead of every other night. Tonight, Marty told him, "Make a list of all of the things you'd like to do on the weekends for the next two months to make up for the two months that we've been gone. Movies, games, food . . . you get to choose what you want to do with us."

Then I got on the phone with Sue—I heard her ask Keenan to go start his homework in the other room. "Chris," she said, "I wanted to give you an update about Keenan . . . you don't need to worry, but he keeps asking not to go to basketball, so even though there's only two more weeks left in the season, we've decided to let him quit the team."

With overwhelming exhaustion pressing in on me, it was difficult to process this. "Is he bummed about it?" I asked.

"No, I think he's relieved. Lately he seems tired . . . not just of basketball. I think he's starting to get worried about you and Marty. Your recent blogs are less upbeat, and the notes you left him mentioned you'd likely be on your way home by now."

"How long has he been like this?"

"Probably the last few days, since Frank and I took over again."

"Okay, thanks for letting me know."

It felt surreal to be dragged back to the responsibility of parenthood as I struggled to stay present in Antarctica.

There were 20 miles left to the Pole.

While 20 miles seems like a breeze for endurance athletes, it was still a surprisingly long distance to swallow when my mind had already pushed my failing body beyond its end point. Back in 1911, Scott and his polar team froze to death in their tent only 13 miles from their next food depot.

Distance in Antarctica can be deceptive.

DAY 47. AS we skied out into the bright sun and low wind, I glanced up into the morning sky and noticed a spectacular circular rainbow around the sun. Known as a sun halo, it is created by sunlight shining through ice crystals in the atmosphere. Nature's art set a positive tone for the start of the day.

As I looked out at the horizon, I could see farther into the distance than usual. The cobalt-blue sky beckoned me forward, and I fell into a steady pace. It felt strange to feel uplifted after so many drag-you-down foggy days. Three hours into the day, I noticed a speck of shimmering light that jumped off the ice in a way that looked different than sun reflecting off snow. I squinted hard at the area to see if my mind was playing tricks on me. At that same moment, my ski suddenly caught a piece of windswept ice. I lost my balance, and my body slammed onto the snow.

Looking back at Marty, I said, "I think I saw something." I stood up, shook off the fall, and peered forward into the whiteness. I couldn't locate the mysterious spot. *Was it a mirage?* I skied faster, chasing the idea that I'd seen something other than the never-ending blanket of white. My heart raced with the pulse of anticipation. Five minutes passed.

Then I stopped and pointed toward the horizon. "Marty, I see it again. Can you?" I thought I saw light shimmering off a man-made object.

Marty came in close so that he could look down my arm to see precisely where I was pointing, like a sharpshooter sighting down the barrel of a rifle. It was a small black dot.

"Yes, I see it!"

We looked at each other. I yelled, "It's the Pole! It's the Pole!"

We jumped up and down hugging each other, then fell to the ground tangled up in skis. As I burst out laughing, I remembered what being completely alive felt like.

Marty stood up, stared back at the Pole, raised his arms in the air, and yelled, "We've got this!"

In that moment, I knew that no matter what happened, we were going to make it to the Pole. If we burned down our tent, we would ski through the night and into the morning. If one of us became injured, we'd hobble our way in.

I stood up. It was all suddenly so real. A real part of civilization, a real confirmation that our days of skiing and dragging sleds and sleeping on the ground were almost over. Adrenaline rushed in, pushing out exhaustion. The moment of pure joy united us—and reminded me of what our marriage usually feels like.

Marty turned on the GPS. "We are sixteen miles from the South Pole."

"Wow, incredible that we can see that far."

The object we saw was probably a huge antenna or outbuilding perched at the gateway to the Amundsen-Scott South

Pole Station—the US scientific research facility at the bottom of the world.

I stopped looking at my compass and skied directly toward the black beacon. The dot came in and out of view as the glacier undulated up and down, following the contours of the terrain. When it fell out of sight, I skied with anticipation for it to rise from the ice like a phoenix from ashes. Each time it came back into view, more energy pulsed through my veins. I floated along, hypnotized by its power—I wasn't aware of skiing for the next few hours. All I knew was that after forty-seven days, our finish line was finally within reach.

After nine hours, we stopped at an elevation of 9,293 feet for what we hoped would be our last night. The black dot on the horizon was hiding since our tent lay in a downward dip of the glacier. I piled snow onto tent flaps, jumping up and down every so often to warm myself. The temperature was −45 degrees; I had never been so cold while setting up camp.

Inside our tent, we bundled up in warmer clothes, including puffy down pants. Our evening progressed as usual, but with minimal conversation despite the excitement of seeing the Pole. We both knew we still had to pound out about 11 monumental miles in extremely cold conditions. It was 8:00 p.m. when we lay down for the night, hoping to bank a little extra sleep for our big day ahead.

As the tent fell into absolute silence, my body, like the stillness of cold, lay suspended in the moment. I looked up at the tent wall and reread the quote that said "Silence is also conversation." I had read that quote countless times, but that night, I realized that silence wasn't a wedge between us, it was a bridge. It wasn't to be filled—it was to be felt. I closed my eyes. I had found home in silence.

THE NEXT MORNING, the stove was a bit fussy, like a child hiding under the covers, refusing to wake up and emerge from her warm cocoon into the cold, unforgiving world. In silence,

Marty and I split our last packet of hot chocolate; a mere four ounces each to kick-start our day. Marty's eyes, at half-mast, had the surly look of caffeine deprivation. His dull yet persistent headache probably contributed to the somber vibe in the tent. As we ate raspberry-crumble desserts for breakfast (our oatmeal had run out), I wondered why I wasn't more excited for the day I'd envisioned for three years. *Where is my burst-of-adrenaline, hair-on-fire enthusiasm for being almost done?*

Marty checked the weather. "Crap, the wind meter says fifty below with windchill, our coldest reading to date," he said.

Antarctica had planned a big crescendo of a day for us. With serious weather would come serious focus and hard work. Marty began dressing like he'd done for almost seven weeks, following a series of steps that he'd honed to a mindless state of motions: put on top and bottom thermal layers, a second thermal layer of each, and the wind-protection layer of bibs and anorak; insert snacks into various pockets; put on boots, hat, balaclava, vest, oversized down jacket, liner gloves and finally outer mitts; dive out of the tent.

Outside in the bitter cold, he began the daily routine of digging out tent flaps and pulling up stakes while I packed the remaining contents inside.

Over a stiff wind, I heard, "What the hell is wrong with my pants?" Marty abruptly jumped back into the tent. I made sure to remain calm. Marty said, "I'm waddling around outside like a penguin, can't spread my legs more than a foot apart."

Something was desperately wrong deep inside his protective layers. He peeled off layer upon layer, working his way down to ground zero. While his two thermal pants were pulled up, his underwear—hidden beneath them—somehow remained just above his knees. In a caffeine-deprived state, he had re-dressed in haste after making a deposit into the special human-waste bag, a maneuver that was tricky to complete in the confines of the tent.

Outside, we each packed final contents into our sleds and prepared to head out into the cold wind. Then Marty came in close and said, "Chris, my face is freezing, can you pull up my balaclava over my cheeks? I can't get my hands on it."

I searched through the layers of face mask and hoodie zipped around his face. "You're not wearing your balaclava."

Marty stormed through his sled as he searched for this critical piece of gear. When he found it in his clothing bag, he removed the over mittens from his gloved hands and took off his hoodie, hat, and face mask—leaving his face momentarily exposed to the elements. He re-dressed as quickly as possible, this time with his thick fleece Windstopper balaclava in place. By the time we set off, his hands had turned to frozen claws from fumbling around in the 50-below temperatures. As cold crept through my own layers, I led out at a brisk pace to generate body heat—then settled for a slower pace I could maintain.

After about an hour, my hands finally on the edge of warm, I saw the dot of the South Pole Station beckoning in the distance. As if the cold and wind weren't enough challenge, the predominantly sticky snow slowed me to a plodding pace once more. During our break at two hours, we gulped a few sips of warm soup from my thermos. The bit I spilled froze instantly to my glove.

As we gained on the South Pole Station, the dot multiplied and morphed into discernible rectangular and circular buildings. They gave the station an air of permanence and importance.

When it was my turn to lead again, Marty asked at a short break, "Can you go faster? I'm really cold."

"Sorry, this is as fast as my body can go."

I didn't have another gear. As the day wore on, my fingers felt numb, so numb that I wondered if I'd gone past the point of no return. I worried about where Marty stood on the frozen-finger scale. At a break, I pulled out my puffy blue down overboots and wrapped them around my ski poles to act as mini down sleeping bags that stretched from my hands up to my elbows. Marty had completely lost his finger dexterity to the cold, so I helped him do the same.

At the next break, Marty said, "My hands are useless frozen bricks." I broke off a hard chunk of chocolate bar and shoved it through his face mask and into his mouth. Within seconds, we both felt anxious to get moving.

"Since it's so cold, I think we should push on to the Pole without any more breaks," I said.

Marty nodded in agreement.

I skied ahead, studying the various structures that made up the South Pole Station. The iconic dome-shaped building that opened back in 1975 jumped out from the clutter. Over the years, the accumulation of snowdrifts from continuous winds gradually compromised the structure, and it was eventually decommissioned. The new Amundsen-Scott South Pole Station, which opened in January 2008, was designed to accommodate the harsh conditions of the Polar Plateau. The $174-million structure (paid for by US taxpayers) was built on stilts so that the near-constant wind and snow blew under the building, eliminating problems with drifting. The technological and engineering marvel supported an array of scientific investigations, from astrophysics to seismology. If we were lucky, we might get a peek inside the new structure when we arrived. Historically, the scientific community manning the station hadn't necessarily welcomed adventurers. They were in the business of science, not entertaining or helping adventurers. But more recently, adventurers had reported more friendly encounters with the scientific community.

After a while, I returned my gaze to the full grandeur of Antarctica. The splendor of sunlit snow etched with deep lines and chaotic swirls, a white blanket draped over the continent in all directions, the cloudless ocean of blue above—all of this would soon fade to a distant dream. Then I noticed two black dots far off in the distance to my left, well outside the boundary of the Pole. Over the next 30 minutes, I kept glancing back to those dots and finally realized they were moving. *I bet it's sixteen-year-old Lewis and his guide, Carl, closing in on the Pole too.* We'd soon make our turn away from the Pole to avoid the sensitive scientific equipment and follow the recommended route in. After staring at white nothingness for seven weeks, my depth perception seemed off—I couldn't tell if the structures were 2 or 6 miles away. Then I noticed a row of black flags whipping in the wind.

"This must be the Dark Sector," I yelled to Marty. The off-limits area was marked by black flags, flapping in the wind, that lined the perimeter.

Given our GPS issues, we had planned to make our turn when we had visual confirmation of our location in relation to the Pole. We took a hard left away from the Pole and skied on, keeping the black flags to our right. In whiteout conditions, we'd likely have stopped, set up the tent, and waited out the weather to be safe.

Now the moving black dots became silhouettes of skiers. I skied faster as if chasing the thought of people and civilization. We followed our new route for about an hour until we cleared the line of black flags. We stopped in the bitter cold, and Marty verified our location with the waypoint shown on the GPS. I dug out the satellite phone from my sled and, with freezing fingers barely able to punch numbers, called ALE. The company had instructed us to do this so that they could place a courtesy call to alert the staff at the Pole of our imminent arrival. Before I could speak, the ALE staff person said, "I am going to have to call you back in a few minutes," and then abruptly hung up. *Holy crap! Why do they need to call us back? Don't they know we are standing here freezing!* It was like dangling a sandwich in front of a starving woman and asking her not to take a bite until further notice. My hot frustration couldn't stop the full-body shiver that came over me. Just when we had decided to continue on without permission, the phone rang. Apparently, the communications person had been helping a flight take off from Union Glacier at the moment we had called.

After making our final turn, we stopped and put on our big down jackets that were usually too warm to wear while moving.

Beyond cold, we wanted to savor the last mile to the Pole enveloped in warmth.

I pushed my right ski forward, then my left, and felt Marty's body next to me moving in sync with mine. For the first time since starting on the edge of Antarctica forty-eight days ago, we skied side by side, moving slow enough for conversation.

Marty turned and looked into my goggles and said, "Chris, I love you so much."

With tears pooling in my awestruck eyes, I said, "I love you too."

After three long years of relentless sacrifice, planning, and training, and seven weeks of stretching ourselves and our marriage to the limit, we were on the verge of passing the biggest physical, mental, and emotional test of our lives—together. I suddenly felt reunited with Marty. My veins surged with warmth I'd never known.

"Are you warmer now?" I asked over the sound of skis scraping ice.

"Yes, I'm perfect."

Closing in on our goal, I felt as if Marty and I had merged bodies, and we shared one breath, one heartbeat. Twenty minutes passed with feeling nothing but oneness. My heart expanded like a balloon, full of joy as I floated over the terrain. I felt at once whole and incomplete because Keenan wasn't there with us.

With one hundred yards left, Marty turned toward me and said, "Let's pull out the satellite phone and call Keenan and share this moment with him."

Brilliant. It was Saturday at noon in North Bend; 3:00 p.m. in Antarctica. I labored with feeble hands to dial. After two rings, Sue answered.

"Hi, Sue, can you please put Keenan on the phone?" I wanted Keenan to be the first to hear the news.

Through tears, and in unison, Marty and I yelled, "Keenan, we are at the Pole!"

"We wanted to share this moment with you," I said. "You mean so much to us, and we are so proud of you."

Keenan didn't say much as it sounded like he was crying too—I wasn't sure.

"We will call you back later to talk more after we've had a chance to settle in," said Marty.

On Saturday, January 18, 2014, our forty-eighth day, we arrived at the South Pole after covering the last 10.6 miles in seven hours. Our footnote in Antarctic history: we became the first married American couple to ski to the South Pole unsupported, unguided, and unassisted. We joined a short list of about 100 people who have ever completed such a journey; and I am the 18th woman to accomplish this feat. Our effort would also land us in the *Guinness Book of World Records*.

Just after we hung up the phone and took off our skis, Lewis and Carl (who had arrived minutes before us), along with polar legend and ALE staff member Hannah McKeand, popped out of the ALE tent to congratulate us on our arrival. "You did it! Welcome to the South Pole," said Hannah. There were warm hugs all around. The sound of their voices signaled we were no longer alone. It was both exhilarating and jolting to realize the purity and sacredness of our own expedition was over.

Marty and I had thought we'd have to set up our tent, cook our remaining scraps of food, and hunker down as we waited for the ALE plane to transport us back to Union Glacier the next day.

We were wrong.

As we entered ALE's small industrial tent, it was like leaving the cold land of Narnia and suddenly entering the comfort of home. Inside, I stood in awe of this warm world. The tent was like a small one-room cabin, a sanctuary, complete with actual tables and chairs with legs and a makeshift kitchen in the back. Next to the door hung a colorful assortment of hats, gloves, and coats. Further to our right were four comfortable chairs arranged in a semicircle around a propane stove that warmed the room to a balmy 50 degrees. Toward the back of the structure was a smorgasbord of freshly made noodles, breads, cookies, and hot drinks. The entire scene was more than my tired brain could process.

"Do you want anything to eat or drink?" asked Hannah.

"No, thanks," I said, feeling happy just to be inside, sheltered from the cold and wind. My mind became fixated on sitting down in one of the cozy chairs by the warm stove. More than anything, I wanted to bask in this new feeling of complete warmth and delight that we were done. The allure of the chair was as undeniable as it was at the end of a 100-mile race. After Marty and I shed a few layers of clothing, we sat down next to each other in silence. Marty's face was painted with a sweet smile of satisfaction. My eyes danced with a deep knowing of completion.

I reached over and held Marty's hand, resting my arm on his leg. The warmth began penetrating the layers of mental armor I'd worn to protect myself from the cold. The stress built up over the last forty-eight days, not to mention the three years of planning and training before that, began to melt away. And my heart softened and opened wide, as wide and vast as the expanse of Antarctica, and filled with love from family, friends, strangers, the universe. I knew only connection—to everyone and everything. A feeling of lightness overwhelmed me, as if I might defy the laws of gravity and float out of my chair.

WE LINGERED IN our seats—my face frozen in a smile—for a few hours before rising to sample the spaghetti Bolognese, hot chocolate, and homemade chocolate chip cookies. We briefly chatted with Lewis, who had just become the youngest to complete a full expedition to the South Pole with the assistance of a guide, airdrops of food, and replacement equipment. He was waiting for someone from the BBC to call for a phone interview. After four hours of luxurious lounging, eating, and talking, we bundled up and went back into the bitter cold to organize our sleeping gear in the ALE tent that would be our home that night. While it wasn't a hotel with a fluffy down comforter, dreamy pillows, and steaming shower, I was delighted not to set up our own tent.

Before making any calls, Marty and I stretched out on our sleeping bags, relaxing into our new reality.

I looked at Marty and said, "I still can't believe it's over . . . we skied to the South Pole."

"I know," he said in a soft voice through teary eyes. "We did it."

I rolled over and rested my head and arm on Marty's chest. He wrapped his arms around me and I felt utterly content. I had missed this.

After a while, Marty and I began calling our family and close friends who had already learned through the power of social media that we had arrived at the South Pole.

When we called Leni, she yelled into the phone, "Congratulations!" Sue had already called her with the wonderful news. "You guys did an awesome job. You should be so proud. We love you."

"You'll never know how much you helped us to get here," I said. "We love you too."

While talking to his brother, Mike, and his mom and dad, Marty shed more happy tears. I heard him say in a shaky, emotional voice, "This is by far the hardest thing I have ever done in my life. It's difficult to describe the intensity of it all and how awesome it feels to be done."

He hung up the phone and turned to me. "Man, all of my emotions are coming out now. It's like a faucet has been turned on."

Like he had back on Denali, Marty had held a tight leash on his emotions until he reached his goal.

"Maybe you'll catch up to me," I said, smiling.

"Chris, you were a great teammate." Marty leaned in to kiss me. "Thanks so much for everything."

"We are a great team," I said.

I was grateful—for a slow transition back to civilization, and to be among fellow adventurers in one of the wildest places on earth. And for more toilet paper since we had only half of a paper towel remaining.

The next morning, after breakfast, it was time to take some photos.

Marty and I skied the short distance from the ALE shelter, through the blasting wind to the geographic South Pole—the true bottom of the earth at 90 degrees south—the place where all the lines of longitude converge in the southern hemisphere. Since a moving ice sheet covers the continent, the golden marker must be repositioned every year to account for the roughly thirty-three feet of travel per year. We huddled together, the fur ruff of our coats flopping in the wind as we smiled wide for the camera.

I was reminded of the photo taken at base camp on Denali after we summited back in 1998. Back then, though we had hardly known each other, we had jumped in with both feet and embarked on a new life together. Standing here at the Pole, we celebrated our years of teamwork and devotion, and the new people we've become through adventuring together.

Then we skied a few yards over to the red-and-white-striped pole topped by a silver ball that marks the ceremonial South Pole, an area that commemorates the creation of the Antarctic Treaty, and provides a perfect backdrop for more dramatic photos. Twelve flags from the countries that signed the treaty flapped hard in the breeze. I felt Marty's arm firm around my waist as we squinted at the camera. The American flag snapped right behind us like the triumphant beat of snare drums. We were standing at the bottom of the earth.

CHAPTER 15:

HOMEWARD BOUND

Five days and five flights after standing at the South Pole, we arrived at Sea-Tac Airport in Seattle, exhausted and giddy. It was Thursday, January 23, 2014. It had been nine weeks since our departure, ten days longer then we had anticipated for our entire trip.

As we'd flown from the South Pole back to ALE's base camp, I marveled at the expansive landscape that we'd covered over the previous seven weeks. It felt strange to cross it again in just five hours of flying, with none of the physical grind and emotional battle that we had pushed ourselves through. During that flight, Marty noticed a numb and tingly feeling in his fingertips and faint purple lines streaked his fingernails. Back at base camp, staff treated us to a feast of bacon-wrapped filet mignon, raspberry-soaked sponge cake, and more—after forty-eight days of dehydrated meals with the same soft, mushy texture, I savored every bite. Then we luxuriated in hot showers at the bathhouse. The first glimpse of our naked bodies in the mirror prompted Marty to exclaim, "Chris, you look ripped, and I look like an emaciated prisoner of war." We later found a scale and discovered that I'd lost fifteen pounds and Marty had lost twenty-five. Just as it had for polar travelers before us, Antarctica had completely transformed our bodies. If we wanted to get back into ultrarunner shape, it would take some effort. But for now, I wasn't worried about that—I was thankful our bodies hadn't completely broken down.

As the first one off the plane in Seattle, I rushed down the Jetway and burst through the door. My eyes scanned for Keenan, wondering if he'd made it through security to meet us at the gate. Sue had mentioned that airport personnel were considering making an exception to the security rule so Keenan could meet us right as we came off the plane.

Before I could get my bearings, I noticed a light-blue blur of excitement running toward me. In an instant, Keenan, Marty, and I were entangled in a heartwarming hug, our bodies merging into one six-armed being. I enveloped all of Keenan, feeling the warmth of his face next to mine, his arms wrapped tightly around my neck, his body taller than I remembered. Tears pooled in my eyes, then slowly rolled down my face. I held on tight, as if he might float away if I let go.

I spoke softly into Keenan's ear. "I love you so much."

"I love you, Mama. I love you, Dad," Keenan whispered back. I exhaled a deep breath, then lingered as I soaked in every inch of a moment I had visualized for months.

"We are so proud of you . . . your courage and bravery," I said. "You inspired us every day." More tears.

When I opened my eyes and finally let go of Keenan, I was welcomed into the arms of Sue and then Frank. Around us, people rushed by like a movie played in fast motion—the buzz of civilization overwhelmed my senses. We posed for photos, trying to capture the immensity of the moment, then made our way toward baggage claim. We caught a glimpse of a crowd waiting in an area up ahead, many of them wearing the light-blue 3 Below Zero T-shirts we'd distributed before our departure. Marty, Keenan, and I joined hands and spontaneously began jogging toward cheers and clapping.

A pack of thirty-five excited well-wishers held signs that said "Welcome home to the USA," "You did it," and "History made." Instantly swarmed by our tribe, Marty and I rode the train of hugs. There were Lindsey and Ben; Brett and Becky with their daughters, Emillia and Isabella; my niece Jessie; my neighbors Jill and Lori with their families; Leni's husband, Randy, with Ryo and Simone; and more. *Wait, where is Leni?* I looked up and saw her near the back of the pack, but before we connected, Marty and I were ushered over to a KING 5 newsman who was waiting patiently for a quick interview for the evening news.

We stepped in front of the camera and the glare of a spotlight.

"Welcome back from Antarctica. I understand you completed your expedition in forty-eight days," said the newsman. "What was the toughest part of the expedition?"

"The lack of rest days and the wear and tear on our bodies and minds," said Marty. "And of course, being gone from our son, Keenan."

I chimed in, "And the monotony of skiing eight to ten hard hours every day—in combination with frigid temperatures, relentless wind, and crusty waves of snow that we pulled our sleds through."

At base camp, we had eaten dinner with Vern Tejas, a legendary polar guide and climber who had just climbed Mount Vinson for the thirty-second time, and who had summited Mount Everest ten times. He told us that in many ways what we had accomplished was much harder than summiting Mount Everest. "The day-after-day mental and physical grind of a full expedition to the South Pole is extremely difficult," he said. "You should be proud of your success going unsupported and unassisted to the Pole." This compliment, from such an accomplished adventurer, meant the world to us.

"How does it feel to be home?" the newsman asked.

"It's surreal being back in the civilized world with so many colors and sounds," said Marty. "We loved sleeping in a soft hotel bed and taking a hot shower."

"And seeing all of our amazing family and friends here at the airport," I continued. "This is just awesome."

"Congratulations again," said the newsman. The spotlight turned off, and we got back to catching up with friends.

Finally, my arms wrapped around Leni as I gave her the biggest hug ever. "Oh my gosh, thanks so much for everything you did for us!"

"Of course, it's so great to have you back!"

The crowd began to disperse, but Sue and Frank, the Nunns, and Leni and her family lingered at baggage claim with us. As I chatted with Leni, I spontaneously pulled her into another big bear hug and didn't want to let go. In that moment, there were no words to articulate the complete feeling of gratitude for her unwavering friendship and emotional support, so I just said, "Thanks."

"Chris, you are so welcome," she said.

I hugged Leni again before we went our separate ways, and she laughed.

"Chris, you keep hugging me."

"I know . . . I can't help it."

Keenan talked nonstop as we made our way down I-90 east toward North Bend. Details of the past two months spilled out like chocolate from a wedding fountain. When we pulled into our driveway, the headlights revealed an American flag hanging next to a poster painted with the ceremonial red and white pole. On the windows hung more welcome-home banners that said, "We love you" and "You're awesome." A blow-up black-and-white emperor penguin stood guard over the scene. Even though it was winter in the Northwest, the lush, vibrant greens and fresh aroma filled my senses completely.

I was home.

Marty and I negotiated our way around half-built Lego creations crowding the playroom floor. Swirly silver decorations hung from every inch of the ceiling in the family room and kitchen—making it shine and sparkle. Tiny American flag toothpicks poked out from the edge of chairs and couches and in the corners of pictures and inside plants. Homemade chocolate chip cookies, lemon bars, red wine, flowers, cards, and a framed photo of us at the South Pole crowded the kitchen table and countertops. The refrigerator burst with fresh food donated by our local food co-op, PCC Market (with Leni's help). On the front porch, I discovered another bouquet of flowers, a fine bottle of champagne, and an extra roll of toilet paper—since we'd almost run out in Antarctica.

The next day, Keenan stayed home from school. It was time for our four-day family slumber party. We moved Keenan's mattress, Kiya's bed, and our flat-screen TV into our bedroom, creating a cozy family cave. We watched favorite movies, played card games, and ate pepperoni pizza in bed—lounging, laughing, and loving our way back together as a family.

ON A WARM July morning, Marty and I ran up the familiar Mount Si trail near our house. Pine scented the air, and dirt puffed up as our running shoes ate up the trail. The dense green forest and 70-degree temperature was nothing like Antarctica's vast open nothingness and bitter cold.

"That was so fun giving another presentation yesterday. Each one takes me back to Antarctica," I said.

"I know. Hard to believe it's already been six months."

While we had fallen back into the motions of our daily routine, my life had felt anything but routine. Within a month of our return, we had started to share the stories of our adventure with crowds of kids stuffed into libraries and auditoriums. In between those presentations, we talked to journalists from newspapers and magazines and did radio and TV interviews. It was our two minutes of fame.

I turned the corner of a familiar switchback. "Remember the presentation where the third-grade boy came up afterwards and asked to have his picture taken with us?"

"Yeah," Marty panted.

He had told us, "You are my heroes." After he left, his teacher shared that he had a mild learning disability and didn't usually talk to people.

"That really stuck with me," I said.

"Me too," said Marty. "And what about returning to Saint Joseph School and the roar from the audience?"

"And their questions were so thoughtful." The kids seemed to have followed every blog post and detail of our expedition.

"'Were you worried about running out of toilet paper?'" Marty quoted. "'On Day 39, you didn't sound very good, what was happening?'"

We laughed.

Of all the presentations we'd given to schools, businesses, and organizations, one of my favorites was to the Rotary Club in Hot Springs, Arkansas, the one Dad had organized. Dad, Mom, and all my siblings had watched from the front row—they were in town for Mom's eightieth birthday celebration. At the end of the presentation, fighting back tears, I'd publicly thanked my family for their support and for helping us succeed.

I had learned what was possible with the help of others. It's hard to feel much more alone than when skiing across Antarctica, even though Marty had been by my side. Eventually, isolation had become a motivator for me to seek connection and love from outside our tent—to know I wasn't alone. I felt profoundly grateful for what I had accomplished with my team of supporters.

After the presentation to the Rotary Club, listening to Dad brag about us to his friends had been priceless.

Marty took a swig of water from his bottle and said, "Thinking back, I feel humbled knowing that our expedition inspired people."

"It feels really good."

Our speaking engagements felt especially meaningful because I was hoping to do more inspirational talks for my business in the future. While I knew success wasn't all about reaching goals, our journey had reinforced the idea that true satisfaction in the second half of my life would be about positively impacting others. I wanted to leave something of myself with those I encountered. I could see myself stepping into the next me—fully embracing Passionate Chris, a force of energy who would share nuggets of wisdom learned through adventure, and spark positivity and inspiration in those she met.

"And what about all of the emails from people," Marty said. A group of hikers coming down the trail stopped to let us pass. "I still think about the one from John McAdam."

The CEO of F5 had written, "Marty, I've been following your blog every day and I'm so impressed with you both. Congratulations on an outstanding job making it to the South Pole."

"Does it make it tough to have left there?" I asked as I slipped past another hiker.

"I had a good fourteen-year run," Marty said. "It just seemed right to start fresh somewhere new."

When the time had come to return to work, Marty had taken a job as director of facility management at a smaller tech company in Seattle that didn't require international travel.

"It will be great for you to be able to have even more time with Keenan." I pulled out an energy bar from my pocket and took a bite. "He did really well while we were gone."

"Now he seems to be more confident and independent—sitting down and working on his homework without us pestering him, and asking teachers for help without us playing the middleman."

"And I love listening to him talk to his aunts and uncles," I said. "They all have inside jokes from their time together."

"It looks like he really bonded with everyone and had fun."

None of my worries about our adventure somehow hurting Keenan had seemed to come true. I chalked up his stress at the end of our expedition to being tired of plastering on a happy face all the time. He had been trying hard to keep it together at school and for all of the visitors in our house. But it appeared that the benefits for him had outweighed the stresses. I remembered back to what he had said at one of our presentations—that he had learned he needed to work hard and keep a positive mindset to reach a goal, was inspired by us and proud of what we had accomplished, and hoped he could do something amazing one day.

Through misty eyes, I said, "Keenan makes me so proud."

Marty stopped and turned around on the trail in front of me. "Me too," he said, and kissed me.

After we started running again, we turned onto The Connector Trail. "How do you think Antarctica affected our marriage?" I asked.

Marty thought for a minute, then said, "I think we get closer each time we complete a major outdoor adventure together. I think we definitely deepened our bond this time." He paused, then said, "Also, you have always been a better communicator than me, and you helped me improve along the way."

An electric feeling surged through me. "Thanks," I said, somewhat surprised since I'm usually the one focused on the importance of communication.

We continued running down the gentle trail in comfortable silence. Since Marty didn't ask me what I thought, I asked myself: *How do I think Antarctica affected our marriage?* Because I'm a strong, independent woman married to a strong, independent man, it had become tough at times to connect to our shared love during our expedition, especially when we fell into self-preservation mode. I hadn't felt this difficulty before in our relationship—and I wondered about marriages that struggle in everyday life because they are stuck in what appears to be a never-ending loop of stress.

I broke the silence. "I agree with you that in the end we got closer as a couple, but man, there were times when I felt completely separate from you. Writing about it has shined a light on the stress that the cold and isolation and exhaustion put on us."

"Yeah, but I always blamed it on the environment and didn't think we were stressed at each other."

"But when you're in the middle of it all, I think it's hard to separate the two."

I decided that in the future, if we hit a giant-sastrugi-sized patch of stress in our lives, I would fight to preserve my connection with Marty. A gentle touch or knowing glance could access the love that sometimes lingered in the silence between us.

I jumped over a two-foot-wide gurgling creek. "How do you think Antarctica affected you and your running?"

"At least I'm still running pretty well," he said with a smile.

We were still trying to calibrate the net physical toll of our expedition. Marty had lost twenty-five pounds in Antarctica, and it didn't take him long to gain back ten of those pounds to land at his regular weight. I lost the same amount I had intentionally gained before the trip—fifteen pounds. Despite Marty's brush with frostbite, he had regained full feeling in his fingertips—although they were now more sensitive to cold—and the purple stripes on his nails had disappeared. And the pain caused by his pinched nerve also vanished with the storage of his harness and sled.

Then, in a hushed voice, Marty continued, "You know, I just feel a sense of peace and satisfaction."

"What do you mean?"

"I don't have anything I need to prove; I guess I wanted to prove to myself that I could be like the polar adventurers that I admire. You know—why not me?" Marty stopped, bent over, and stretched his back. "Plus, reaching the South Pole feels like part of my legacy. I can imagine Keenan years from now sharing our adventure with his kids. That makes me happy." Running again, he continued, "And I don't need to have a big 100-mile trail race on the calendar to motivate me to run and accomplish a goal. Trail running is still part of who I am, but I'm okay just running at a relaxed pace instead of racing. I can maintain my strength and enjoy myself."

"I know, I don't miss racing like I thought I would," I said, "and it feels liberating to be free of an intense training schedule." I sensed it would take quite some time to fully recover from the extreme physical and mental effort put into our South Pole expedition—and find motivation to train that hard again.

"I'm sure there's another big adventure out there for us," said Marty, "but for now, I'm content."

I was feeling the same way, loving taking a break from thinking about what was next and really focusing on now—enjoying our life and Keenan, being more present. For most of my life, I'd been in perpetual motion. Now, I was slowing down to find balance between motion and stillness. Time was bent and shaped like origami into something new. I was sitting still; savoring solitude without suffering loneliness. I had begun writing and listening to my deep voice of intuition.

I realized I had learned a few secrets to loving more deeply. I must believe that I am enough, even with all of my imperfections. I don't have to do anything special to be worthy of love and belonging; I can just be. As self-love and acceptance grows, so does my capacity to love and accept others.

Silence softened me, showing me the way to insight and contentment. As I turned down the volume of chatter in my head, I could hear all that people said in the spaces between words.

The trail flattened, and sunlight streaked through the canopy. I thought about the meandering of our trail conversation and said, "I hope we feel satisfied for a long time."

Running through the veins of the forest, I was reminded of the quote my yoga instructor had read at the end of class the other day: "Everything that you are looking for—happiness, joy, and peace—is already within you." I had come to believe that Antarctica hadn't changed who I was, it revealed who I was. Shattered open, I peered into my soul and felt connected to everything. My bold, strong side would no longer block the light of my soft, vulnerable side—because vulnerability is never a weakness, it is simply a truth of being completely human.

And just like our universe is expanding, so are we humans. The further I adventured into the outer world, the more my inner world expanded. Adventuring into the unknown had taught me that I could grow and learn and love to infinity.

AFTERWORD

Since the Antarctica expedition, our journey has taken unexpected turns. Dad rallied to see us reach the Pole, but two years after we returned from Antarctica, his heart stopped beating for good. He was eighty-three years old. I'm saddened to know that he didn't live to read this book, as each time I'd give him an update on its progress, he'd say with pride, "I can't wait to read it."

After Dad passed away, my siblings and I decided to move Mom from Hot Springs Village, Arkansas, to North Bend, Washington, into an assisted living home nestled in a lush green forest 2 miles from my house. Just after I returned from Antarctica, Mom had officially been diagnosed with Alzheimer's, so she couldn't live by herself.

Three years after returning, in February 2017, Marty started immunotherapy treatment for advanced squamous cell carcinoma, a form of skin cancer that had spread from his lymph nodes in his neck to his lungs, where he has nine small tumors. He is taking a drug called Keytruda every three weeks for up to two years. Luckily the drug has caused few side effects other than fatigue—nothing like the physical wrath that can be caused by chemotherapy. In fact, cancer hasn't caused any physical symptoms for Marty beyond an occasional rash, so he is still active: running, strength training, and working at his job.

A few months after the diagnosis that the cancer had spread to his lungs—before starting treatment—Marty returned to Mount Rainier and completed a solo 95-mile run around the mountain on the Wonderland Trail. A few months after that, Marty, Keenan, and I celebrated Christmas 2016 in Nepal in the shadow of Mount Everest, after hiking together to Everest Base Camp at 17,600 feet.

When we first told fifteen-year-old Keenan about Marty's cancer advancing to his lungs, he calmly said to his dad, "I know that I'm lucky to already have done so much with you. I've gone places and done things that some people will never get to do with their dad. I'm grateful for those times."

Marty and I looked at each other, both holding back tears. Our little boy had grown into a wise young man.

Not long after that, a few months before Mom sadly passed away from Alzheimer's and joined Dad, I talked to her about how Keenan was growing up—beyond how he was handling Marty's cancer. I told her how I was excited for Keenan's freshman year in high school. He was already dreaming of spending time during summers working for our friend Simon in Tanzania, or landing an internship in Washington, DC, or white-water rafting down the Grand Canyon with his friends (no parents), or planning a gap year when he graduated high school to travel internationally.

Mom said with a grin, "Good. Now you'll know what it feels like to be a mother of someone like you." While Mom was probably referring to all of the worry I caused her when I headed out on adventures, I took her comment as the ultimate compliment.

Marty and I have raised a child who at the age of fifteen loves adventure—who is wide open to possibilities. I want adventure to live at the center of our family story, and at the center of his life.

But at this moment, Keenan is taking a different adventure with his dad, through cancer. While we don't know how this story will end, as a family, we know from our experience with past adventures in the wild how to handle challenge and adversity. *One day at a time. Be strong. Be true. Stay united. Let love surround us.* With determination, perseverance, grace, love, and hope, we will keep moving forward.

Through all of it, I've learned there is an intimacy between life and death. Death puts a laser focus on all that is present right before us, this moment—reminding us to keep living and loving every day.

ACKNOWLEDGMENTS

First on my list of people to thank is my son, Keenan, for his courage and resilience during our absence. He made me proud beyond words. Thanks, too, to the surrogate team of parents who cared for Keenan while we were away: Sue and Frank Mocker, Lindsey and Ben Larson, Leni and Randy Karr, Becky and Brett Nunn, Melodie and Mike Fagan, Jean McGuire, Pat Keenan, and Jim Keenan. We could not have embarked on this adventure if not for this amazing tribe, whose presence with Keenan gave us peace of mind.

Some of those who cared for Keenan also held important roles on our expedition support team. A standing ovation to Brett and Lindsey, who worked tirelessly to transcribe and post our daily audio blogs and update our social media channels. Thanks to Leni for being our school liaison and funneling kids' questions to us, and for providing invaluable pep talks via satellite phone while we were in Antarctica. Hooray for Sue, who oversaw all of the moving parts of our Keenan support network.

Thanks to our parents—Jim and Helen Keenan, Tom and Vicki Sheskey, and Dean and Ann Fagan—for your unwavering encouragement of every crazy adventure we've undertaken, and for enduring sleepless nights along the way. To all of our extended family, thank you for showing us that a united, connected family enriches our lives.

Thanks as well to our special group of close-knit neighbors and cheerleaders: Laura, Ted, TJ, and Jack Mandelkorn; Lori, Randy, Nate, and Ian George; Jill, Jeff, Kari, and John Orth. Living down the street from these kind and generous families makes our little corner of North Bend a special place I hope to always call home.

Thanks to my tribe of ultrarunning friends, with whom I've shared countless hours of joy and struggle on the trails over the years—particularly Leni Karr and Wendy Wheeler-Jacobs. A hearty thanks to Susan Geiger for inviting me to join her Denali climbing team back in 1998, and for her enduring friendship.

Thanks to the staff at Saint Joseph School in Snoqualmie, especially Principal Peg Johnston, who supported our expedition from the beginning, and for introducing the entire school community to our journey. To Keenan's sixth-grade teachers, who kept a special eye on him in our absence: Emily Castle Bemis, Roseann DiBianco, Carmen Sanchez, and Leah Weitzsacker. I knew Keenan would continue to thrive with you by his side.

To all the students who followed our daily blog—especially the fourth through eighth graders at Saint Joseph School, Sharon Piper's third-grade class at Optad Elementary School, Meredith von Trapp's fifth-grade class at North Bend Elementary School, Mary Jo Williams sixth-grade class at Weber Elementary, Sommer Powers eighth-grade Language Arts class at West Cottonwood Junior High, and Penny Perkin's eleventh-grade American Literature class at New Hampton High School. You gave us a reason to keep striving every day.

To the strangers who cheered us on as we dragged tires on the Snoqualmie Valley Trail, and everyone worldwide who followed along on social media during our journey to the South Pole. You celebrated our successes, sympathized with our struggles, and became a valued part of our team.

This book would not exist had it not been for my publisher, She Writes Press, especially Brooke Warner and her team. I am eternally grateful for their enthusiasm and guidance in ushering me through the publishing process. A special thanks to developmental editor extraordinaire Kirsten Colton, who masterfully helped sculpt and shape early drafts of my manuscript. Thanks to Erin Cusick for her keen eye and superb copyediting skills.

Thanks to my council of writing group friends—Pamela Denchfield, Nancy Logan, Anne Sisson, and Maren Van Nostrand—whose collective wisdom and insight have helped me to become a better writer. A big thanks to all of my manuscript beta readers, including Lynne Curry and Michelle Conrad, for providing constructive feedback that strengthened the book.

I'd like to express my sincere gratitude to Keith Heger of Polar Explorers, who was instrumental in helping us prepare to venture to the South Pole without a guide or resupply. A heartfelt thanks to all of the folks at Antarctic Logistics and Expeditions (ALE), especially Steve Jones, who answered our countless preparation questions, and who read every word of my manuscript and offered suggestions to improve the historical accuracy. A special thanks to polar explorer Hannah McKeand, who selflessly offered her firsthand notes from skiing the Messner route.

Thanks to Christian Eide, Helen Thayer, and Scott Jurek for sharing their expertise about expedition food, cold-weather travel, and endurance training. And to our strength coach, Courtenay Schurman, for helping us learn how to build strength while maintaining stamina. Thanks to naturopath Dr. Alyssa DiRienzo and massage therapist Dina Gosse for all the years of helping me to maintain a healthy body.

A final thanks to Antarctic legends Roald Amundsen, Sir Ernest Shackleton, Reinhold Messner, and others, whose pioneering quests into the cold unknown inspired us to chase our own dream.

ABOUT THE AUTHOR

Author photo © Mary Miller Photography

Chris Fagan and her husband became the first American married couple to ski without guide, resupply or other assistance to the South Pole. She has summited Denali, in Alaska; run 100-mile trail races through the mountains; canoed the hippo-laden Zambezi River, in Zimbabwe; and biked through remote Tanzania. Her adventurous spirit shines through in her work as a consultant, trainer, speaker, and writer. For over two decades, Chris and her company, SparkFire, have helped Fortune 500 companies develop innovative new products and services. Along the way, she's trained hundreds of people in creative thinking processes. A popular keynote speaker, Chris consistently gains praise for her dynamic style and natural spark. She lives in the Pacific Northwest with her husband, teenage son, and two labs, Winston and Kiya. *The Expedition* is her first book.

www.chrisfagan.net | www.sparkfireinc.com

 chriscfagan | 🐦 @chriscfagan

📷 @chriscfagan | in. linkedin.com/in/chriscfagan

EXPEDITION STATS

Day on Trail	Date	Latitude	Longitude
1	12/2/13	S82°23.582	W065°14.296
2	12/3/13	S82°27.488	W065°58.731
3	12/4/13	S82°32.388	W066°54.473
4	12/5/13	S82°39.618	W067°16.709
5	12/6/13	S82°48.113	W067°44.448
6	12/7/13	S82°57.564	W068°17.080
7	12/8/13	S83°06.691	W068°50.690
8	12/9/13	S83°14.019	W069°20.777
9	12/10/13	S83°23.353	W070°07.820
10	12/11/13	S83°32.151	W070°55.589
11	12/12/13	S83°41.314	W071°45.850
12	12/13/13	S83°50.141	W072°38.456
13	12/14/13	S83°59.176	W073°35.853
14	12/15/13	S84°08.421	W074°46.339
15	12/16/13	S84°17.366	W075°58.838
16	12/17/13	S84°25.978	W077°06.446
17	12/18/13	S84°35.126	W078°29.772
18	12/19/13	S84°45.062	W079°27.313
19	12/20/13	S84°55.244	W079°55.552
20	12/21/13	S85°07.818	W080°37.244
21	12/22/13	S85°07.818	W080°37.244
22	12/23/13	S85°20.853	W081°10.521
23	12/24/13	S85°31.474	W081°30.565
24	12/25/13	S85°43.917	W081°40.877
25	12/26/13	S85°55.979	W081°48.835
26	12/27/13	S86°06.346	W082°10.186

Hours Traveled on Trial	Distance Traveled in Miles	Altitude in Feet
2	2.3	542
7	8.6	710
8	11.3	950
8	9.5	1050
8.15	11.25	1219
8.5	12.5	1532
8.5	12.1	1776
8	10	2030
9	13.1	2400
9	12.6	2755
9.25	13	3117
9	12.5	3353
9	12.6	3466
9.5	13.5	3535
9.5	13.4	3562
9	12.5	3725
9.5	14.0	4090
9.5	14	4268
8	12.7	4382
9.5	15.1	4440
Rest day		4440
9.5	15.3	4455
8.5	13	4750
9.5	15	5055
8.5	14	5230
9	12.5	5657

(continued on next page)

(continued from previous page)

Day on Trail	Date	Latitude	Longitude
27	12/28/13	S86°18.866	W082°16.909
28	12/29/13	S86°30.714	W082°27.561
29	12/30/13	S86°41.029	W082°31.809
30	12/31/13	S86°50.826	W082°21.100
31	1/1/14	S87°01.812	W082°26.462
32	1/2/14	S87°09.257	W082°25.063
33	1/3/14	S87°20.359	W082°27.614
34	1/4/14	S87°30.520	W082°23.940
35	1/5/14	S87°41.281	W082°36.114
36	1/6/14	S87°53.423	W082°34.146
37	1/7/14	S88.03.914	W082°11.548
38	1/8/14	S88°16.375	W082°10.856
39	1/9/14	S88°25.669	W084°14.724
40	1/10/14	S88°36.114	W082°23.371
41	1/11/14	S88°46.754	W82°34.147
42	1/12/14	S88°57.898	W083°10.554
43	1/13/14	S89°09.043	W083°23.920
44	1/14/14	S89°19.400	W082°53.613
45	1/15/14	S89°30.794	W082°42.587
46	1/16/14	S89°42.299	W082°29.409
47	1/17/14	S89°52.759	W083°15.140
48	1/18/14	S90.00.000	

Hours Traveled on Trial	Distance Traveled in Miles	Altitude in Feet
9.5	14.5	5732
9	14	6088
8	12	6221
8	11.5	6563
9	13	7093
6	9	7292
9.5	13	7561
9	12	8000
9.5	13	8271
10	14.5	8392
9	13	8615
10	14.3	8821
8.75	10.7	8930
8.5	12	8990
8.5	12.3	9022
9	12.9	9046
8.5	12.9	9091
9	11.9	9150
9	13.1	9114
9.5	13.2	9209
9	12.1	9213
7	8.75	9301

BOOK CLUB QUESTIONS

1. Why did Chris and Marty ultimately make the difficult decision to go on an expedition to Antarctica? How do you feel about their decision to leave their son, Keenan, for two months? What difficult choices have you made to chase a dream?

2. What themes did you detect in the story? Did any of them remind you of topics that are relevant to your life?

3. In the book, the author writes, "Adventure expands who you are. Adventure helps us step out of the ordinary to realize the extraordinary qualities that we all possess." What does she mean by this?

4. Why do Chris and Marty want adventure to live at the heart of their family? How do your values manifest in your life?

5. In what ways do you think Chris and Marty are coming to terms with middle age and their own mortality throughout the story? How do you think middle age will affect, or has affected, your life?

6. How did extended family and close friends play a role in the story? What impact did the students and strangers following along during the expedition have on Chris and Marty?

7. Which parts of the book stood out to you? Are there any quotes, passages, or scenes that you found particularly compelling, unique, or thought-provoking?

8. What do you think about the various challenges and stresses that impact Chris and Marty, individually and as a married couple, while they are in Antarctica? Think about the following: being away from their son, foggy goggles, faulty skis, relentless wind, 40-below temperatures, whiteout conditions, bumpy sastrugi, isolation, lack of sleep, only one rest day, menstruation, and hot flashes. How has intense stress in your life impacted you and your relationships?

9. What did you learn about the continent of Antarctica by reading this book?

10. In what ways were you able to identify with the characters— think about their personality traits, motivations, and values—while reading this book? What adjectives would you use to describe Chris and Marty as individuals?

11. In reading about the planning and expedition phases, what thoughts or feelings did you have about the author's son, Keenan? How well did he appear to cope with the absence of his parents? Did you detect any changes in him once Chris and Marty returned home?

12. Later in the journey, Chris reveals that she didn't like feeling weak and sometimes wore her "strong woman" armor. What purpose did this serve her? What happened when she put down her armor and became more vulnerable? Could you relate to the tension between being strong and being vulnerable?

13. By the end of their journey, how do you think Chris and Marty had grown or changed?

14. How did this book impact or change you? Do you have a new perspective as a result of reading it? Did you learn something new?

15. If you could talk with the author, what would you want to say to her or ask her?

SELECTED TITLES FROM SHE WRITES PRESS

She Writes Press is an independent publishing company founded to serve women writers everywhere. Visit us at www.shewritespress.com.

Gap Year Girl by Marianne Bohr. $16.95, 978-1-63152-820-0. Thirty-plus years after first backpacking through Europe, Marianne Bohr and her husband leave their lives behind and take off on a yearlong quest for adventure.

Blue Apple Switchback: A Memoir by Carrie Highley. $16.95, 978-1-63152-037-2. At age forty, Carrie Highley finally decided to take on the biggest switchback of her life: upon her bicycle, and with the help of her mentor's wisdom, she shed everything she was taught to believe as a young lady growing up in the South—and made a choice to be true to herself and everyone else around her.

Naked Mountain: A Memoir by Marcia Mabee. $16.95, 978-1-63152-097-6. A compelling memoir of one woman's journey of natural world discovery, tragedy, and the enduring bonds of marriage, set against the backdrop of a stunning mountaintop in rural Virginia.

Postcards from the Sky: Adventures of an Aviatrix by Erin Seidemann. $16.95, 978-1-63152-826-2. Erin Seidemann's tales of her struggles, adventures, and relationships as a woman making her way in a world very much dominated by men: aviation.

The Longest Mile: A Doctor, a Food Fight, and the Footrace that Rallied a Community Against Cancer by Christine Meyer, MD. $16.95, 978-1-63152-043-3. In a moment of desperation, after seeing too many patients and loved ones battle cancer, a doctor starts a running team—never dreaming what a positive impact it will have on her community.

Fourteen: A Daughter's Memoir of Adventure, Sailing, and Survival by Leslie Johansen Nack. $16.95, 978-1-63152-941-2. A coming-of-age adventure story about a young girl who comes into her own power, fights back against abuse, becomes an accomplished sailor, and falls in love with the ocean and the natural world.